LIVING the DREAM

LIVING THE DREAM

AN INSIDE ACCOUNT OF THE 2008 CUBS SEASON

JIM McARDLE

TRIUMPH
BOOKS

Triumph Books and colophon are registered trademarks of Random House, Inc.

Library of Congress Cataloging-in-Publication Data

McArdle, Jim.
  Living the dream : an inside account of the 2008 Cubs season / Jim McArdle.
    p. cm.
  ISBN 978-1-60078-158-2
  1. Chicago Cubs (Baseball team) I. Title.
  GV875.C6M43 2009
  796.357'640977311—dc22

2008055266

This book is available in quantity at special discounts for your group or organization. For further information, contact:

Triumph Books
542 South Dearborn Street
Suite 750
Chicago, Illinois 60605
(312) 939-3330
Fax (312) 663-3557

Printed in U.S.A.
ISBN: 978-1-60078-158-2
Design/editorial production by Prologue Publishing Services, LLC

To my father, Frank L. McArdle,
who coached me into becoming a Cubs fan and
shepherded me to follow my love of writing.
This work is a marriage of those two passions.

CONTENTS

FOREWORD

WHEN I FIRST HEARD THAT Jim McArdle was leaving his job as the editor of *Vine Line*, the Cubs' official monthly magazine, to write a book chronicling the 2008 season, I thought he had picked the jackpot of all years to write about the Cubs. They had gone from worst to first the year before only to sputter in the first round of the playoffs in a 3–0 sweep versus the Arizona Diamondbacks. Two thousand eight represented the 100th anniversary of the last World Series title for one of sports' most popular franchises that continues to sell out Wrigley Field on a yearly basis. The club and ballpark were in the process of being sold, adding uncertainty to the future of the team and its historic home.

Essentially, 2008 was set up to finally, really, be *the year*. And from my standpoint, no matter how it played out, Jim would have a fascinating story on his hands.

Who better to tell the daily chronicle of the 2008 Chicago Cubs than Jim, whose father, Frank, introduced him to the Cubs in the 1960s? Jim would watch the games on WGN on his dad's lap. Frank grew up near Wrigley Field during the Depression. He and his buddies would hang around the park until the seventh inning, when they would be allowed in for free to watch some very good Charlie Grimm–led ballclubs.

Jim's first clear memories of the Cubs came during the infamous 1969 season when the Cubs blew a big division lead and lost out to the Miracle Mets in the old NL East. His first trip to Wrigley Field came the following year, and all he could think about was watching Ernie Banks play in person. Unfortunately, Mr. Cub would sit out that day, but Fergie Jenkins pitched a complete game, and the Cubs won 2–0. Jim had one more chance to see Banks later on, but alas, he was given yet another day off. The consolation that day was watching Atlanta's Hank Aaron give the Wrigley Field fans a moment of anxiety on a deep fly out late in a game won by the Cubs 6–5.

Who would have guessed that three decades later, Jim would be regularly rubbing elbows with the likes of Banks and Jenkins and another Hall of Famer, Billy Williams? To this day, Williams won't let Jim forget a surreal scene in the late 1990s when Billy needed a ride back to the ballpark from a *Vine Line* photo shoot. Jim was excited beyond belief to have the chance at some one-on-one time with one of his heroes, but he had forgotten one minor detail as they walked up to his two-door Dodge Daytona hatchback—the passenger-side door didn't work. So the Cubs legend could either drive or climb through the window to get in the car. He ended up getting in the driver's side and climbing over the center console to the passenger seat. Fortunately for Jim, Billy thought the whole thing was hilarious and to this day still kids him about it.

A key moment in Jim's professional career came in his early days on the job with the Cubs. He had gone into the Cubs' clubhouse to pass out some copies of *Vine Line* when longtime clubhouse manager Yosh Kawano, who protected that room like it was his own, starting firing questions at him: "Hey, what number was Paul Popovich?"

Jim said, "Twenty-two."

"What number was Ken Holtzman?"

Jim replied, "Thirty."

On and on it went, until Kawano finally said, "Hey, you're pretty good." Jim had passed the test, and from that day forward, Yosh treated him like he belonged.

Mike Huang, a *Vine Line* colleague of Jim's and a close friend, sums up nicely what it's like to hang around Jim McArdle: "He'll always offer to buy you a beverage at his favorite neighborhood watering hole. And if you can't get along with Jim, you can't get along with anyone."

So pull up a stool next to Jim and enjoy the story of the 2008 Chicago Cubs.

—Len Kasper

FOREWORD

GROWING UP IN SEATTLE, I would watch the *Game of the Week* on television on Saturdays. When the Cubs played, there was something about Wrigley Field and Ernie Banks. It was like I knew that was where I was supposed to be.

And then I got signed by the Cubs, and when I got called up in June 1960, we won a doubleheader in Pittsburgh. I had two wonderful games and drove in five runs. In those days, the team did not talk to you when you first came up. There were only 400 major league ballplayers—eight teams in the National League, and eight teams in the American League. So I had to prove myself, because I was taking one of their teammates' jobs. Ernie was the first guy who talked to me and made me feel good.

The next day I walked out onto the field at Wrigley for the first time to take batting practice. Nobody was in the stands. We had our clubhouse down in the left-field corner back then, so I was walking down the foul line with Ernie, and I stopped to look around. The ivy was in full bloom. It seemed smaller, cozier than on TV. I just felt like King Kong. It felt like home, and I literally had the sensation I was floating. Ernie was just watching me, to see my reaction. He knew what I was feeling. It still feels that way. You feel good when you go there; I think everybody does. So I wasn't wrong on either one of them, Ernie or Wrigley.

From 1960 to 1966, we averaged a little more than 700,000 fans each season, and we didn't have Wrigleyville. There were only a few bars around. On occasion, Fergie Jenkins would go over to Ray's Bleachers, which is now Murphy's. A lot of players in my day went to Ray's. Ray Meyer (not the DePaul basketball coach) was the owner then, and their patrons were part of the Bleacher Bums. We knew them by their first names.

My place was Bernie's Tap & Grill. I used to park on Clark Street just south of there, where a family named the Rizzos owned the lot. Billy Williams and other players parked there, too. Sometimes I'd pop into Bernie's for a cup of coffee before going to the ballpark. How I got to know them was through Linda Dillman, who worked in the front office at Wrigley. Linda used to help me answer all my fan mail. Her husband Donnie's father was Bernie. After Bernie died, Donnie and Linda took over the bar, and that's how I was always over there. I watched their boys grow up. They are like a second family.

The first year I played for the Cubs I rented a home in Elmwood Park. Then I had a house built in Park Ridge. I started following Berteau Avenue back home from the ballpark around 1962. It's a side street north of Irving Park Road and was kind of a back-road way of getting west out to the expressway. A lot of the kids, I'd run into them on Berteau, and I'd stop at corners and sign autographs. It was wonderful.

After I retired in 1974, I was in the business sector for several years. Then in 1989 they invited me to throw out a first pitch in the playoffs. I'd never been at Wrigley for a night game, and I'd never been on the field for the postseason. When I walked off the mound, I thought, *Boy, I'd sure like to be a part of this one day.* And then the next year, WGN Radio hired me to do color.

For my first game, we were ready to go on the air. I had my scorecard, I had my coffee sitting there. And Tommy Brennaman got up and said, "Hi, everybody. This is Thom Brennaman with Ron Santo and Bob Brenly." All of a sudden the wind came, hit my coffee, and spilled it all over my scorecard, and I went, "God dammit!" Thom looked at me, speechless. I said, "That's it. I'm through." Well, I continued to struggle that first year, because when I got behind the mike I became somebody else. I was trying too hard. Finally, they urged me to just be myself. I've learned to become a part-time broadcaster, but I'm really more of a fan. I came here when I was 20 years old, so the majority of my life I've lived in Chicago. It's my home. I've become what the fans are out there. I don't even realize I'm doing it, but I react emotionally to the moment. That's me, because I care so much.

I've dealt with diabetes since I was a teenager. I've had just about every problem that comes with it, and I would have never gotten through that adversity if it weren't for this game and these fans. Once I walked into Wrigley Field, not once did I think about any of these things. For the 40,000 Cubs fans who come here on any particular day, it's an outlet for them. I take baseball that way. I played hard, but I enjoyed it. Whenever I put the uniform on, if I had a problem someplace else, that problem was gone. I was in my happy place, where I was always meant to be.

—Ron Santo

PREFACE

NLDS Game 3 • October 4, 2008

DERREK LEE CAME UP IN A seemingly benign situation: two outs,
nobody on base, Cubs down 2–0 but with time left in the fifth
inning. This was the 2008 Cubs, whose 97 wins were the most by
the franchise in 63 seasons. The 6′5″ Lee was the biggest Cub in
stature and an unofficial team captain with 12 years in the majors.
Like Frank Chance, "the Peerless Leader" of the Cubs' last championship club 100 years before him, D-Lee played first base. Lee
was the guy who would stand up in front of a roomful of teammates when words were necessary. And they listened when D-Lee
spoke. On this night, he had doubled and singled in his first two
trips to the plate, and his .556 batting average for the series shined
in white lights on the right-field scoreboard at Dodger Stadium. "It
doesn't seem like anybody on the Cubs is hitting that well," my
friend Willy B noted.

Lee struck out on a slider down in the zone, angrily whipped
his bat aside, and slammed down his helmet, which went bouncing toward the Cubs' dugout. The Dodgers added a run in the bottom of that inning, and the score remained that way until
pinch-hitter Daryle Ward singled home D-Lee with the Cubs' soli-
tary run in the eighth. Cubs Nation was there, but their team never
did much to get us out of our seats.

Los Angeles disheartened us in the first inning—by inches. Russell Martin doubled just fair down the left-field line, and moments
later, he slid into third base a whisker ahead of Alfonso Soriano's
throw on Manny Ramirez's single. One out later, James Loney

doubled both runners home, and the chants of "Sweep! Sweep! Sweep!" started up again.

From our seats high behind home plate, we observed the body language in both dugouts. The Dodgers stood up front, hanging on every pitch at the rail, while all we could see of the Cubs were their legs sprawling lifelessly off the benches.

The day had started out innocuously enough, with Willy B and me flying into LAX that morning. One of his friends invited us to stay at her home in the foothills of the San Gabriel Mountains. I'd never met Jill but knew of her from Cowboy Mouth, a band Willy B used to tour with that wrote a song named for her, in which everything she owns is red and "everybody loves Jill," so says the refrain. We parked outside her home, and everything seemed to check out with her song: red car, red porch, red window trim. And then she opened her *red* front door…wearing Dodger *blue*. Ugh!

We spent the afternoon doing Hollywood things: star-searching down Rodeo Drive and the Sunset Strip, lunching at a beachfront café in Malibu, and people-watching on Venice Beach. Will's television-executive friends regaled us with celebrity stories. One showed her cell-phone photo of a tyrannosaur skull in the house foyer of one of Hollywood's leading men and invited us to a premiere party for Christian Slater's new television series that night. But we had a date with Chavez Ravine.

On our way into the parking lot in Jill's convertible, we were the targets of many taunts. "Our fans are kind of thuggish," Jill warned. No kidding. I had made a wager with Willy B—a beer to the first one who spotted a celebrity—and on our way through the parking lot, he hollered "Tonight's the night!" to a guy wearing a Cubs cap. The guy replied, "No, Tuesday's the night!" Will turned to me. "You owe me a brewski," he said. "That was Jeff Garlin."

But it wasn't the night at all, and Game 5 on Tuesday would become superfluous. With two outs in the ninth inning, I was desperately rubbing my fingertips over the etching of my father's name on his World War II dog tags hanging around my neck. Should've gone to the Christian Slater party, I thought, as Soriano futilely checked his swing on strike three of 100 years.

Dad always hated the Dodgers for leaving Flatbush, a community not unlike where he grew up on the North Side of Chicago. I had new reasons to hate them. On my way out, a Dodgers fan got in my face and screamed wildly, "CUBBIES SUUUCK!" Another taunted, "Maybe next century!" I passed a mural of Johnny Podres at the top of my section and wondered if any of these goons knew who he was or that a "dodger" was a trolley-car dodger native to Brooklyn on the other coast. Two guys paraded past with a bedsheet on which they scribed, "100 years and counting." I said to Willy B in a hushed tone, "I bet they'd drop-kick a baby here."

Packing to leave on Monday morning, I came across the *Chicago Tribune* sports section that I'd picked up for the Saturday flight out. TO LIVE AND DIE IN L.A. read the bold headline, a play on words from a mid-1980s film by the same name. The movie starred William Petersen, a Cubs diehard who in 1980 cofounded the Remains Theatre Ensemble down the block from Wrigley Field, in what's now the Gingerman Tavern. Petersen's character was a corrupt Secret Service agent who got his comeuppance in the end of that movie. I know I was in Tinseltown, but that wasn't supposed to be the end of my story. Mine would be a Cubs version of *Fever Pitch*, and the amazing comeback was supposed to start here.

Instead, the *To Live and Die in L.A.* theme song by British new wavers Wang Chung played irrepressibly in my mind as I walked to my gate at the airport, its gritty overture and heavy bass pounding like a migraine headache. Somehow, my memory played back the opening line of lyrics, which seemed to speak directly to me as a Cubs fan facing a cold, empty winter for the 100th time:

> *In the heat of the day*
> *Every time you go away*
> *I have to piece my life together,*
> *Every time you're away*

This time it was magnified exponentially. I had quit my job with the Chicago Cubs six months earlier, set up shop 460 feet from home plate at Wrigley Field to write a book, and bankrolled on the century anniversary. No team really *could* have a bad century, right? This just *had* to be the year, and I set about documenting it every step of the way. I was living the dream, people said, but it ended here, in a hostile environment, 2,000 miles from the Friendly Confines. I wasn't wearing any skivvies, had my last 20 bucks in my pocket next to my lucky 2008 penny, and some jackass was taking more joy in my misery than his team's playoff survival. This was not a dream. This was the same recurring nightmare that quakes Cubs fans awake every autumn.

Reality. Wait 'til next year. Again. But that Cubphrase illustrates our battle-tested resiliency. We will be back. Even the broken-hearted fan who auctioned his allegiance on eBay in the waning days after elimination. Who's he kidding? He can no more sell off his allegiance than he can his ancestry. Cubs fans are incorrigibly loyal. We'll pick up our same routines next season: enjoying a pregame meal at our favorite Wrigleyville watering hole, ballhawking out on the streets during batting practice, denoting an "H" for "hopped" after P7 on a scorecard every time Soriano hops while making a catch in left field, and unfurling the mother of all W flags while singing "Go Cubs Go" in chorus after a win.

We're loyal because it's never been solely about reaching a destination. It's about having experienced the journey—that long, long journey—together, with our "family," that will make reaching that destination worthwhile. Someday.

ACKNOWLEDGMENTS

THANKS TO THE CHICAGO CUBS organization; it was an honor to serve the Cubs for 12 years. To Executive Vice President of Business Operations Mark McGuire, who accepted my resignation with the entrustment to tell an accurate and fair story of a 2008 season that had a sensitive centennial backdrop. To my former colleagues in the Cubs' publications department—Lena McDonagh, Mike Huang, Juan Castillo, Joaquin Castillo, Jen Dedes, and Sean Ahmed—for inspiring me to be the best I can be. And thanks to Mitch Rogatz and Tom Bast of Triumph Books, who believed in my concept and ability to deliver, and to Don Gulbrandsen, who took me by the hand, patiently and professionally, through the scribing of my first book.

Gratitude, as well, to all of Wrigley's rooftop owners, for sharing their stories, their tasty eats, and their unique "views." Special thanks to the research assistance of Ed Hartig, Brian Bernardoni, Pete Scales, and Kathleen T. Knorr—I helped you give birth to your baby; you helped me give birth to mine. To those who served as my ragtag but crack editing staff (you know who you are), your sounding board was invaluable to a rookie author. Thanks to the photography donated by Will Byington, John "Nunu" Zomot, and longtime Cubs photographer and friend Steve Green. Much appreciation to the regular fans at Wrigley Field, who opened their lives and "their living rooms" to me in 2008. And lastly, I am fortunate to have a large cache of family and friends, who supported me in more ways than they'll ever know. "No man is a failure who has friends," Clarence the angel told George Bailey in *It's a Wonderful Life*. In that regard, this book can only be a huge success.

LIVING the DREAM

1

WRIGLEYVILLE

IN 1937 THERE WAS A 10-year-old boy living in a neighborhood known as Old Irving Park about five miles directly west of Wrigley Field. In adolescent insubordination against his mother, he stormed off one day. His sister Kathleen came home. "Where's Frankie?" she asked. "He ran away," her mother shot back, busy setting the table for supper. "Off that way," she added, dismissively flipping her wrist to the east, "toward the Cubs."

Kathleen caught up to her brother, who was walking resolutely down Addison Street with his baseball mitt in hand. "I'm going to join the Cubs. Maybe they need a batboy!" he exclaimed. She talked him down from joining the traveling baseball circus, and they headed back home. He never did get a job in baseball, but almost 60 years after that juvenile standoff with his mother, Frankie's son came to work for the Cubs in the organization's publications department. In 12 years as editor of the monthly magazine *Vine Line*, one of the highest-regarded team publications in pro sports, and 11 years as a regular Wrigley Field tour guide, I came to know more about the Cubs and the ballpark than my dad or his father ever could have imagined. And that's saying something.

My grandfather and namesake, who immigrated in 1915, initially became a White Sox fan. He came from Northern Ireland and settled on the South Side of Chicago, noted for its Irish population. Since the Catholic Comiskey family owned the Sox, and the Protestant Wrigleys owned the Cubs, it was a natural. However, soured by the Black Sox scandal in 1919, and since he eventually settled his family on the North Side, where he was running garages like the one in which Al Capone staged his infamous St. Valentine's Day Massacre, he switched allegiances.

Like many fans, I attended my first Cubs game with my family. It was in 1970, and I don't remember much except that Fergie Jenkins shut out the Phillies 2–0. But I do recall fixating on the homes across the street and thinking how cool it would be to live there, to look out my living-room window and watch Cubs baseball every day.

The story is bittersweet how I came to live 460 feet from home plate. When the Cubs went to the National League Championship Series in 2003, a charter was booked to fly front-office employees to Games 1 and 2 of the World Series at the AL site. That plane, obviously, never flew. With another weekend to apartment hunt, my roommates, Rudy Vorkapic and Dan Long, and I found a place on Sheffield Avenue. Our apartment was the home of Kathleen Turner's private dick character in the 1991 film *V.I. Warshawski*. In fact, the building was nearly destroyed from a stunt in the movie that set the building on fire. The place was right across from the bleachers, in fair territory. From my bed, I could wake up to see the flags waving from the right-field foul pole. Who else in Chicago could say that? We procured an excess hunk of bar from our favorite watering hole on what's known as the "Southport Corridor" just west of Wrigley, put in some fancy-colored track lighting and started referring to the place as the Love Swank Lounge, or "Swank," for short.

All three of us grew up rooting for the Cubs in Chicago-area suburbs: I in Des Plaines, Dan in McHenry, and Rudy in Bellwood. I graduated from Chicago's Columbia College with the quick-witted 43-year-old Rudy, known as "Dude," whose Serbian genealogy gave him olive skin, wiry black hair, and a keen predisposition to drink schlivovitz. Early in my journalism career, I met Dan, another writer who started on the preps sports beat. The 44-year-old has a stocky build, shaved head, goatee, and a cynical sense of humor. Think David Wells. I came to call him "Crankshaft," derived off a name-calling rant we found amusing that was spewed by vile nightclub performer Tony Clifton in the Andy Kaufman biopic *Man on the Moon*.

Rudy moved to New Orleans after the 2004 season, got married, and launched a satirical *Onion*-like newspaper called *The Levee* in the wake of the Hurricane Katrina fiasco. A new friend named Will Byington took up residence. He has short, black hair and a goatee, and in a knit skull hat without his glasses, the 30-year-old looks like U2's The Edge. Born in west suburban Naperville, Illinois, "Willy B" picked up a southern accent (he calls us "y'all") in four years of college at the University of Alabama. Coming off a few years of touring with a rock band called Cowboy Mouth, he was launching a new career in photography, and thought shooting his favorite team and sports venue would be a great place to start. Operating on the top of our three-flat was a rooftop business called Skybox on Sheffield.

A new city ordinance with regard to these rooftop businesses passed in February 2006. Among other things, it mandated that every rooftop owner install emergency lighting and sprinkler systems throughout their buildings by January 2008. The two blocks began to have a feeling of abandonment as leases weren't renewed, and apartments went unrented while properties could be brought up to code. We became victims in November 2007, when we were forced to leave Skybox on Sheffield. They were going to tear up drywall to install sprinklers, rip off the back of the building to put in an elevator, and were considering converting our apartment into a place where corporate guests could conduct meetings before games. One of my friends called it, "Cubtrification."

"You gotta leave?" my buddy said. "All so some fat cat doesn't have to use his legs to climb the stairs?"

Actually, it was the Americans with Disabilities Act, which all legitimate businesses have to comply with. The rooftops had grown from a cottage industry to a respected Chicago tradition in 20 short years. For me, however, in the middle of making arrangements to write this book, the timing couldn't have been worse. Imagine the limitations of an apartment hunt in a total of 21 buildings on two streets—about 70 flats by my count, many of which were occupied or unavailable for the same reason I was in the housing market.

Astonishingly, we found quite a few, but nothing that would accommodate all three of us. So Willy B took a one-bedroom place

The author's first apartment across from Wrigley, home of Skybox on Sheffield.

Photo by Will Byington / www.willbyington.com

right next door, where residents routinely hang around on the front porch before, during, and after games. With his second-floor flat right across the gangway, we chaffed on moving day that a conveyer belt from window to window would have come in handy. Dan and I found a two-bedroom apartment in a brown brick six-flat on Waveland Avenue with a spectacular second-floor view looking directly down the left-field line at home plate. We'd essentially moved from foul pole to foul pole. If a home run ever crashed through our window, we could do the umpires a favor and make the call, because half of our living room is in fair territory, and half is in foul. In fact, one of our windows was broken a few years back during the filming of *Rookie of the Year*, but they cheated and were hitting from third base.

It's a different perspective of the stadium, busier and more intimidating. The end of the left-field upper deck looms high overhead, with erect light standards towering 150 feet above like a dorsal fin, and staggered concrete rows on the lower grandstands appearing like sharp teeth on an open jaw of a massive predator fish about to pounce. At ground level across the street, concessions deliveries go into Gate K, and garbage trucks tow away dumpsters. Players drive past on the way into their parking lot for home games and board busses in front of our building for road trips. Then there are the loud comings and goings of Engine 78 and Ambulance 6 at a firehouse that's been four doors to the west at 1052 Waveland since 1894.

I marked it off one day; we actually had moved closer. Where it used to be 390 paces from my front stoop to the office door at Clark and Addison streets, I had trimmed it to just 285 (230 if I cut through Gate K!). When we first moved in, Crankshaft's mom somehow got our street address mixed up, and he wasn't getting mail from her. He asked where she was sending it, and she told him 1040 West Addison Street. "Well, no wonder," he told her. "You're sending it to first base!"

Ours is the only building on Waveland and Sheffield that isn't making a buck off the Cubs. There are no rooftop bleachers, no billboard advertisement. It's just a flat, tarred roof. Since 1989, the 50-year-old owner of the property has lived on both sides of the top floor, which was converted into one giant apartment by her father, an attorney who purchased the building for $30,000 in 1971. "Landlady Lara" grew up around the corner on Kenmore Avenue in a building she and her brother still own. Needless to say, she loves her Cubs. Her dogs are named Ryno and Fergie, and almost every time I see her out walking them, she's wearing some sort of Cubs apparel.

Even more, perhaps, she loves her neighborhood and hates how it's transformed from the days when she'd set up a lemonade stand at the corner of Waveland and Kenmore as a little girl. More fans meant more riffraff and years of cleaning puke off the front steps. After fans tore off the downspout while chasing after a Cubs home run in the 2003 playoffs, she put in a wrought-iron fence around the front of the building. "I hate that fence. I feel like I'm in jail," Lara said. "It used to be a neighborhood. I don't get that sense anymore. There are no kids. When's the last time you had a trick-or-treater? I don't like that part. It's very transient. People live here two or three years, and then they move."

Until the roof started leaking and needed repairs around 1992, she used to have friends over for rooftop parties, enjoying all the playoff games in 1984 and 1989, Opening Night in 1988, and the 1990 All-Star Game much the same way other rooftops were operating at the time—with lawn chairs, coolers, and a charcoal grill.

"Going up to the roof is really a pain in the ass. You've got to carry all the stuff up, and if somebody comes late, you've got to go downstairs and buzz them in," Landlady Lara said. "It's not an easy thing to do, and when you think about it, how many friends do you know who will have a party more than once or twice a year? People say, 'Oh, I'd have people over here all the time.' Well, at first you would."

She constantly resists lucrative offers to sell the building from those who want to convert it into another rooftop monstrosity. It's her home, and I admire her for literally holding her ground.

•   •   •   •

A MISCONCEPTION ABOUT Wrigley Field is that it hasn't changed in 90-plus years. Granted, the addition of the upper deck in the late-1920s brought its capacity up to roughly what it is today, and its backyard character was created in 1937 with the addition of the bleachers and towering center-field scoreboard, and the planting of the ivy. Consider that the scoreboard originally was a rusty-looking reddish-brown, the green doors on the outfield walls were barn-door red as late as the 1970s, and the red marquee at Clark and Addison streets was a bluish-green as recently as the 1960s. And that's not even mentioning the lights that were added in 1988, relocating the press box to accommodate the addition of mezzanine suites in 1989, or the bleachers' renovation completed in 2006.

Even the term "Wrigleyville" is relatively new. The ballpark dates back to 1914 and originally was called Weeghman Park, after Charlie Weeghman, who built it for his team in the upstart Federal League. After that league folded in 1915, chewing gum magnate William Wrigley was an investor in the Cubs when Weeghman purchased them and moved them into the park in 1916. Wrigley bought out Weeghman as principal owner in 1918, changing the stadium's name to Cubs Park in 1920 and to its present name in 1926.

Wrigleyville won't be found on a Chicago neighborhood map, because it's actually an enclave of Lakeview, which was settled in the mid-1800s and was incorporated as a township in 1857. After refugees from the Great Chicago Fire of 1871 began to settle in Lakeview, the population boomed from 6,500 in 1880 to more than 52,000 in 1890, a year after it was annexed by the city of Chicago.

In 1891 the Lutheran Church announced plans to develop an eight-acre parcel of property bordered by Addison, Sheffield, Clark, and Waveland for a church and seminary. Soon, however, Lakeview became a loud, bustling community. Alongside what would become the western wall of the ballpark, the Milwaukee Road Railroad moved coal, sand, and gravel to local builders, and ice and milk to residents. Noise from the rail area, the rumbling of the nearby elevated train, and the clanging of the trolley car bells on Clark Street drove the seminarians out, and they sold the land for $175,000 in 1909 to Milwaukee investor and hotel owner Charles Havenor, who planned to build a baseball stadium for an American Association team. While that never materialized, Weeghman signed a lease for the property and had a 14,000-seat, single-story ballpark constructed.

The migration of middle-class America from the cities to the suburbs in the 1950s and 1960s preceded the recession of the 1970s. A sign of the times, many major league teams moved from aging, intimate inner-city ballparks to massive, multipurpose, concrete coliseums. Wrigley Field endured due in large part to Philip K. Wrigley, who took over ownership of the Cubs after his father, William, died in 1932. Often criticized for spending too much on the stadium and not enough on his team, P.K.'s legacy lives on in baseball's second-oldest venue. It's a throwback to the days of Ebbets Field, Shibe Park, and Forbes Field, when fans could walk down to the park to enjoy a hot dog and a few innings of baseball during their lunch break. "It's one of the few ballparks that's actually right in a neighborhood," said future Hall of Famer Greg Maddux. "Most of the ballparks are built right next to an interstate."

When Maddux came up with the Cubs in 1986, players all lived in the suburbs. Ryne Sandberg and Rick Sutcliffe, teammates on the 1984 and 1989 division-winning teams, tell stories about carpooling together to the ballpark. Billy Williams spent 1959 to 1974, most of his Hall of Fame career, with the Cubs. He returned as an instructor, and in 1980, he and another coach, Gene Clines, took an apartment on Addison Street just west of Wrigley. One day they were headed to the stadium, but for some reason Williams had reservations and brought some of his valuables along.

"When we got back, our television and a lot of things were gone. They had broken into the place and stole a lot of stuff," Williams said. "This place over here was run down. They put the lights in the ballpark, and a lot of people started buying these buildings, redoing them, fixing them up, because they knew when they put the lights in that Wrigley Field was going to be here."

Indeed, the installation of lights ensured the Cubs' longtime commitment as tenants at a time when prime-time baseball was harvesting increasing advertising revenue. As yuppies began populating inner cities like Chicago again, so did players. On game days during the 2003 playoffs, Crankshaft and I made a habit out of touching Eric Karros' mailbox a few blocks away for good luck. We even left a thank-you note the night the Cubs advanced past the NLDS.

During his tenure with the Cubs, from 2004 to 2007, catcher Michael Barrett lived in Lakeview and Lincoln Park. He often would have breakfast at Sam & George's Restaurant on Lincoln Avenue or Anne Sather on Belmont, and dined with his wife at Strega Nona on the Southport Corridor, among other places. Perhaps more than any Cub in recent memory, Barrett gushed about his experience on the North Side.

"After I got involved more with the team, I realized the community was involved, dating all the way back to the early 1900s," Barrett said. "It was about taking pride, not just in being a member of the Cubs organization, but in being a member of this community. I sort of felt like that carried over into my attitude going out on the field every day."

Of the guys on the 25-man roster in 2008, only one lives in the suburbs, and 60 percent live within a couple miles. Like in the days of sandlot ball, Ryan Dempster and Ted Lilly have about a five-minute walk from their homes to the ball yard, and Ryan Theriot spent the 2007 season living across the street. Wrigleyville truly has become home of the Cubs.

·   ·   ·   ·

WATCHING THE CUBS FROM THE rooftops of Chicago's historic Greystone buildings is a tradition that dates back to the West Side Grounds, where the franchise played from 1893 to 1915. A May 1898 *Chicago Daily Tribune* article reported that owners of buildings across an alley south of the ballpark were charging fans 10¢ to come up top and watch games at a time when admittance to the stadium was 50¢. The article intimated it wasn't the first time this was a issue: "New fences and high grand stands which were erected around the Chicago ball park at Polk, Wood, and Lincoln streets this year have cut down materially the number of suburban grand stands. Three still remain, however, to give distress to the managers of the park."

The Chicago building commissioner, the *Tribune* noted, aimed to put these enterprisers out of business by forcing them to buy amusement licenses that would be denied to resident dwellings. Apparently, however, the rooftop businesses continued, because in

Fans watch a Cubs game from the rooftops overlooking the right-field bleachers.
Steve Green photo courtesy Chicago Cubs

1908, a 14-year-old boy named Willie Hudson was watching from a roof at 451 Wood Street when Cubs shortstop Joe Tinker hit a drive into center field. Jumping up to see if Tinker would score on an inside-the-park home run (he did), Hudson fell off the edge and dropped 50 feet to his death.

A Chicago Historical Society photograph shows fans watching the first game ever played at Wrigley on April 23, 1914, from what's now the Ivy League Baseball Club at 3637 Sheffield Avenue. The *Chicago Tribune* noted the next day, "The windows and tops of flat buildings across the way from the park were crowded with spectators." The home team that day was called the Whales, an appropriate moniker since the old ballpark has come to be the big whale of the neighborhood, supporting an economic ecosystem of plankton. The plankton include souvenir stands, parking lots, ticket scalpers, fast-food joints, bars, and guys walking around selling anything from T-shirts to women's underwear to, in 2008, Japanese hachimakis (headbands). Authoring a book on the Cubs from a building that's the last bastion of the old Wrigleyville, I've become one of the plankton, as well.

By far, however, the most profitable species of Wrigley plankton are the rooftop businesses. Though they didn't fully evolve as an industry until the last quarter century, a *Tribune* article of September 29, 1932, stated the Internal Revenue Service would tax building owners who charged more than 40¢ for admittance to their rooftops or upper windows during the World Series, when Babe Ruth hit his famous "called shot."

A year after graduating from Southern Illinois University in 1973, Chicago native George Loukas and his brother, Angelo, bought a large building with three entrances on the northwest corner of Waveland and Sheffield for $135,000 and started renovating its 18 rental units. His mostly Puerto Rican tenants were baseball fans who would go up top to watch Cubs games. Loukas and his friends started joining them, and a few years later, after purchasing the Cubby Bear Lounge and The Sports Corner, he would bring along burgers, hot dogs, and beer from his two neighborhood saloons. By the end of the 1970s, he had extended a staircase on the back porch to the rooftop; and in the early 1980s, he installed bleachers that had been discarded by the park district. "We first started charging $5 or $10 about 1979 or 1980. My friends would just reimburse me," said Loukas, 59. "Basically, that's how I started in the rooftop business."

Jim Murphy purchased a three-flat at 3637 Sheffield in 1973 for $18,000. Murphy, a Chicago policeman, moved in and would carry his gun to take out the trash in a neighborhood pocked with gangs and tenement-like housing. In 1976 Murphy sold that property for $36,000 and rolled his profit into a building erected in 1898 three doors down at 3649 Sheffield. His future wife, Beth, was a tenant from 1979 to 1987 and remembers when Murphy installed a bathroom, spread Astroturf over the tar roof, and put up bleachers. In the 1984 playoffs, Nike and Hilton Hotels rented the deck for corporate outings. "I think they paid with barter—

gym shoes, that kind of thing. But it was business-y; it wasn't just family and friends sitting on lawn chairs," said Beth Murphy.

The rooftop was used for a brief scene in the 1986 film *About Last Night...*, with Rob Lowe and Demi Moore climbing the stairs of a wooden porch around back to reach the rooftop deck. Today, it's distinguished by Harry Caray's likeness on a large pinwheel that's attached to a dormer on the rooftop. The pinwheel, from the old exploding scoreboard at Comiskey Park, was donated to the Murphys by popular Chicago shock jock Steve Dahl.

Before he died of cancer in 2003, Murphy purchased three more properties to the north, including a tavern called Ray's Bleachers in 1980. What originally was known as Ernie's Bleachers, selling hot dogs and sodas out of a sidewalk window in the 1930s, Murphy's Bleachers has expanded to become a thriving sports bar and a popular game-day meeting place.

In 1977 three University of Illinois fraternity brothers pooled together $135,000 to buy a three-flat that was constructed in 1916 at 3639 Sheffield. They began renovating that winter despite the absence of a functioning furnace. Lying in bed in the middle of the night during his first week in the third-floor apartment, one of the owners, Steve Woodruff, heard a noise. He immediately thought of the roughly 30 people they had just evicted. "I thought, 'The sons of bitches are coming to get me,'" he said. "I reached around the corner to flip the light switch on, and opened the door, yelling and screaming. There I was, stark-ass naked, waving a cowboy boot around in my hand—because that was the only weapon I could find on my floor—and there were about 300 mice. And there probably were more cockroaches than mice."

Woodruff was a trader at the Chicago Board Options Exchange when he lived in the building from 1977 to 1980. Since the markets closed at 1:30 PM, he caught a lot of games. There was a trapdoor entrance from a ladder in his apartment, and they'd have friends over for barbecues on the rooftop, which they enclosed with brick posts and one-by-six boards built up around the parapet perimeter.

In the 1980s independent contractor Bob Racke was buying and restoring several old, dilapidated buildings in the neighborhood.

Some owners of the developing rooftop businesses hired him to put in bleachers and run plumbing for water fountains, bathrooms, and outdoor showers. A fringe benefit was enjoying Cubs games there with his two young boys, Tony and Mike, who loved baseball and started pressing their dad to get a rooftop building of their own. When a run-down three-flat that had been erected in 1908 at 3633 Sheffield became available, Racke scooped it up for $250,000 in 1988. "This floor right here," Mike said from what's now the third-floor lounge, "was up to your knees in garbage."

"There was mold on the windowsills. It was borderline condemnable," Tony added. "There was a family of 30 living on the third floor. They were cooking in the bathroom. The police had to kick them out. It was gang, Latin Kings stuff and all that."

Bob Racke renovated in the summer of '88, during which time he successfully petitioned the city to establish the first legally recognized private rooftop operation. The Lakeview Baseball Club opened to its first paying crowd on August 8, 1988, the night the lights went on at Wrigley for the first time. He lived on the second floor for a few years and ran the rooftop operation, eventually retiring and turning the business over to his sons, who are now in their early thirties. They proudly note that two of their great-grandfathers played for the Cubs: Bill Traffley (1878) and Larry Hoffman (1901).

LBC has developed a unique culture, with two highly visible signs. One reads EAMUS CATULI!, which is Latin for "Let's go Cubs!" The other has a series of annually changing numbers and starts with an AC (*anno catuli*, which is Latin for "in the year of the Cubs"). The numbers are a running total of the years since the team's last division title, last NL pennant, and last World Series appearance. At the beginning of 2008, it read AC006299.

Today, LBC has nearly 100 members who pay an annual membership fee and is the only private club among the rooftop businesses. That's because shortly after LBC opened, the city council passed an ordinance banning the opening of private clubs within 2,000 feet of any open-air stadium.

Nevertheless, a new type of plankton was thriving in the whale's wake. The ecosystem was changing.

· · · ·

AT FIRST, THE ROOFTOPS WERE a slow-developing venture. During a major league baseball umpires' strike in the 1980s, longtime crew chief Larry Young recalled going up on one of the buildings to picket during a game. "There were about 20 of us," he said. "This was before they had all the seats up there. I remember going through somebody's bedroom to get up there."

Loukas originally had designs on becoming a prep football coach, but his Wrigleyville bars and properties were prospering. In the mid-1980s he purchased a six-flat constructed in 1917 at 3643 Sheffield for about $425,000. In 1988 Loukas was content earning advertising revenue on that rooftop from Budweiser's giant Spuds MacKenzie balloon. It wasn't the first, as Old Style had mounted an inflatable on his other property, and Rusty Jones was perched atop a large walkup building constructed in 1921 at the northwest corner of Kenmore and Waveland. When the city banned the inflatables that summer, the owner of that nine-unit Kenmore/Waveland property decided to sell. Loukas gave him a deposit on the building, which he later purchased for $725,000, and started another rooftop operation. "Basically, we had two groups of people: his tenants and my customers. We ran that whole first summer with that deal," Loukas said. "In that first year we probably grossed about $20,000 worth of rooftop revenue."

Loukas obtained a permit to put an observation deck on top of his new Sheffield property in 1989. Off the rooftop of that building, Reds pitcher Tom Browning famously dangled his legs while in uniform during a couple innings of a 1993 ballgame. In the meantime, Loukas ended his partnership with his brother in December 1988, selling their original property at 1010 Waveland. It eventually sold again for $5 million in 2000 to a family-owned real-estate investment group headed by Jamie Purcell. In time, Loukas got back to having three rooftop properties in Wrigleyville when he acquired a three-unit 3609 Sheffield building in 1999 for $725,000 and had bleachers put up a few years later.

For years he's had season tickets in Section 17, right behind home plate, but Loukas prefers to watch from his rooftops. "It's my own personal skybox," he said. "It's like I'm a farmer, and I'm looking over my field."

Dave Abrams, who used to take the El to Cubs games with friends from his boyhood home in West Rogers Park, was working for a real-estate investment company in suburban Oak Brook in 1990 when he teamed with two partners to purchase a then-92-year-old building that was in foreclosure at 3627 Sheffield for $425,000. While they renovated the building, several film productions shot on location from the property, including *The Babe*, *Blink*, and *A League of Their Own*. When Skybox on Sheffield opened in 1993, they had innovated several new ideas, including an indoor lounge on the third floor with a pool table, stadium-style seats on the roof, catered food service, and a business center with a printer, computer, and Internet service.

"I would wear a suit and stand out on the front stairs, find a guy walking in a business suit and say to him, 'Hey, buddy, you wanna come up and watch a game?'" said Abrams, who's now 48. "We started with the idea of entertaining corporate people. The rooftops weren't as posh as they are today. We had blind faith teaching businesspeople this new concept of trying to enjoy a ballgame from across the street."

Abrams eventually bought out his associates with a new partner named Marc Hamid, owner and president of a North Side ticket-scalping business. What had started as a cottage industry with a $20 handshake was starting to turn big-time profits as a viable option for corporate entertainment. In 1998, 44th ward alderman Bernie Hanson sponsored a bill that created a tax, annual licensing fee, building inspections, evacuation plans, and food regulations for rooftops that sold admission to watch Cubs games. The city and state were recognizing them as legitimate businesses, but the Cubs still weren't getting a cent of the new entrepreneurs' profits. Then the organization announced plans to add 2,100 seats to the bleachers in June 2001. Animosity was brewing. A lengthy legal and political chess match ensued, with the Wrigley Rooftop

Association led by Jim Murphy trying to block the bleachers expansion project, and the Cubs filing a lawsuit in December 2002 against the rooftop owners in U.S. District Court for unjust enrichment and copyright infringement.

Meanwhile, Sammy Sosa's epic race to Roger Maris' home-run record, the arrival of Kerry Wood, and the Cubs' push to the postseason in 1998 brought fans who had been soured by the 1994–1995 players' strike back to the ballpark. Wrigley Field averaged 2.2 million in attendance from 1996 to 1997, and that number spiked to nearly 2.8 million from 1998 to 2003.

The 1998 season was the last for two single-family frame homes on each side of Landlady Lara's six-flat. In midsummer, Sosa belted a homer onto the open second-floor deck of a little pink-sided house to the east. For the rest of that season, there was a sign on that porch with a big red bull's eye and the words "Sammy was here." The property was sold in 1998 to real-estate developers, who leveled the structure that off-season and raised a three-story orange brick building in its place. The same fate befell a yellow-sided home to the west. Mark Schlenker, who's now 45, bought that house for $385,000 in September 1998. He finished construction of "Brixen Ivy" at 1044 Waveland a couple months ahead of what originally was named "Skybox on Waveland" to the east of Landlady Lara's at 1038 Waveland. That building changed ownership in 2004 for $1 million, becoming the third rooftop business in the Purcells' "Beyond the Ivy" group. The Purcells acquired another property just west of Brixen Ivy at 1048 Waveland for $2 million in October 2000. Its gabled roof had been converted into a flat rooftop ready for staggered rows of seating in 1996.

Schlenker, who lived in his building from 1999 to 2005, initially had a hot tub on the roof deck. But with the need to be reinstalled by union plumbers, have a lifeguard on duty, and have it pass inspections, it proved too much bother.

"I was the first one to buy a piece of land and design a [rooftop] building from the ground up, and that's what threw the city off, because they didn't know what to do," Schlenker said. "Usually, people build buildings, and they have commercial on the bottom and residential on the top. This was the first time that they'd ever come across anything that had commercial stuff on top and residence below.

"They said, 'Build a normal three-flat, but make the stairways commercial width, make them out of steel, have two exits, one in front, one in back, and make it really strong.' That's kind of what I did."

After graduating from suburban Niles West High School, the University of Illinois, and Georgetown Law School, Tom Gramatis scalped tickets during the Chicago Bulls' run to six NBA championships in the 1990s. In 2002 he purchased Murphy's original rooftop business at 3637 Sheffield for $2.5 million and eventually moved into the three-flat. Gramatis, who is 39, went to his first Cubs game in the mid-1970s, and an idea was planted. "I remember being with my dad and looking out in right field and noticing people up on the buildings," he said. "I wanted one of those. I thought it was cool, and it looked like a good business."

· · · ·

IN EARLY 2004 THE ROOFTOP OWNERS and the Cubs reached a settlement on a 20-year agreement calling for the owners to give the ballclub a share of their gross revenue (approximately 17 percent). Estimates at the time put that annual dollar amount as high as $1.5 million. In exchange, rooftop owners would be compensated if their views were compromised by the bleachers project. But the Cubs weren't interested in changing the Wrigleyville skyline, and their project reflected that by maintaining the bleachers' tapered look and the ability to take in the neighborhood view from the grandstands. "The rooftops are part of the cityscape," Mike Racke said. "It's part of what Wrigley Field's all about—the charm of the neighborhood and the view. The view from inside the park out is almost as good as from outside of the park in."

In April 2005 the Chicago City Council signed off on the Cubs' bleachers expansion plan, which would add 1,800 seats and improve amenities in the outfield concourse by the following Opening Day. The city also approved the Cubs' plan to construct a five-story "triangle building" that would include parking, retail shops, office space, and an improved home clubhouse on a parcel of land bordering the western wall of the ballpark to the corner of Waveland and Clark.

A year later, Chapter 4-388 of the Municipal Code of Chicago was passed, concerning the "rooftops in the Wrigley Field adjacent area." For the first time, harmony existed among the Cubs, their enterprising neighbors, and the city. Meanwhile, the Cubs drew 3 million fans for the first time in 2004 and started a waiting list for season tickets that four years later has grown to include 95,000 names. Wrigleyville was booming, and a new wave of development began.

Many of the rooftop owners built up since the new ordinance raised their maximum height limit from 61 feet to 69 feet above grade. Relevant to any rooftop commercialism on properties west of the alley between Addison and Waveland and south of the alley between Sheffield and Seminary, the ordinance also created licensing ($500 per year), an amusement tax, occupancy limitations of 100 (up to 200 for clubs with a roof level exceeding 1,600 square feet), and specific safety code requirements such as steel-frame, concrete-interior shells, and wide metal staircases.

After the 2007 season, the three owners of 3639 Sheffield tore their building completely down, except for the front façade, and rebuilt. Gramatis did the same with the Ivy League Baseball Club next door.

"Your choice was to either stay the way it was and just kind of run the operation, or if you're going to do anything you have to do this major renovation, which we did, where you basically just gut the building and take all the wood out. So it's a huge investment to do that," said Jim Lourgos, a real-estate attorney who estimated their costs to redo 3639 Sheffield at close to $4 million. "That's the decision every rooftop owner is facing now....Once you do something and it hits this trigger point, you then have to do everything."

The Racke boys are in the middle of a $2.5 million renovation that widened the interior staircase, and will convert the first floor into a greeting area and the second floor into a cigar bar. The Purcells, who converted an apartment into a third-floor lounge and built new washrooms on the roof when they bought their first building at 1010 Waveland in 2000, expanded the lounge and rebuilt the rooftop bleachers in 2007. Gramatis negotiated a lease with a building owner to run another rooftop operation on a wide nine-apartment walkup building at 3621 Sheffield (where Willy B eventually moved). His cousin, Lee Gramatis, helped run that business as well as Ivy League until they split in 2007. Lee took over the lease in 2008 on the 3621 location, renamed Wrigley Done Right.

For the first few years I lived in Wrigleyville, my pregame routine included a stop at a folding table set up in the parking lot immediately south of that building for snacks and small talk with a kindly old man we came to call "Jerry the Peanut Guy." But the ecosystem was changing, and only the strongest plankton survived. Tom Gramatis fronted a group that purchased that parking lot in 2006. The presence of Jerry the Peanut Guy was replaced with construction crews in 2007. By Opening Day 2008, the second of Gramatis' twin rooftop buildings would be ready to open, bringing the total of rooftops entertaining for Cubs games to 16, although two of them were closed for renovation. *Crain's Chicago Business* estimated the rooftops' collective revenue from 2000 at $7 million, and the Cubs put that number at $10 million in one report two years later. Rooftop owners reported a 20 percent increase in revenue in 2004, the first year of the agreement with the Cubs, and in 2006, *Crain's* reported their collective revenue at $17 million. When the Cubs filed a lawsuit in 2002, they estimated the rooftops attendance totals at 1,690 per game. Today, in addition to the capacity crowd of 41,160 that can witness a game across the streets, the rooftops can accommodate nearly 2,500 fans.

The final tally on Gramatis' concrete castles was $15 million, including the property. Both rooftops serve champagne, have carving stations, and feature tiered pricing that limits access to night-club-like third-floor lounges to its highest-paying customers. "I spent $600,000 just on the build-out of that room," Gramatis said of the lounge at 3617 Sheffield. "I generate the most money of all the rooftops, and I sort of innovated a little bit more than some of the other guys did, the way I priced it, the way I run it."

That included kegs in the basement piping beer up to the rooftop. To anyone who's carried case after case of suds up multiple flights

RONNIE "WOO"

Some Chicagoans spend their summers playing volleyball and sunning on the beaches; some join cycling groups and convoy up and down the 18-mile bike path on the lakefront; some spend their weekends at the numerous neighborhood street fairs. And then there are the regulars at Wrigley Field. Like him or not, Ronnie "Woo-Woo" Wickers probably sticks out the most. A staple around Wrigleyville for decades, he roams Lakeview on game days wearing a full Cubs uniform, whooping in his trademark "Cubs! Woo! Cubs! Woo!" cheer. First-time visitors start wooing right along, while season-ticket holders and ballpark workers cringe and turn a glaring eye. Sometimes he'll ride his Pee Wee Herman–looking red Cruiser bike with 38-inch wheels around the stadium, waving to anyone and everyone.

"I get on a lot of people's nerves. I make a lot of noise, but it's all in fun," he said. "They say, 'Ronnie, turn it down.' I just do it because I want the Cubs to win, and I know they can hear me. I don't get paid, but I feel like I'm part of the team."

Born premature, Ronnie spent the first few months of his life in a South Side hospital incubator. Today, the 66-year-old black man is a retired custodian, living off social security in a nearby retirement community. His grandmother took him to his first Cubs game in 1949. He was seven years old, and his favorite player, Jackie Robinson, was in town. Ronnie would always come when the Cubs played the Dodgers, and Jackie would sign autographs for him and his twin brother on his way into the park. Ronnie shows off the Legend wristwatch that Negro Leagues star and former Cubs coach Buck O'Neil gave to him off his own arm. While Woo-Woo may have followed his African American heroes at first, his love of all things Cubs came to transcend all boundaries.

Then in 1984 he came home and found his girlfriend dead. "I just left," he said. Ronnie Woo was homeless off and on for six years. He used to sleep in the stairways of the Palmer House Hotel and in a booth at the restaurant where he delivered pizzas. "God and the Cubs kept me going."   ┄┄┄⟩

Having a few friends didn't hurt, either. Today, Ronnie gets taken care of with tickets and a hot dog all the time. One guy even saves a guest room in Arizona for spring training every March. A few years back, friends pooled their money to get him a set of dentures. It's a prime example of a generous Wrigley fan culture, but Ronnie Woo is hardly the only ballpark regular.

of stairs—like Willy B when he worked on our old building one summer—this is a welcome improvement.

Elsewhere in the neighborhood, one developer who had bought up real estate on the south side of Addison between Clark and Sheffield was proposing to build a 105-foot, nine-story building on a footprint of 94,000 square feet that would include apartments, hotel rooms, a health club, retail space, and parking. His initial plan and a revision both were rejected by the neighborhood, which the Cubs learned in the 1980s could be a strong and organized entity. The proposal to add lights wasn't unanimously welcomed by any stretch. The Citizens United for Baseball in the Sunshine (CUBS) organized and fought hard against it, with their yellow signs stating their "No Lights!" stance posted in many Wrigleyville windows.

When the Cubs first announced their bleachers renovation plan, neighborhood groups again mobilized. So Tribune Co. made Crane Kenney its principal executive in charge of Cubs operations in 2003 at a time when they were negotiating an increase in night games in addition to the rooftop partnership, and bleachers expansion. He attended his first community meeting at LeMoyne School just east of the ballpark on Waveland.

"What I came away with was the neighborhood really didn't like us," Kenney said. "We had a really ineffective community outreach program."

In May 2004 Kenney appointed Michael Lufrano general counsel of the club. Lufrano, 43, grew up in Lakeview, two blocks north of Belmont Avenue between Broadway Street and Lake Shore Drive, and remembers spending his birthdays at Wrigley Field every year. After graduating from Harvard Law School, he worked on Bill Clinton's presidential campaign, and from 1993 to 1995 did "presidential advance," mapping out strategy and logistics of the commander-in-chief's busy travel schedule. He returned home in the mid-1990s and joined Tribune Co.'s law department in 1997. With Lufrano massaging through issues the community had with the effect Cubs games had on parking, behavior, littering, and traffic congestion, relationships improved.

"This is my community; this is where I grew up," Lufrano said. "I don't think you can tell the story of Wrigleyville without talking about the history, and I don't think you can understand some of the people who are here without knowing where they came from, and what it was like here 10 years ago, 20 years ago, 30 years ago. The neighborhood's radically different now than it was when I was growing up.

"The neighborhood's different west of Clark than east of Clark Street, too. West of Clark, you've got people who are building $2 million homes. I assume that means they're going to stay in the community a long time," he added. "It's a little more transient east than it is west."

For his part, Kenney, 45, has taken note of the Red Sox's recent success. Born in Quincy, Massachusetts, just across the Neponset River from Boston, he learned to do long division by calculating the batting averages of his favorite Red Sox players.

Kenney compares the Red Sox closely with the Cubs. Both are storied ballclubs that play in historic venues, and harvested tremendous nationwide fan bases during long championships droughts. Boston ended its wait due in no small part to the approach John Henry and Tom Werner took after they purchased the franchise in 2002. Under the direction of President Larry Lucchino, the Red Sox increased sponsorship revenue by more than 380 percent and premium licensing revenue by 590 percent. A February 2008 newspaper article reported that $100 million had been poured into Fenway Park since 2002.

"They put some substantial money into the stadium to create some club space, new seating on the [Green] Monster, like we did with our bleachers, and improve the quality of the park experience inside. All of their suites were rebuilt," Kenney said. "As a result, they generate significantly more money inside their ballpark than we do, even though we're in a larger market....They've capitalized on the character and the charm of Fenway, which is similar to Wrigley, in a way that we haven't done here. That's basically why I'm in my job—to make sure that happens."

The construction of the triangle building west of the stadium would enable the Cubs to do a lot of that and more. The organization has the second-smallest front-office staff in baseball, but Wrigley has limited space to add to its 90 full-time employees. The home clubhouse is one of the smallest in the league, and there is no access to a batting cage while a game is in progress. A Cubs player preparing to pinch hit has to bat off a tee into a net that's dropped down from the ceiling of the clubhouse.

Between the triangle building and the ballpark, the ballclub could build an enclosed street-level, tree-lined, cobblestone walkway that could provide fan amenities for use before, during, and after ballgames.

Kenney has gone so far as to suggest the Cubs might have to consider playing a season at the White Sox's U.S. Cellular Field or another site so that Wrigley's grandstands and upper deck could be completely torn down and rebuilt. But when it was announced on Opening Day 2007 that billionaire real-estate mogul Sam Zell would take over Tribune Co. in an $8.2 billion sale, the Cubs were put on the market in order for Zell to finance some of the debt to take the media conglomerate private. Although Kenney and general manager Jim Hendry still had the wiggle room to add payroll and commit to long-term player contracts, construction of the triangle building and any major capital projects were put on hold. The future plans of Wrigley would certainly weigh on offers for the team and ballpark, which would be coming in as the 2008 season progressed.

· · · ·

IN THE 1960S BLEACHERS FANS who attended games every day wore yellow hard hats, sang amusing limericks, and raced along the top of the outfield wall, necessitating the pitched baskets that now catch home-run balls—and occasionally, people. The unique culture inspired a 1977 play called *Bleacher Bums*, conceived by Joe Mantegna and put on by Chicago's Organic Theater Company.

Fans are still out there in the bleachers today, only they are hardly bums. They are lawyers, doctors, nurses, salespeople, teachers, and other professional types. They arrange their schedules to be at as many games as possible. Some make all 81; others might miss a handful. Many have season tickets, but they still have to arrive early to reserve their favorite seats. With capacity for 4,960 in the bleachers, Wrigley by far has the most general-admission seats in baseball, creating a unique culture of fans who become family to one another. "If there's one place you don't mind being two hours before the game, it's Wrigley Field," one of them told me.

The Cubs have a season-ticket base of 15,000 and another 8,000 on a partial plan, many of them having shared their seats and experiences with friends since as far back as the 1960s, and having passed tickets down from generation to generation.

Without a doubt, Cubs fans are the biggest enigma in sports. Why keep coming back, year after year, for more heartbreak? It's like taking back a lover who's betrayed you. The relationship cycles through the seasons of hope in the spring, love in the summer, heartache in autumn, and forgiveness in the winter.

Jack Brickhouse, legendary Cubs announcer from 1940 to 1981, once said in jest, "Any team can have a bad century." Yet, as 2008 opened, the Cubs were embarking on that very truth. Their last World Series championship came in 1908, just before William Howard Taft was elected the 27th president of the United States. Eight years later, Taft's cousin would sell the Cubs to Weeghman and a group of investors who would move them to the North Side of Chicago.

The Chicago National League Ball Club Inc. won six National League championships in the 1800s before there was a World Series and appeared in three of the first five fall classics, winning two. Most people have heard of the famed "Billy Goat Curse," but that only dates back to 1945, when tavern owner Billy Sianis brought his pet goat to Wrigley for the World Series. (Why anyone would want to bring a goat to such an event is way beyond me.) The goat was denied entry, and Sianis supposedly said, "Them Cubs, they aren't gonna win no more." At that time, they had appeared in 10 fall classics; only the Yankees (14) and Giants (12) had been to more, and the Dodgers, Phillies, and St. Louis Browns (today's Orioles) never had won a championship. Through 2007 the expansion Astros, Padres, Pilots/Brewers, and Rockies never had won a World Series, and the Expos/Nationals, Senators/Rangers, Mariners, and Rays never even had been to one—a collective 266 seasons of futility.

Despite years of heartbreak, ever-optimistic Cubs fans fill the seats at Wrigley Field season after season. *Steve Green photo courtesy Chicago Cubs*

So why does everyone say it's the Cubs who are cursed? It's because our only defense is falling back on a history our grandparents don't even remember. And yet the fan base grows boundlessly each year, spreading literally into the neighborhood skies and figuratively across the globe. As editor of *Vine Line*, it amazed me how far our subscribers were spread—Japan, Germany, South Africa. Everyone seems to be RSVPing for a party we know is coming soon.

Just when did the invitations go out? Was it 2003, five outs away? Cubs fans seemed to turn a corner with that season, culminating in the team winning its first postseason series since 1908. A feeling of entitlement permeated, and fans started doing something rarely heard at the "Friendly" Confines. They booed their own. The Red Sox ended an 86-year championship drought in 2004, and the White Sox snapped their 88-year dry spell in 2005, serving to intensify the "when's our turn?" sentiment.

·   ·   ·   ·

EARLY IN HIS TENURE AS team president, Andy MacPhail came to an epiphany of the burden that comes with running the Cubs. Anyone who ever sat in his chair—or came aboard as a general manager, field manager, or even a player, for that matter—could justifiably claim no responsibility for the years of failure that preceded them. And many do just that when they become a Cub. But somewhere along the way, they inherit the losing legacy like a parrot or a set of luggage.

When MacPhail resigned following a dismal 2006 season, John McDonough moved up from his chief marketing post to become president and promised, "The Cubs are going to win the World Series" over and over at his introductory press conference. At the Cubs Convention that winter and in the 2007 marketing campaign, McDonough made the blue *W* a focal point. Per Wrigley tradition, following a victory a white flag with a blue *W* flies over the center-field scoreboard like a majestic whale breaching the sea. Fans seemed to run with the idea in 2007, with more and more waving W flags as the Cubs shook hands on the mound after the final out.

But there's another side to that culture—a blue flag with a white *L* that flies after a loss. Nowhere are fans more uneasy, wondering what oddity will befall their team next. Blame gets passed around sensationally and irresponsibly. It was the black cat that ran onto the field at Shea Stadium and cursed the 1969 Cubs, not the Miracle Mets' 38–11 finish. It was Steve Bartman's "fan interference" on that foul ball in the NLCS that caused the 2003 Cubs' unraveling, not Alex Gonzalez botching that potential inning-ending double-play grounder moments later.

Lou Piniella, a man with a winning résumé, even sensed the pessimistic feelings in the Chicago media. "They tend to be a little bit apprehensive....They sort of hope for the best but expect the worst," he told me during an interview midway through his first season as Cubs manager. "This is a much tougher job than what I thought coming in here. I'll be honest with you, it's a little more daunting. I don't know why—the high profile of this team or the expectations on this team or the fact that they haven't won in such a long time. It sort of surprised me a little bit."

During his third week on the job, Piniella witnessed perhaps his first couple of "Cubbie occurrences," a term he would later coin. During a 2–1 loss to St. Louis at Wrigley Field that dropped the Cubs to 6–10, Henry Blanco popped up a bunt, and the ball nearly went down his shirt in a bizarre play that saw Cards catcher Yadier Molina seem to catch the ball and Blanco's head all at once. Ruled a Cardinals triple play initially, Piniella won that argument with the umpiring crew. But in the ninth inning, Ronny Cedeno was tagged out when he tried to steal on a pitch and overslid second base—despite the fact that the pitch was ball four, automatically advancing Cedeno to second! Crankshaft was working on a story for me the next day when he overheard Piniella talking with Ron Santo on the field during batting practice. Santo anchored third base for the Cubs from 1960 to 1973 and has been the radio color commentator since 1990.

"I've been around the game long enough," Piniella told Santo. "Sometimes things happen, and you go, 'God damn!' But here, things happen and you go, 'GOD DAMN!'" Dan, standing next to Hall of Fame Cub Billy Williams, nudged him and whispered, "He's learning!"

Like any Cubs fan, I know the score. I know about the goat and the cat and the fan in the hat. But I fixate on the photos of Bartman and see at least a dozen other hands reaching for that foul ball. Bartman making contact was the only thing separating his infamy from their obscurity. It's shameful to place blame on results and not intent, but I'm afraid the only thing that will liberate Bartman, black felines, and cloven-hoofed mammals is a Cubs championship.

It's not that I believe in curses, because I don't. I believe in bad baseball. From 1947 through 1966, the Cubs had only one plus-.500 season, and from 1973 through 1992, only two more. A corner has been turned since then, and they've been knocking on the door. Sooner or later, serendipity has to answer. I was about to turn 45, and my job had sort of run its course with the Cubs. No room to move up, and I'd gotten what I was going to get out of my time and experience. My tools have always been words, and baseball was merely what I used to screw, hammer, and tighten them. I had come to a fork, and rolling the dice on poetic fate, I gave notice to the Cubs that I would be leaving my job at the end of March, set on telling the best story ever told.

The Roman numeral for 100, after all, is the letter C.

2

CONSTRUCTION SEASON

THERE ARE TWO SEASONS in Wrigleyville: baseball season and construction season. Working through the winter in the Cubs' front offices—one floor up from the concourse, tucked under the terrace reserved seats behind home plate—is sometimes like working in a dentist's office. The jackhammers and heavy machinery reverberate in your head and shake the walls.

It's been the same in recent years with the rooftop buildings across the street. Renovations, rehabilitations, and reconstructions start in October, and in some cases extend into the season. The second building north of Waveland on the west side of Kenmore, where late-night talk show host Conan O'Brien once lived with comedian Jeff Garlin during Garlin's Second City salad days, was torn down shortly after we moved in. Across the alley from our backyard, a new brick three-flat was largely completed by Opening Day.

In January 2008 the Ivy League Baseball Club and the 3639 Wrigley Rooftop, neighboring businesses on Sheffield Avenue, had construction fences surrounding their completely gutted structures. Workers at Beyond the Ivy, next door to Crankshaft and me, made a daily habit of waking us, even on Saturdays. On the first business day of the year, I crossed Waveland Avenue and entered Gate K on my way to work. In a rare quiet moment, I could hear my footsteps echo in the ballpark concourse. It's a pretty cool sound—*cool* being the operative word when it's 7 degrees. They say Wrigley's concourse in the winter is the coldest place on earth, and I wouldn't argue.

A forklift sped past, and workmen bundled in layers continued the task of making the 94-year-old ballpark the modern marvel that it is. "Hey, Paulie, ya got a one-inch drill bit?" one asked another.

Installation of the new playing field had been completed before the end of 2007. White Sox head groundskeeper Roger Bossard designed it. That may sound blasphemous to Cubs fans, but "the Sodfather" counts Fenway Park and Busch Stadium among 19 major league stadiums using his patented system. Look what it did for the Red Sox, Cardinals, and White Sox. Plus, the flatter surface and modern drainage would prevent rainouts and injuries. There were four feet more of outfield warning track that extended along the brick grandstand walls where foul lines butt up against tapered pads. If only it had been there five years earlier, Bartman would've heard Moises Alou coming and ducked out of the way.

I took a quick peek at the new field. Blanketed by snow, it seemed as if it might sag or even collapse. I had to remind myself it was built on solid ground, and maybe without the warped "crown," our story's heroes would start playing like kings (as they did in 1908).

The daily newspaper clippings assembled by media relations interns reported that we also were embarking on the centennials of the first Mother's Day, the first passenger to take flight in an airplane, the first horror movie—*Dr. Jekyll and Mr. Hyde*, which opened in Chicago—and the founding of General Motors.

Hot topics in the news included the loathsome idea of selling naming rights to Wrigley Field, and Chicago Mayor Richard M. Daley backpedaling on his ardent opposition of a proposal to have the state-run Illinois Sports Facilities Authority (ISFA) purchase and renovate the historic ballpark. Sam Zell, who in December finalized an $8.2 billion deal to purchase Tribune Co. and take it private, came up with the proposition. Reportedly, he would receive a huge up-front payment for Wrigley, and the ISFA would issue tax-exempt, long-term bonds at a reduced interest rate that would be retired by a 30-year-lease commitment from the team's new owner.

Zell's personal fortune was estimated by *Forbes* magazine at $5 billion in 2007, and he has a knack for acquiring depressed assets just before they turn around. They don't call him "grave dancer" for no reason. While taking in a game with Cubs chairman Crane Kenney late in the 2007 season, he asked why Tribune Co. didn't have the foresight to purchase any of the rooftop buildings across the street. "There's no such thing as missed opportunity," Zell told him. "There's only a price."

•   •   •   •

THE CUBS CONTINUED to fill the business section in January, as the recent exodus of veteran front-office leadership continued. Jay Blunk resigned as senior vice president of marketing to join John McDonough, his former boss, who'd become president of the NHL's Chicago Blackhawks in November. The two had been around for every Cubs Convention since they helped conceive and develop the winter gala. The January fan fest would seem odd without them.

So it was good that the Cubs Caravan offered some levity, although it didn't seem so at the time for those involved. The Caravan is a traveling road show that precedes the convention. Players, coaches, broadcasters, and front-office staff visit area schools, hospitals, and communities on a goodwill mission that raises money for charities and encourages children to read, among other things.

On the way back to Chicago, one of the buses ran out of fuel 10 feet from a gas pump. "It was right there; we just couldn't get to it," bench coach Alan Trammell said. "We got out and pushed. There was ice and everything there, but even on an 80-degree summer day we wouldn't have been able to budge it."

Another bus was dispatched to drive them back to the Hilton Chicago, where WGN Radio play-by-play man Pat Hughes kicked off the convention the following evening as emcee of opening ceremonies. "It's 20 degrees outside," Hughes said. "Just perfect for Opening Day!"

Fortunately, the love of thousands of fans was heartwarming inside the hotel's Grand Ballroom. A chorus of "LOOUU" echoed when manager Lou Piniella emerged on a balcony overlooking a sea of fans below. All the Cubs legends were introduced—Ernie Banks, Billy Williams, Fergie Jenkins, Ryne Sandberg, Ron Santo, and on and on. On the balcony, 1960s–1970s-era second baseman Glenn Beckert took a cell phone call and cupped his hand over his ear in a fruitless attempt to listen. TV announcer Len Kasper remarked to me, "This is my fourth [convention], and this is the most juiced I've seen it."

Introductions complete, shortstop Ryan Theriot stepped to the podium to introduce Dustin Eglseder. The young man from Iowa who'd won the *American Idol*–like competition to conduct the seventh-inning stretch on the final day of the 2007 regular season was back to do so again. Only this time, Eglseder, who was fighting bone cancer, was without his right arm. "Thank you for inspiring us," Theriot proclaimed to Eglseder.

A one!...A two!...A three!...

Coming off a division title, the mood was in stark contrast to recent conventions. But front-office bosses had to answer tough fan questions about naming rights, the sale of the team and ballpark, the future of the multipurpose triangle building proposed for construction adjacent to Wrigley's western wall, and any final player personnel moves that might be forthcoming. Kenney explained to one ballroom full of fans how the payroll had started at $85 million when he became chairman five years earlier and had gone north since. Sitting alongside Kenney, a wide-grinning Piniella cut in. "Let's get a little further north," Piniella said, and the room exploded. Next, "Sweet Lou" boldly stated the team's goal was a fast start and 92–93 total wins.

Where players past and present are concerned, the fan fest is mostly a love-in. Mark DeRosa, a second baseman whose three-year, $13 million free-agent signing raised eyebrows a year earlier, received huge applause. General manager Jim Hendry revealed that Kerry Wood turned down multiyear contracts for more money from other teams in order to return for his 11th season as a Cub. "Pay me what you think is fair," Woody told Hendry. Absent to prepare for the birth of his second child, Kid K received a huge ovation.

Things sped up around Wrigley over the next month. On February 5 at 8:30 AM, an 18-wheel tractor-trailer was parked outside Gate K. Wearing layers of sweatshirts and jackets, full-timers from the ground crew loaded the team's essentials for spring training.

Dustin Eglseder leads Cubs Conventioneers in singing "Take Me Out to the Ball Game." *Steve Green photo courtesy Chicago Cubs*

"This is like the official bell ringing," said head groundskeeper Roger Baird with his usual friendly smile.

Pitchers and catchers would be reporting eight days later, so when I saw Ted Lilly at the Hilton Chicago accepting an award at a Comcast banquet on February 11, I wondered how he logistically was going to make it on time. Lilly explained he was flying back to Sacramento, California, the next morning, where he'd load his truck and drive the 10-hour trip to Mesa, Arizona, with his agent.

Relief pitcher Scott Eyre already was on his way. Recruiting rookies Sean Gallagher and Nate Spears as passengers, Eyre made the drive from his home in Sarasota, Florida, in a 40-foot motor home. The RV had four slide-outs, three televisions, and a shower, which Gallagher discovered was difficult to use in traffic. With assurances he wouldn't be throwing any wild parties, Eyre was allowed to park his springtime home in a trailer park for people age 55 and older.

There already had been enough misbehaving in Mesa. A day before report day, a local man was arrested and charged with stealing more than $10,000 from several locations, including three farmhands' lockers while they were working outside at the Cubs' year-round training complex at Fitch Park.

Moods took a positive turn quickly. On Valentine's Day, pitcher Ryan Dempster was declaring his love. One of the more outgoing and fun-loving personalities in the clubhouse, the red-goateed Canadian prepared all winter to make the switch from the bullpen to the rotation. Having come to camp in the best shape of his life, he bumped into Piniella on his way to run up nearby 2,700-foot Camelback Mountain. Piniella cracked he'd join him—in his truck. "Demp"'s confidence extended to his teammates, too. He flatly told reporters the Cubs would win the World Series.

In a season in which the 100-year anniversary would be thrown at them time and time again, was he crazy?

"I think it's funny when people make predictions or they say things, and people are like, 'Oh, how can you say that?'" Dempster responded when reminded that ace Carlos Zambrano had guaranteed the same thing the previous spring and was roasted for it in the press. "You believe it. You really do. Enough of all the...the curse this, the curse that, the goat, the black cat, or the 100 years. Maybe we need some more guys saying that. Honestly, it's like anything—if you believe it you can achieve it. I know it's a corny saying, but it's true." The next day, "Madam Cleo" was added to the nameplate above his locker, a ribbing reference to the tarot card reader.

Piniella didn't think his pitcher was off his rubber. With two World Series rings as a player with the Yankees and one as manager of the Reds, he knew a thing or two about credence. In his second year of camp, familiar now with the personalities of his main weapons and how to play them, the skipper was just as self-assured. "There's swagger here, there really is," Piniella said.

"Swagger is confidence. That's all it is. It's a confidence that we're good, and we intend on playing good. That's all it is. There's swagger in this camp. They have to back it up on the field, but these kids feel good about themselves."

• • • •

WHILE FANS ACROSS the country toasted Budweisers on February 18 to remember broadcast legend Harry Caray on the 10th anniversary of his death, position players filtered into camp in Arizona. It was a different-looking Cubs camp, with rookie Kevin Hart wearing the No. 22 that used to have the name "PRIOR" stitched above.

There was a getting-to-know-you period that extended to media and front-office staff, who were getting to know an additional press corps from Japan, along with interpreters, and an outfielder named Kosuke Fukudome. It would have beeen fun to hear Harry Caray try to enunciate this one: *Koo-zook Fooka...Foo-quad...frick-a-do...oh, the hell with it!* (For the record, it's pronounced *KOH-skay foo-koo-DOUGH-may*.) The 10th Japanese position player to sign a major league contract was the first to do so with the Cubs, a team that hadn't been to a World Series since a month after V-J Day.

Fukudome batted .305 with 192 home runs and 647 RBIs in nine seasons with the Chunichi Dragons, capturing Central League Most Valuable Player honors in 2006. He signed a four-year $48 million contract in December and appeared in Wrigley's Stadium Club with two members of the Japanese consulate six days before Christmas to meet the Chicago press corps. Hendry hoisted a Cubs jersey over Fukudome's shoulders for the first time, and he lowered his head to button the blue pinstripes. Fukudome, seeming to perceive a gaffe in his posture, snapped erect and smiled, confident.

"Hi. My name is Kosuke Fukudome," he said through an interpreter. "I'm very happy to sign my first major league contract and play with this historic team. I'm also looking forward to playing in such a historic ballpark with such ecstatic fans." Fukudome and his wife, Kazue, had welcomed their first son three days before his visit. They named him Hayato, a combination of the Japanese words for "windy" and "number one." The name was derived from Chicago's nickname ("Windy City") and Fukudome's new uniform number.

At the onset of spring training, Piniella was asked for his initial impressions of his new right fielder: "I love the fact he took the No. 1 on his back," he responded. "That tells me a lot about the individual. I don't think a player takes No. 1 if he has doubts."

On the day Fukudome arrived, Zambrano wore a blue headband and Fukudome's tight-fitting No. 1 jersey, teasing his next-door locker mate that "I'm No. 1 here." Stacks of seven dozen baseballs were left next to each player's chair to sign for charitable and promotional use. When "Big Z" wasn't looking, Fukudome pushed his tower over one locker. The rookie walked away, and the Venezuelan veteran returned, grinned, and moved both stacks to Fukudome's locker. Big Z later had a Japanese reporter write Zambrano in Japanese script on the back of his spikes.

First baseman Derrek Lee, whose father played and scouted in Japan, and outfielder Alfonso Soriano, who signed with the Yankees out of the Japanese minor leagues, tried speaking to Fukudome in his native tongue. Yoshi Nakazawa, a trainer with Fukudome's

Fans line up around the block to get to the ticket windows (inset) on the first day of sales.
Steve Green photo courtesy Chicago Cubs

old team in Japan who was hired by the Cubs, cooked Japanese dishes. A six-page cheat sheet of Japanese words was circulated. His new teammates clearly were trying to make Fukudome feel at home and ease the pressure of close to 30 reporters and photographers following his every move. The extra press prompted Piniella to compare the first full-squad workout to Opening Day.

The enthusiasm was mirrored in Chicago, where fans lined up for the first day of ticket sales. The Cubs sold 516,957 tickets that day. It didn't break Major League Baseball's record, which the Cubs set in 2004 and broke in 2006, with 597,571 tickets sold. But the organization continued to set the bar in single-day ticket sales. Three days later, the Cubs announced plans to auction off three rows of 71 season tickets in a new section abutting the Cubs bullpen. It was sponsored by the Chicago Board Options Exchange, whose somewhat innocuous CBOE, painted in the same gold as the outfield distance markers, would adorn the brick wall in front of the section. The auction closed March 13 with bids as high as $400 per seat per game. "I've been wanting to auction seats off for a long time, in part to raise the money, but also to educate ourselves on what's the market value of our tickets," Kenney said.

The organization also was trying to grasp the value of naming rights. Considering the Mets' 20-year, $400 million deal with Citigroup for their new stadium, Zell contemplated renaming the whale—for a price.

The plankton got busy producing a variety of T-shirts that would become prevalent around the ballpark all summer, like "Keep it Wrigley" and "It's Called Wrigleyville for a Reason." An ESPN.com poll named Wrigley hands down over Lambeau Field and Fenway Park as the most untouchable name in sports venues. Defiantly, Zell told CNBC, "The idea of a debate occurring over what I should do with my asset leaves me somewhat questioning the integrity of the debate."

• • • •

THE LAST PLAYER TO ARRIVE in Mesa was third baseman Aramis Ramirez, the team's RBI leader in three of the previous four seasons. "Rammy" reported in tremendous shape, hopeful that trimming

10–12 pounds would save his legs from nagging injuries of past seasons.

He adeptly disarmed the media from turning him into the next Michael Vick. Ramirez had been featured prominently in a Dominican Republic cockfighting magazine, which reported that he raises roosters to compete in a sport that is legal in Ramirez's native country. "I'm not even going to let you finish that question," he said when the topic was broached. "I'm not going to talk about that. That's personal. That's a different culture down there."

Piniella addressed the team when it was fully assembled for the first time on February 20. He told them not to concern themselves with the constant questions about the 100-year anniversary. His message was simple: don't put that pressure on yourselves; let this team stand on its own merit.

"What has happened in the last 99 years? Hell, I've only been here one, so I'll take responsibility for only one," Piniella said.

Hendry, sitting next to him at the spring's first news conference, quickly chimed in. "I'm good for five [years]."

Ernie Banks was there for 19 of them but always has been allowed more condolence than accountability for never getting to a World Series. The 1957 and '58 NL MVP and the Cubs' all-time leader in games, at-bats, total bases, and extra-base hits, "Mr. Cub" has been the best ambassador a team or a sport could ever want. Every now and then, he drops in on the front office to take us into his world.

In his twilight years, Ernie gets around slower, the result of many knee surgeries. But his jovial spirit is boundless. He has his own way of looking at life, and I rather fancy seeing it through his eyes. I learned from years of getting to know Ernie that he is much more comfortable talking about you. He's modest about his own amazing path through bigotry to the National Baseball Hall of Fame. So he tends to dictate the conversation, and his thoughts are all over the place: "Are you married yet?" "I think they should rename Wrigley the Hanging Gardens of Babylon." "Mr. Wrigley used to say the Cubs made money while going broke." Your brain feels like ol' Ern reached in there and scrambled it, but you have this amazingly refreshed sensation.

On February 28, while our story's heroes were playing their Cactus League opener in Arizona, Ernie stopped by Wrigley after receiving an award as African American of the Year from Jesse Jackson that afternoon. Dressed to the nines and wearing a rose boutonnière, Mr. Cub held court in the community relations office.

Outside, we took a photograph of him standing on a peninsula in the construction area where his statue would be unveiled on Opening Day. He was hamming it up with his black fedora like he was Cab Calloway. Traffic nearly stopped.

When pressed about his feelings about the statue, he became humble. He'd talked to friends like Stan Musial and Hank Aaron about having their effigies erected at ballparks in St. Louis, Milwaukee, and Atlanta. Statues, Ernie said, were for soldiers, poets, and dictators...guys named Plato and Socrates.

"But you're *Mr. Cub*," I said. "Don't you think you should have a statue here where the *Cubs* play?"

He didn't answer. Ernie once told me the Cubs didn't need to spend the money; he'd stand there himself. Then he froze mime-like in a pose. I half believed him. He was fixated on how much the statue cost and kept asking if I knew.

"Ernie, I don't have my hands on the purse strings around here," I said.

We ran into VP of business operations Mark McGuire a moment later. Surely, he would have that information. But Mark cleverly skirted the question by saying he hadn't gotten the bill yet.

The following Monday morning, Ernie wore his own custom-made trading vest in the Cubs' red-and-blue colors when he rang the opening bell for trading at the CBOE.

• • • •

THE JULY 15 ALL-STAR GAME in the final year of Yankee Stadium, the House that Ruth Built, seemed a long way off. Snowstorms and arctic freezes were tag-teaming Chicago in one of the most brutal winters in memory. Yet, Opening Day was only a month away.

On March 5, McDonough, the former Cubs president, and NHL Commissioner Gary Bettman held a press conference about the possibility of hosting a Chicago Blackhawks game at Wrigley Field in

Ernie Banks, "Mr. Cub," hams it up near the site where his statue would be erected. *Juan Alberto Castillo photo courtesy Chicago Cubs*

2009. Heck, with a few inches of ice from the shortstop area out to the outfield, why not strap on the skates right then and there?

Better yet, courier the ice down to Arizona. The athletic trainers could use it. Ramirez was sidelined with shoulder soreness. Relief pitcher Jose Ascanio was given a black eye in a scuffle with a would-be mugger outside a convenience store. Eyre had a cortisone shot for a bone spur in his elbow, Soriano fractured his right middle finger, and Daryle Ward strained a butt muscle.

Even coaches Trammell and Matt Sinatro were healing from knee surgeries, and longtime clubhouse man Yosh Kawano was hospitalized with cellulitis in his foot. And farmhand Casey McGehee complained of allergies to grass, of all things!

But nobody had a worse spring than DeRosa. First, he was asked continually about persistent rumors the Cubs were going to acquire Baltimore second baseman Brian Roberts and turn DeRosa into a super sub. Matters turned real serious in the first week of camp at Fitch Park. "DeRo" was taking grounders with other infielders when Theriot noticed he seemed to be gasping for air. DeRosa, who had a history of irregular heartbeats dating to his teenage years, merely was employing breathing techniques he had learned to control it. Nevertheless, feeling faint and weak, DeRosa left the field. After being examined by a team doctor and given an EKG, DeRosa was sitting upright on a stretcher when EMTs took him to a local hospital.

"I was scared and worried," Theriot said. "But he was fine throughout the whole thing. I know he was joking around inside right before he left."

"I don't think I was scared," DeRosa said. "[But] the looks on everyone's faces make you nervous."

DeRo spent a night in the hospital and was diagnosed with atrial dysrhythmia. Facing a decision, he flew back to Chicago two days after his 33rd birthday and had an hour-long procedure performed that uses electrical energy to destroy tissues in the heart that were causing rhythmic disturbances. After returning to camp and working back into the lineup, DeRosa fouled a ball off the cheek of teammate Alex Cintron, who was standing in the on-deck circle. With just five games under his belt, DeRosa was sent home with the flu later in the month. He returned two days later and was scratched from the lineup with sinusitis.

It didn't end there. While packing for the move north to Chicago, his wife had spilled water on a computer—fried. A rock skipped up, ricocheting off the windshield of her car—busted.

"It's going to be a good year," DeRosa said. "I'm getting it all out of the way."

Then there was the controversy over who would take over Dempster's role as closer and the verbal sparring between Piniella and one of his pitchers. The closer's job was a three-man race among second-year man Carlos Marmol, veteran Bob Howry, and Wood. The threesome and Piniella were asked about it daily.

MEDIUM AT LARGE

On the afternoon of March 3, the supernatural came to Wrigleyville as a former Cub was summoned back on the 11th anniversary of his death. Writer Dave Hoekstra organized a gathering at the Sheffield Hotel for a piece he was doing in the *Chicago Sun-Times*. Back in the day, the building at 3834 North Sheffield Avenue, a few relay throws north of Wrigley's bleachers entrance, was known as the Hotel Carlos. The name still is carved into the stone archway of the terra cotta entrance.

Cubs shortstop Billy Jurges was shot twice here by a jilted lover July 6, 1932, in an incident that helped inspire a scene in Bernard Malamud's baseball novel (and later Hollywood film) *The Natural*. Hoekstra brought out a medium named Rik Kristinat to channel Jurges into Room 509, a dank corner lodging where the shooting occurred.

With course salt-and-pepper hair and a bushy mustache, Kristinat, 52, is a sturdy Chicagoan who grew up in south suburban Tinley Park. His mother is a descendent of immigrants from Southern Italy. Kristinat spent lots of time with his grandparents, who lived in Chicago's famous Little Italy neighborhood. His grandfather taught him to love the Cubs. He followed his Lithuanian father into the occult. "I'm a mingling of my father's side, which was all spiritual, and my mother's side, which was all Cubs," Kristinat quipped.

My friend Mike Reischl, a Chicago cop and baseball historian, brought a short biography on Jurges and a bottle of gin. Jurges' lover, "Mike the Cop" told us, had blamed the shooting on "too much gin." We toasted with a cup of white gas, and Kristinat, who claimed he had no prior knowledge of the incident, turned his attention to Jurges. Sitting in a chair in the corner by a window, he rubbed a photograph of Jurges, who coincidently was born in 1908.

Kristinat closed his eyes and began describing how it happened. Jurges had gotten the woman a glass of water from the bathroom sink. She followed him, and the gun went off during a struggle at the adjacent door to the hallway. Kristinat held his left rib cage with his right hand and repeatedly clenched his left hand into a fist, which had ached all day. He asked if these were the locations of Jurges' wounds, which they were. There was another spirit in the room. "She's very ⤳

present here," he said of the assailant. "There wasn't love there, but there probably was a relationship."

Kristinat searched for her name. She wouldn't give it to him. He smelled Lily of the Valley, a perfume his grandmother wore. "I figure it was Lilly or it was Rose or Scarlet," he said, "because why would she give me Lilly of the Valley? That's why I'm assuming it was a floral name."

Arm hair stood up straight. Jurges' former inamorata's name was Violet Valli.

Questions turned to 1932. With Jurges recovering from the shooting, the Cubs acquired infielder Mark Koenig from the Yankees for the pennant run. Jurges and eventual Hall of Famer Billy Herman dissented on appropriating Koenig a full share of the team's World Series money, and the former Yankee had to settle for a half-share. It angered Koenig's former teammates, whom the Cubs met in the Series. Many believe Babe Ruth's renowned "called shot" in Game 3 was misinterpreted body language as the Bambino and Cubs players traded barbs.

Kristinat channeled Jurges' agitated explanation: Ruth had mocked the Cubs and was pointing at Jurges, who was playing shortstop that day, not at the center field bleachers. If only the Babe had been in this room on that fateful day.

"Billy is feeling bad about [slighting Koenig]. He's looking for redemption," Kristinat said. "That's what I do as a medium, I give them their redemption. Billy, you can move on. You're forgiven for taking Mark's money."

I asked Kristinat to get Jurges' thoughts about today's Wrigleyville. "When he was here it was a better neighborhood," Kristinat relayed. "It's starting to be the neighborhood he remembers again."

Then the 2008 Cubs came up. March was prognostication time. Would Cubs fans be embarking on a 100th wait 'til next year in six months?

Kristinat relayed Jurges' words: "We played for love, and that's why we got as far as we did. If they play for love, they'll be okay."

"I'm talking fast because he's talking to me," Kristinat continued. "He's really getting mad, and he wants them to win, too. By the All-Star Game, they'll start realizing they're going to be winning and playing for love."

Veteran starting pitcher Jason Marquis, upset with his uncommitted role, suggested he would "take my services elsewhere." Surprised when relayed those comments, Piniella charged: "He can go somewhere else right now if he wants. How's that?...I'm not pleased with that comment."

Piniella later apologized to Marquis, but he was growing impatient. By the time mid-March approached, the Cubs had lost nine of their first 13 Cactus League games. DeRosa missed the first 11 games, Ramirez was out the first eight, and Soriano missed a week. Felix Pie was sidelined with what was originally termed a "twisted testicle," giving baseball bloggers good fodder and male Cubs fans cause to snugly cross their legs. Pie, who was ahead of rookie Sam Fuld in the battle for the center-field job, had surgery March 10 to correct the problem.

"We don't have much longer," Piniella said. "We're way behind schedule. I like 60, 70 at-bats for everyday players, and we're not going to be able to do that. So we better get 50, 60."

Meanwhile, media reports began shooting holes into the proposed sale of Wrigley to the ISFA, even though former Illinois governor James Thompson, the chairman of the ISFA, said a proposal would be coming to the Cubs shortly. "We're continuing to talk with them, but the longer something goes on without a deal being reached, the less likely a deal is," Kenney admitted.

Kenney suggested if a government agency purchased the ballpark, the 2004 landmark designation bestowed on Wrigley should be relaxed. Among other things, landmarking applied to the famous red marquee at Clark and Addison, although Cubs executives believed the First Amendment gave them the right to change the words on the sign. Hence, the supposed legal grounds to rename the park to the highest bidder—in the minds of Tribune Co. suits, at least.

It almost seemed like an olive branch when complimentary gum holders and packs of Wrigley's brands arrived for every front-office employee one March day.

The *Sun-Times*, always eager to lob cannonballs across Michigan Avenue at Tribune Tower, had a contest with a $1,000 prize for the best video about Wrigley Field naming rights. *Chicago Tribune* intern Katie Hamilton punked the competition by winning the award with a video filmed in large part right in front of my apartment building with a soundtrack "twist" to Twisted Sister's 1980s hit song "We're Not Gonna Take It."

Things were on schedule on the other side of Waveland. Like an eyelid struggling to pry itself free from sleepers in the morning, message boards, lights, and all the other doohickeys at the ballpark started going off as electricians tested equipment.

The Cubs already had sold 2.95 million tickets and were well on their way to a fifth straight season of 3 million in attendance. Beer trucks started showing up with pallets and pallets of cans and kegs. A day later, the ice machines arrived.

On March 18, workers began putting brick pavers into what Cubs executives were starting to refer to as Marquee Plaza. By Opening Day, the area beneath Wrigley's famous red marquee at the corner of Clark and Addison streets would have a red-brick flooring with fans' messages and Mr. Cub's effigy looking over them like a proud papa bear.

As the Cubs collected for pregame stretching that afternoon in Arizona, Ramirez asked strength and conditioning coach Tim Buss what his car was doing on a ramp near the right-field corner of HoHoKam Park. "That's not my car," said Buss, who then did a double take. "Dude, that's my car!"

Actually, it was his wife's car, a 1995 Nissan with more than 100,000 miles on the odometer. The windows had been smashed, and the hood, trunk, doors, and quarter panels were dented like an overripe peach. A couple of bats and balls were lodged strategically in the windshield. Suspects ran rampant through Buss' mind: Woody, Demp, Big Z, DeRo... The Cubs have a love-hate relationship with the man who pushes them in the weight room and stretches them seemingly beyond limits. They tease him incessantly. Demp came over and handed Buss the keys to a 2008 Nissan Xterra compact SUV parked outside the clubhouse, saying: "Quit pouting and get in your new car."

"I thought they'd lost their minds," said Buss, who later discovered his wife "was in on it. They called and told her what they were going to do."

As the second-to-last week of camp concluded, Rich Hill, an 11-game winner in 2007, continued to struggle. Woody's sore back and outstanding spring performances by Dempster, Marquis, Jon Lieber, and Sean Marshall delayed Piniella's key pitching staff decisions.

"By Monday," Piniella said of a day that would be a week from Opening Day, "unless there's an injury, a 'Cubbie occurrence,' I think we'll be in good shape to announce some plans." Writers ran with the new phrase, using "Cubbie Occurrence" to explain everything from the billy goat to black cats to Bartman.

Piniella often thought out loud as he played with numerous possibilities over the final week. Every starting position player was subject to his whimsical musical batting orders. Fukudome, for one, was considered for the first five positions in the lineup with the exception of the cleanup spot.

An early cut in each of the previous three spring camps, Geovany Soto was just happy to still be catching big-leaguers. Soto took a look around a clubhouse designed to house as many as 60 players when the team first moved into HoHoKam in late February. "Wow," he thought, "I've never seen this locker room so empty." It was to be Soto's official rookie season, even though the 25-year-old Puerto Rican had been a late call-up in each of the previous Septembers. Venezuelan backup Henry Blanco, a 10-year veteran, lockered next to Soto. With a dead-on impression of a pit bull's bark, Soto would call out to his mentors Blanco and Daryle Ward on the practice field.

Lieber, the Cubs' last 20-game winner in 2001, barely lost out on the final rotation spot. Piniella named Dempster and Marquis to join Big Z, Lilly, and Hill as his starting five on the same day he gave Wood the nod as closer. Woody didn't pitch on back-to-back days until the last week in Arizona but had yielded no walks in 10 innings of Cactus League play. After 11 career visits to the disabled list and surgeries on both his elbow and shoulder, Kid K's once-golden arm was ready for a new task.

"Less than a year ago, I didn't think I was ever going to be playing again," Wood said. "By far, it's probably the best I've felt in several years."

The next day it was announced that Eyre would open the season on the disabled list, meaning the final spot on the pitching staff would go to either Marshall or Carmen Pignatiello. Cintron was released, and Piniella ambled up to infielder Mike Fontenot near the hitting cage. With boyish looks, thick blond hair, and listed generously at 5'8" in the media guide, Fontenot had been mistaken for the batboy by Soriano the previous May when Fontenot entered the visitor's clubhouse at Shea Stadium after being recalled from Iowa.

"Have you got a place in Chicago?" Piniella asked.

"No," Fontenot replied.

"Well, you can get one," said his manager. Fontenot had made the club.

Less than a week before Opening Day, Hendry signed 31-year-old Reed Johnson to a one-year $1.3 million contract moments after the former Toronto Blue Jays outfielder cleared waivers. He had a reputation as a scrapper who wasn't afraid to take one for the team, having been hit by 80 pitches since 2003, second most in the majors. Johnson, a California native, showed up for the Cubs game in Scottsdale sporting a shaved head, goat-looking chin mullet, and a recharged manner. "You don't know how bad I wanted to be here. This is awesome," he said.

The roster was coming together. Piniella, sizing up his chess pieces, liked the versatility of his defense. DeRosa could play just about anywhere. Ronny Cedeno, Fontenot, and Ward could back up every infield position. Johnson could play every outfield position and play them well. Blanco was there to tutor Soto and fill in when needed. But the Cubs still didn't string more than two wins together until the final week of camp, and the bullpen had blown several late leads.

Piniella remained anxious.

"This is not like a spigot, where you turn it on or off," he said. "You have to get into a rhythm, get into the habit of winning baseball games, holding leads, so you feel you can do that comfortably when the season starts."

Back in Chicago, printers and construction workers finished up projects. Employees of Levy Restaurants, which operates the ballpark's concessions and souvenir stands as well as the Stadium Club,

Bill Murray singing with sportswriter Rick Telander at the Cubby Bear just before Opening Day. *Photo by Will Byington/www.willbyington.com*

reported to prepare food and test out equipment. Cubs security employees picked up uniforms and prepared the stadium's gates with equipment, paperwork, and wheelchairs, among other items.

The ground crew set up two long white tents over the infield and had giant heat blowers going 24/7 inside. "It's about 85 degrees inside there right now," Baird told me. It looked like a family picnic at the forest preserve, and with Pink Floyd's "Welcome to the Machine" being tested over the public-address system, it seemed a bit like a party...to everyone except the ground crew. They were weary after working all weekend and until 9:30 the previous night.

The Cubs finished Cactus League play March 27, leading the majors in spring-training attendance for the ninth time in 12 years. Eleven of their 15 games were sellouts. HoHoKam sold $2.8 million worth of tickets and another $2.8 million in food, beverage, and merchandise, an increase of more than $400,000 over the 2007 season.

Anybody who says Wrigley Field is the key to the Cubs' popularity should heed these numbers.

Our story's heroes headed to Sin City for two final exhibitions against the Seattle Mariners. Eyre dispatched his RV to Chicago. He wasn't going to live in it. Rather, it would be stored and hopefully put to good use for a parade in October.

Piniella was playing the ponies at the team's Las Vegas hotel casino, where the sports book listed the Cubs as second favorites to win the World Series. "I noticed that," he said. "I like our team. We've got good young guys and veteran counterparts."

Wrigleyville went through its final non-baseball weekend and braced for Opening Day. The Banks statue was put in place on Friday as I finished my last day of official employment with the Chicago National League Ball Club Inc. Fittingly, my brick paver was installed that very afternoon. In the middle of the Glenn Beckert section, with Mr. Cub towering just feet away under a blanket, it read:

McARDLE FAMILY

CUBS FANS

SINCE 1919

On Saturday night, *Chicago Sun-Times* columnist Rick Telander and publishers of *The Heckler*, a free satirical sports newspaper circulated around the ballpark, hosted the 100th Annual Next Year Day Party at the Cubby Bear, kitty corner from the final touches being applied to Marquee Plaza.

They had a bad Harry Caray impersonation contest, played a game of "pin the mullet on the Sox fan," and passed out chef hats from the Billy Goat Tavern and "Party Like It's 1908" T-shirts. There was a countdown with balloons and confetti dropping at the stroke of midnight like it was New Year's Eve. Sam and Bill Sianis, the owners of the Billy Goat Tavern and Grill, assured the crowd: "The curse is dead! No more curse. The goat is dead."

"Next year is here!" Telander proclaimed, as his band, the Del Crustaceans, broke into "Go Cubs Go," joined by the family of Steve Goodman, who composed the song in 1984 shortly before his death from leukemia. Piniella mistakenly referred to the tune as "Go Cubs Win," but the anthem took hold during the 2007 season when the organization started playing it at Wrigley after the final out of a victory, and television crews piped it into their broadcast as the Cubs shook hands on the mound.

The party went into the wee hours, with Hollywood star and Cubs fan Bill Murray joining the band on stage to sing "Honky Tonk Woman," "Hang on Sloopy," and, most appropriately, "Devil in a Blue Dress."

The next morning, the Cubs checked out their new home playing surface for a final workout before Opening Day. Piniella emerged from the dugout in the chilly, moist air and walked out near third base, surveying the ground beneath him. He headed over to the new bullpen with Kenney, pitching coach Larry Rothschild, and assistant GM Randy Bush. Baird joined them with a tape measure, and they reaffirmed the distances from mounds to home plates at 60′6″.

Zambrano peeked his head out among a throng of media rubberneckers, declaring, "All right, guys, here we are…the Cubbies!" And they came out in sweatshirts and knit skull hats.

With the ground still frozen, the grass hadn't begun growing. Short grass equals ground balls that get through the infield quickly. Pitchers complained, "You've got to grow this grass out." Hitters endorsed, "This is great; keep it short!"

Ramirez, Soriano, and some other Latino players stood at third base and chattered in Spanish about the closeness of the new CBOE seats. Then Rammy grabbed a baseball, whipping it straight down at his feet. It deadened in the sponge-like dirt. They checked out the new pads on the dugout benches and noted that the visitors' side was left with the hard wooden slabs.

Surrounded by the media, Lee, a leader by example known more commonly as "D-Lee," said all there was left to say: "We're ready to go. It's finally here. I think we're better on paper [than last year]. Now we have to go out and prove it."

The Cubs made their final roster cut of the spring. Marshall was dispatched to Iowa so he could stretch out his arm and be prepared to return as a starter, if needed. Pignatiello, a local product from New Lenox, Illinois, would be in the bullpen on Opening Day. It was a just reward for a guy who had toiled for eight seasons in the organization's farm system.

All the preparations were complete. It would be cold the next day, for sure, but the games would start counting.

Tucked in the concrete-walled labyrinth behind the dugout in Wrigley's catacombs, the interview room has come to be called "the dungeon" by media members. Piniella met them there for the first time in 2008.

"[Opening Day] should be special for anybody who puts on a uniform," he concluded. "You still get goose bumps, get nervous. They're fun. You work hard all spring for this, and the fans are excited; the ballpark's electric. I like the idea of opening at home."

With that, Piniella's spring training was complete, and he left for the day. Piper Mead, an account executive in the Cubs' marketing department, stayed with her camera. When Piniella finished, the moment she was waiting for was upon her. A second backdrop was pulled down with a Nippon Life Insurance Co. logo interspersed with that of Cubs.com.

Kosuke Fukudome checks out the backdrop that would frame his press conferences all season. *Piper Mead photo courtesy Chicago Cubs*

Mead had sold the sponsorship and was anxious to send a photograph of Fukudome in front of the backdrop to her client. On the eve of his Cubs debut, Fukudome answered questions from American and Japanese press alike, about everything from the climate, Wrigley's ivy, and the close proximity of the bullpen mounds.

When the advertisement behind him was brought to his attention and he was asked if he had an endorsement contract with Nippon, Fukudome tilted his head back and peered over his shoulder to see the backdrop. He grinned while responding, "No."

I leaned over to Piper and whispered, "I hope you got that."

Interviews continued in the clubhouse, and players got the same questions they had all spring—about 100 years, Tinker, Evers, and Chance, black cats, billy goats, and Bartman.

"The only thing I'd heard before coming here was the moniker 'Lovable Losers,'" DeRosa said. "I didn't know about the black cats and billy goats and the 100 years. I really didn't know the severity of the situation. And I think that's a good thing. The clubhouse doesn't buy into it."

Walking out of the concourse, I found Lieber dragging a bag to a car waiting outside Gate K. "Leebs" was one of my favorites during his first tenure with the Cubs. We caught up for a minute and wished each other well on our new jobs. Then I suggested he might want to lose the tag with the Phillies logo that was affixed to his duffle.

"Good idea," he said with a wink.

3

APRIL

I WOULD DESCRIBE SUNRISE at 6:35 AM on March 31, Opening Day, but the day came sans the sun, which rose later in the afternoon in the form of Japanese import Kosuke Fukudome.

There was a light rain, and flags atop the grandstands flapped west. From my sun porch, I could see WGN-TV's *Morning Show* crew stirring on my old rooftop, and there was activity and lights on in the press box.

On the radio, disc jockey Lin Brehmer played a knockoff of Elvis Costello's "Allison" to the lyrics, "*Aaadd-i-son...our time's overdue.*" Brehmer and WXRT were broadcasting live at Yak-Zies on Clark Street like they do for every home opener. Tubs of ice and beer sat idle until legal serving time. "Let's get a time check," Brehmer said at precisely 7:00 AM, followed by the cracking sound of can tabs.

Another deejay, Marty Lennartz, did his traditional invocation in his alter ego, "the Regular Guy," complete with Chicago accent. He impressively dropped the names Steinfeldt, Overall, and Reulbach with the obvious 1908 alumni Tinker, Evers, and Chance. "Dat team won because of Merkle's boner," he said, "and dat meant something diff'rent in doze days."

The Mix's Eric and Kathy were at Harry Caray's, where Willie B and I were handed free Budweiser products. ESPN Radio broadcast from Murphy's in the morning and Red Ivy during the game, US99 was at Casey Moran's, and The Score was at Sluggers.

Wrigleyville was awake and ready to immortalize Ernie Banks, its greatest ambassador.

I stopped home and found a package from the company that prints Wrigley's scorecards. I'll be darned! Opening Day scorecards leaned against our building entrance amid the Waveland Avenue bustle. It would be the first of 26 deliveries, one for each home series.

Politicians and VIPs were joined at marquee plaza by Ernie's teammates Ron Santo, Billy Williams, and Fergie Jenkins.

Hammerin' Hank Aaron was there, too, and said of his slugging contemporary: "He certainly paved the way for a lot of us African Americans. He showed the way we should carry ourselves, not only on the field but off the field, as well."

A blue sheet was slipped off, and Ernie fixed his eyes on the statue. "Is that me? Is that me?" he asked, borrowing an umbrella and mimicking the effigy's pose. In his speech, he talked about how his parents raised 12 kids on $10 a week. He wondered how he ever got to Addison and Clark streets from those days of poverty in Dallas.

"Seeing this statue makes me think of my dad, who only made it through the third grade, and my mom, who only made it through the sixth grade," Mr. Cub said. "They may not have been educated, but they were wise. They taught me the greatest lesson of my life, and that is to be satisfied."

He never coveted. He never considered it his right to be a champion. He was content playing day baseball "under God's light," for what he called the world's best fans.

"Long after I'm not here," he said, pointing up at his bronze likeness, "I'll still be here!"

•　　•　　•　　•

ERNIE'S WERE THE ONLY HANDS on a bat that morning. Batting practice was canceled. So were traditional player introductions. First cheers of the season were reserved for the ground crew when they charged onto the field at 1:03 PM to remove the tarp.

The game started 40 minutes late, but fans welcomed Fukudome with a standing ovation as he came to the plate in the second inning. They hadn't gotten back into their seats before he ripped the first big-league pitch he ever saw off the base of the center-field wall for a double.

Fans camp outside the bleachers gate for the opening of the 2008 season.
Photo by Will Byington/ www.willbyington.com

Still stretching in the seventh inning before Fukudome's third at-bat, I was a row below groundskeeper Rick Fuhs in the press box. Fuhs, who's been on the crew for more than 30 years, mans the 71-year-old control panel that operates the magnetic-eyelet system in the middle of the center-field scoreboard. "Scoreboard Rick" asked for a hand.

I reached up, and he guided me. "Hit this button here," he said, "and then the one to my right....You just put Fukudome's number up!"

Single!

Despite Fukudome's hitting and my right index finger, the game went scoreless into the ninth. Kerry Wood strode in from the bullpen to AC/DC's "TNT," selected for the occasion by teammate Ryan Dempster. But the lyric "watch me explode" became literal when Wood hit the first batter and gave up three runs.

In the bottom of the inning, Fukudome came up with two men on, and the crowd chanting, "*FOO-koo-DOUGH-may.*" He blasted Milwaukee pitcher Eric Gagne's 3–1 pitch to the right of the center-field shrubbery for a game-tying home run. As Derrek Lee and Aramis Ramirez rounded the bases with their right arms raised in fists, a Japanese play-by-play man, his voice bound for Far East radio, chattered loudly in the press box.

Almost instantly, Wrigley's souvenir warehouse was flooded with emails and calls for Fukudome merchandise.

Kosuke Fukudome (right), Aramis Ramirez, and Derrek Lee return to the dugout after Fukudome's dramatic game-tying homer on Opening Day.
Steve Green photo courtesy Chicago Cubs

Konnichiwa to Cubdom, Kosuke. They lost anyway.

The press corps posed that he'd been sandbagging in spring training, where Fukudome hit .270.

"My approach was the same as it was at spring training, but this was Opening Day, so maybe mentally there was something extra," he said. "Since we lost the game, it values a little less."

On the patio at Bernie's on the corner of Waveland and Clark, friends gathered for the season's first postgame beverage. The ringleaders are Joe Scheidler and Tom Peak.

At 6′3″, broad-shouldered, and bald, "Big Joe" wears unbuttoned Cubs jerseys over a T-shirt and stands out in a crowd. He works his job in sales so he can attend most home games. Like many Cubs fans, he's got his eccentricities. He always carries a $2 bill and usually has odd-denomination coins.

Joe grew up in the northwest-side Edgebrook neighborhood, where his friend "Moose" used to force him to sit inside on beautiful summer days watching Cubs baseball.

After returning from grad school out East, he and his wife, Amy, bought bleacher season tickets in 2001. They split them up when they divorced. However, they still live in the same house and sit together in the top row of the bleachers in right-center field, Big Joe in Section 312, Row 14, Seat 110, next to girlfriend Christie, and Amy with her beau just down the row.

Tom and his wife, Ginger, have sets of season tickets in the upper deck and the bleachers. Tom is from south-suburban Chicago Heights, but his dad grew up blocks from Wrigley and used to load the kids into the family car for Cubs outings every summer. Ginger also is from the South Side and started coming to more games after college.

They've been married 10 years, both are in their forties, and they started their own document-copying company a few years back. Dedicated to their business, they never had kids and spend their free time traveling, which includes lots of Cubs road trips.

With a bright smile, warm face, and great knowledge of baseball, Ginger is a Cubs fan's perfect wife. Tom admits it all the time. She is the Abbott to his Costello. Tom's nose tells you he was a rugby player. He wears bowling shirts and for special occasions a homemade Cubs fez over his thinning blond hair.

He had this leftover bag of peanuts from Game 7 of the 2003 NLCS. Per tradition, I shelled and ate a single stale nut from the bag. Ugh! Thankfully, "Peanut Tom" was saving the rest for that October we'd all been waiting for.

For the next day, April Fool's Day, Harry Caray's was a perfect place for shenanigans. The Wrigleyville tavern opened on the southeast corner of Addison and Sheffield in mid-March, but this was the official opening night, and celebrities like Ernie Banks, Jim McMahon, Bill Kurtis, and Ron Kittle, as well as Ramirez and teammates Geovany Soto and Felix Pie came by.

I showed Mr. Cub my BlackBerry screensaver. It was a photo he'd once sent me of his face doctored onto a greased-up bodybuilder in an email titled, "I'm comin' back!"

He bellowed and ran off with my phone, showing it to his wife, former Bear Richard Dent, the bar staff…anybody.

Proprietor Grant DePorter reminisced about he and Harry first patrolling this neighborhood in 1993, at what was then dark-and-dingy Hi-Tops. They were looking for a place to spread the business from its original Kinzie Street steakhouse. "I think it's appropriate that we ended up here, in Harry's first choice," DePorter said.

·   ·   ·   ·

CHICAGO CONVENTIONALLY offers cold, gloomy weather for the opener and blue skies for the second game. Such was the story the next time the Cubs took the field.

The irony is that these are the bargain dates for tickets, and they're typically not sellouts. There were scattered empty seats, a bare section in the left-field upper deck, and only three rooftops were operating.

After batting practice, Carlos Zambrano called on Fukudome, sitting three lockers away in the clubhouse, to autograph a baseball for a guest. "My dad," Big Z said, gesturing to introduce the two. Fukudome signed, bowed, and shook Saulo Zambrano's hand.

On a nearby flat-screen television, Fukudome was being interviewed on a Comcast segment taped in Arizona during spring camp. "Hey, Fookie, why do you talk so serious?" Zambrano teased, crumpling his brow.

"Because of the sun," Fukudome replied through translator Ryuji Araki, who grinned as he continued: "And he [Fukudome] says it was *my* voice that was so serious."

I punched in Fukudome's number again on the scoreboard for his first at-bat. He didn't get a hit, but he did reach base with a walk. In the superstitious world of baseball, I now had a daily ritual.

Solo homers by D-Lee and Soto meant that the Cubs' five runs for the year all had come off long balls. They made two errors, were late covering bases, and missed cutoff men. These were the frustrating Cubs of the previous April–May.

Ted Lilly was without a serviceable fastball, and Rickie Weeks hit the game's first pitch onto our next-door neighbor's new brick

LOST IN TRANSLATION

During the Opening Day game, placards with the words IT'S GONNA HAP-PEN had what were supposed to be the same words in Japanese on the back. Fukudome stared confused, as he deciphered, IT'S AN ACCIDENT.

Word also spread across Chicago talk radio that Mr. Cub's catch-phrase on the base of his statue was missing an apostrophe and read: LETS PLAY TWO.

Sculptor Lou Cella came out and punctuated it, literally.

"I've never seen something so trivial get so much made of it, espe-cially because it was so simple a thing to fix. It took on this crazy life of its own," said Cella, who took the public editing in stride. "I talked to more people about that than the statue itself."

sidewalk. "Yesterday we got beat. Today we didn't play well," manager Lou Piniella said after the 8–2 loss. "It's only two games, but it's certainly not a good start. I told my baseball team they'd better be ready to play, and I meant it."

Piniella was grilled in his pregame briefing the next day about flip-flopping Alfonso Soriano and Ryan Theriot in the lineup. It continued in casual conversation among a few media members on the bench during batting practice.

"I was going to move Soriano to number one on Opening Day, but I didn't feel like answering the questions," he quipped, leaving them laughing as he ambled away.

In the clubhouse, Theriot came over with two cups and handed one to Mark DeRosa, his next-door locker mate and double-play partner. The veteran DeRo looked into the cup while the young-ster giggled.

"Is that Red Bull? With my heart? Are you trying to kill me?" DeRosa groused.

A Milwaukee fan held a "Miller Park South" sign, and their team continued to be the aggressor. Weeks bulled over Soto to score on a first-inning fly-out. Where Weeks could have slid around the back side of the plate and scored, knocking the ball away allowed another run to score.

"Yeah, it could have woken us up a bit," Piniella said after the Cubs fought back for a 6–3 victory. "I looked at the replay after the ballgame. The catcher was inside the line a bit. I'm not saying it was intentional, but it could have been avoided."

Players were careful not to charge Weeks with dirty play, either. Piniella attributed seven batters hit by pitches in the series to cold weather and numb pitching fingers. Nevertheless, the NL Central preseason favorites reacquainted themselves.

"I can speak for a few other guys in our clubhouse when I say we've come up playing these guys a lot," said shortstop Theriot. "In the minor leagues, we always seemed to have the Brewers in our division."

Trading places, Dempster picked up his first win as a starting pitcher since April 2005, and Wood recorded his first career save.

Piniella joked that afternoon that he would call media members to consult on his lineup for the next day. Before the first game of the Houston series, one writer asked if Piniella had telephoned any reporters last night.

Skip laughed: "No, but I'm going to ask that you call me before you write your articles. And then we're even."

Soto tied the Astros with a clutch hit in the seventh, but a DeRosa error and a ball Soriano misplayed in left field gave the Cubs their third loss in four games.

. . . .

THE FOLLOWING DAY under a cloudless sky, fans gathered on marquee plaza for the season's first Saturday. Intermixed with the bustle of fans trying to get into the stadium and vendors hawking their wares, others stood entranced, looking down. Trying to find their brick pavers without a location map would lead to many collisions, and cricked and sunburnt necks.

I made my first rooftop visit of the season, to Beyond the Ivy on the northwest corner of Waveland and Sheffield. They were having an annual "roof-raiser" for the Michael P. Gordon Memorial Foundation. John Gordon and his wife, Heather, wore pinstriped Cubs jerseys with the No. 18751 stitched onto the back, the badge number of Gordon's brother, Michael, a Chicago police officer who was killed in the line of duty by a drunk driver in August 2004.

Fortunately, growing up on the South Side as Cubs fans had toughened the Gordons. John Delcassen, a Cubs fan who was filling in for Michael's partner and drove the squad car that fateful night, was there. So was Gordon's regular partner, Mario Mendoza, a White Sox fan whose namesake accustomed him to being teased. The night he died, Gordon sent Mendoza a late-night text message to tease that the Cubs had won while the Sox had lost. "I came all the way from Midway Airport to pay respect to him," Mendoza said. "It's the one Cubs game I come to all year."

Mendoza's partner would have been thrilled with the results across Waveland Avenue. D-Lee went 4-for-4, Fukudome had a clutch two-run double, and Wood pitched a 1-2-3 ninth in a come-from-behind 9–7 win.

The homestand finale on Sunday was Katelyn Thrall's last game day, as she had resigned her media relations post. She was wistful as we chatted during BP. Piniella came over, gave her a gentle kiss on the cheek, and wished her well. "I'm going to be a mess after the game," she said.

Maybe a pirate could rescue this damsel in distress. Johnny Depp was coming to his first Cubs game that day. He was in town portraying 1930s gangster John Dillinger for the filming of *Public Enemies*.

On a sun-baked afternoon, bleacherites unleashed a winter's worth of cabin fever during a 3–2 victory. I'd forgotten a hat, a rookie mistake given the weather, but it was April. Confident in my masculinity, I borrowed my girlfriend Sandra's pink Cubs cap. Peanut Tom reasoned that the roof of the center-field batter's eye should be covered in sand, so fans could watch from a beach chair. "That's when it would be okay to wear a pink hat," he said.

One long-standing Wrigley tradition is that fans in the left-field bleachers shout, "Right field sucks!" across the batter's eye. Those in right taunt back, "Left field sucks!" In the eighth, a few novices next to the juniper bushes in low center field tried to start the wave, long forbidden in these parts. The result was a two-front war, as fans from both left and right ganged up: "Center field sucks! Center field sucks!"

• • • •

FOR THE ROAD OPENER, I felt it necessary to wear away grays and watch in enemy territory. I tried without success to find a pirate in Chicago, but the closest thing to it was Johnny Depp, aka Captain Jack Sparrow. Many Chicago bars cater to specific fan bases, like Michigan football, Kansas basketball, and the Green Bay Packers. Was there such thing as a tavern for Pittsburgh Pirates backers? The Dark Horse near Clark and Sheffield had a Steelers following, so I headed there. Closed. I telephoned Durkin's, another Steelers bar about a mile away on Diversey. A fax machine screeched in my ear.

Next, I went to the Newport Bar & Grill a few blocks away on Southport Avenue, where my friend Matt Richmond tends bar. He grew up in Buffalo, New York, but his family hails from the Steel City. "Pirate Matt" went to his first major league game at Three Rivers Stadium. He attended his only playoff game there in 1990, and his dad once threw out a first pitch at PNC Park. Matt had the beginnings of a beard growing—very pirate-like!

"But I'm really more of a Cubs fan," he insisted.

This would have to do.

The Cubs jumped out to a 7–0 lead; then two errors in the fourth inning led to five Pittsburgh runs. The Pirates eventually sent it to extras before giving back two runs by walking five in the twelfth inning. These marauders were givers rather than pillagers, but we'll take it.

The drama really unfolded two nights later. Losing is the foundation for the tragedies that have been selling since the days of *Oedipus Rex*. Consequently, the Cubs are the subject of many books and blogs.

So Don Evans, who authored *Good Money After Bad*, a sports gambling novel set in Wrigleyville, started the Lovable Losers Literary Revue, a buddy system for writers lost in Cubs macabre. They meet at El Jardin, a Mexican restaurant about a quarter-mile north up Clark Street from Wrigley.

"Hey," Crankshaft said in his best Harry impression as we arrived, "look at the guy in the sombrero!"

"We're going to celebrate and mourn this season with the Cubs," Evans said as he opened the inaugural gathering, proposing a toast to the death of hope and "to all Cubs fans who are no longer suffering...and to those of us who still are."

A band named "Dummy"—with a lead singer by the name of Mark DeRosa—played "Hey! Hey! Holy Mackerel," theme song of the 1969 Cubs. Dave Hoekstra, the *Chicago Sun-Times* writer who brought the medium out to the Sheffield Hotel in March, read about his dooming "sentence with the Cubs." They played the unbleeped version of manager Lee Elia's 1983 tirade against fans and listed things that happened on April 9 in Cubs history, including Sam Sianis' hex-removing parading of a goat around Wrigley on Opening Day in 1982.

They had a trivia game on Cubs injuries. Mike the Cop got into the finals against Miss Illinois, who had performed with a drag queen dancing quartet called the "Big Wig Dancers." She beat him on the cause of Big Z's carpal tunnel injury in 2005 (over-emailing). "Not only did I lose a Cubs trivia game to a girl, but it was a girl drag queen. That's emasculating," Mike lamented.

We watched on TV as the Cubs took a 2–1 lead into the ninth inning, where Woody gave up a game-tying homer to Jason Bay.

We got through Jose Cardenal trivia and a lengthy reading to which we were instructed to drink at every mention of Don Young (just like the Bob Newhart game in college).

Ramirez hit a two-run blast to put the Cubs ahead. Hoekstra closed the meeting with a prayer that began, "Our Piniella, who art in heaven..."

The game outlasted the literaries. Adam LaRoche's two-run homer tied it again, 4–4. "This is perfect!" gleamed Harry, our lone Sox fan in attendance.

On the game went, with Evans telling me about growing up on Belmont Avenue near the ballpark in the 1970s: "You could walk around the neighborhood and not miss a play. Everybody had the game on. Why am I a Cubs fan? I never remember having a choice."

Pie sent the wordsmiths home with rare glee by singling in two runs in the fifteenth inning.

Starting pitcher Rich Hill lasted just three innings the next night, and it was "there goes the neighborhood" for a bullpen that already had eaten up 16⅓ innings of the last two games. The topic of conversation was the same for a group of regulars at Bernie's as we watched Jon Lieber bar the door with 4⅓ shutout innings of relief. To wit, here's what I learned: it wasn't that long ago that the Latin Eagles patrolled the Sheffield/Newport area toward Belmont. For years, a black eagle hood was spray-painted on a building on the southwest corner of Addison and Fremont. The Latin Kings congregated at a White Castle on Clark and Sheffield, where an Einstein Bagels now stands. In the 1960s, '70s, and early '80s, one didn't dare wear black and yellow south of Newport—or black and gray north of Newport. There were the Kenmore Boys and the Wilton Boys, named for streets in the 'hood.

Landlady Lara knows this. So does Ray Meyer, whose father was proprietor of Ray's Bleachers (now Murphy's) from 1962 to 1980, and Rob Castillo, who is Ryno's and Fergie's veterinarian and grew up in a building his grandfather owned just west of the Lakeview Presbyterian Church east down Addison at Broadway.

Back when these forty- and fifty-somethings were kids, Bernie's, Cubby Bear, Sports Corner, and Ray's were about the only bars around. There was a Franksville at Addison and Clark, and a Tastee-Freez where a McDonald's now pushes Big Macs.

"Rob the Vet" still can hear the noises of yesteryear west of his boyhood home. "You got to know the cheers," he said. "You knew if it was a base hit. You knew if it was a little more than a base hit or if a run was scored after it."

He and his friends played fast pitch against the wall of the church. The strike zone boxes they painted are faint but remain. They climbed a fire escape to retrieve balls hit on rooftops and found a nearby group of kids against whom to play a home-and-away schedule.

Ray's buddies created a unique set of rules in the confines behind his dad's tavern, under the El tracks. "If a fly ball hit the El, you were out," he said. "You learned how to hit low line drives." Those were the best days of the neighborhood, as far as they all feel, when the street lights illuminating Wrigleyville in the summer signaled time to go home.

Rob the Vet bemoaned the irony of his dad, a realist, brainwashing him to become a Cubs fan and then mocking his son's blind faith. Once, when Rob got all excited after the Cubs tied up a game, his dad told him, "It's just the prelude to the heartbreak."

A Fukudome walk and Soto homer gave the Cubs a 4–3 lead. Prelude to the heartbreak? Not this time, as three more runs put it away. The Cubs' 7–3 victory was their fifth in a row and completed a sweep as they headed to Philadelphia.

At the start of the season, I knew I'd get to 81 home games. If I could get to 19 road games, it would be an even hundred. I liked the symmetry of that: 100 years; 100 games. Moving toward that measure, Sandra popped for flights and a hotel so we could get to a pair of games in Philly. On our way in from the airport, we passed an exit for Valley Forge, which got me Googling. The memorial arch there is inscribed with George Washington's observation:

NAKED AND STARVING AS THEY ARE
WE CANNOT ENOUGH ADMIRE
THE INCOMPARABLE PATIENCE AND FIDELITY
OF THE SOLDIERY

Inspired by his embattled troops during the trying times of our country's revolution, I found it strikingly evocative of Cubs fans.

If the Cubs were a college football team, there'd be no shortage of bowl invitations. They may never win the big game, but they travel well. Before one of the games, I was talking on the field with Mark O'Neal, the team's director of athletic training. As we scanned the crowd, he remarked that Cubs fans are prevalent to varying degrees in every place they go. Why? There are a multitude of reasons, but WGN-TV's superstation status had a lot to do with reaching fans throughout the country in the 1970s and '80s.

The Cardinals experienced a similar phenomenon before baseball expanded west in the late 1950s and '60s. Until then, they had a monopoly on fans in that region because of their radio network on KMOX. O'Neal grew up in Arkansas and worked as an athletic trainer in the Cardinals' system. "I remember after dark in the minor leagues up in Buffalo, you could get KMOX," he said.

There would be safety in numbers, but this was Philly, where they'd "boo a cure for cancer," as my dad used to say—and Mike Schmidt. Abuse was expected and started while we waited in our Cubs garb for the Broad Street Line to the stadium.

"Cubs fans always travel with their team, even though they suck," blurted Brian, a beer vendor on his way to work. He turned out to be a good kid, though, with recommendations for ballpark food: the pulled pork at "the Bull's BBQ" and something called "the Schmitter."

We met Greg Luzinski, the "Bull" in the Bull's BBQ. The former Phillies star is always there, chatting, signing autographs, and posing for photos. He grew up in the Chicago suburb of Prospect Heights. A Cubs fan, right? "Yeah, I was," the Bull admitted. "Banks and Santo and those guys were my favorites. It was tough because I ended up playing against them."

There was a smattering of cheers from Cubs Nation, but we still could hear D-Lee's and Ramirez's hands slap from our seats behind the dugout as they high-fived teammates after hitting back-to-back jacks in the first inning.

About mid-game we were joined by Josh, a six-year-old hoping to get a ball. Josh was from New Jersey but rooted for the Cubs because his dad was in business with Cubs pitcher Jason Marquis' father. Josh came in handy when Soriano tied the game with a solo homer in the sixth, as he gave the four obnoxious teenage Phillies fans behind us the raspberries. Josh got his ball from Soto, but the Phils got two runs in the sixth to win 5–3.

The next afternoon, Piniella was asked about Big Z. His pitcher the previous night had taken his frustrations out on a tray of bubble gum in the dugout. Piniella, who admitted to pulling a Don Quixote on a water cooler or two in his day, could identify. But those days were in his past. A kinder, gentler Piniella looked for Cubs TV announcer Len Kasper. He wanted to have his wife, Anita, wished a happy 45th anniversary during the broadcast.

"That's all you have to do?" a reporter asked.

"I called her and sung her a little song. I'll take her to dinner in Chicago, too, and got a gift. You know the whole deal," Sweet Lou answered with a wide grin.

The Cubs were one-hit through seven innings by Cole Hamels and lost 7–1. We sat next to John and Jay, two young guys from South Jersey wearing the maroon Phillies colors of the 1970s and '80s. They explained New Jersey's split loyalties to the teams of New York City and Philly. New Jerseyans do, however, agree on musical tastes, singing along as native son Bon Jovi's "Livin' on a Prayer" blared out the stadium's loudspeakers. "They play that song in the delivery room," Jay quipped. "I knew the words when I was two."

In the bottom of the sixth, John and Jay showed no shame in joining in the wave, looking to me for conformance. All I could think was, *Center field sucks! Center field sucks!* Their participation in the wave notwithstanding, they turned out to be good guys. So much for the notion of the brooding Philly fans, although we were lucky enough to get out of town before their team gave away the chance at a sweep by making an error that gave the Cubs a 6–5 victory in 10 innings on Sunday.

City of Brotherly Love, I hardly knew ye.

· · · ·

THERE ARE MANY ALLEGED CURSES associated with the Cubs: the goat, the black cat, Steve Bartman. Why not add another? Call it Dusty's Curse.

On the night in which Dusty Baker made his return to Wrigley Field, the man who took his No. 12 pulled up lame after catching a routine fly ball on the third batter of the game. After the game, Soriano was getting an MRI on his right calf as writers grilled the media relations staff to know if anyone had been dispatched from Triple A Iowa. Piniella met with the media after the Cubs' 9–5 victory, and the outlook looked bleak. The topic turned to Sori's habit of hopping as fly balls arrived, and Piniella chuckled a bit. "What do I think about it?" he asked rhetorically before pausing. "He catches the ball that way. It seems like a natural move for him."

Unnaturally, Piniella had to pinch hit for his leadoff hitter in the first inning. He asked second baseman DeRosa if he could play left field. "Absolutely," answered DeRo. Mike Fontenot went in at second, and DeRosa went out to left field, telling bleacherites, "It's not going to look pretty, but I'm going to get the job done." DeRo then made a play in the second inning that prevented runners from advancing—and possibly later scoring—on what turned out to be a long single. In the bottom of the inning, he hit his second career homer as a left fielder. D-Lee hit another bomb into the upper rows of the left-field bleachers to get the lead for good, and Dempster picked up his second win.

After the game, with The Who's "Won't Get Fooled Again" blaring on the clubhouse stereo, DeRo was asked about his versatility and said, "I've never donned the tools of ignorance. I'd love to give center field a shot, but I don't think I've got enough range....I have no problem moving around and doing what's best for the team."

But the story of the night was homecomings. Corey Patterson was playing his first game at Wrigley since the embattled former first-round draft pick was traded in 2005. Juan Lopez, Chris Speier, and Dick Pole, coaches on Baker's Cubs staff, were with him again on the Reds, as were ex-Cubs players Paul Bako and Kent Mercker. But Baker was the only one meriting a press conference.

A polarizing manager in his Chicago days, Dusty spent much of pregame shaking hands, hugging, and greeting old friends from the Cubs organization and the Chicago media. The muted boos when he came out to exchange lineup cards before the game became more fervent when he walked to the mound later to pull pitchers. Baker still gets blamed for not removing Mark Prior in Game 6 of the 2003 NLCS and charged with allowing the inmates to run the clubhouse toward the end of his tenure.

On a night in which baseball celebrated Jackie Robinson (Baker, D-Lee, Ken Griffey Jr., and others wore the legend's No. 42 on the 61st anniversary of his big-league debut), Baker took the high road. "You can play what-ifs all your life. You can say what if I would have married this girl and not that one," he said. "Gotta leave that back there."

Meanwhile, wildlife experts were trying to determine how a 150-pound wild cougar had wandered into nearby Roscoe Village. The animal was put down by police about a mile and a half west of Wrigley.

Maybe it was following warmer weather or the wind, because 70-degree temperatures finally arrived in Wrigleyville the next afternoon. So did proof of Chicago's label as the Windy City. Pinstriped flags bearing the retired uniform numbers of Banks and Santo flapped wildly on the left-field foul post, and our sun porch windows rattled. Ground crew regulars attempted to raise the flags on top of the scoreboard, but the pulley lifting the NL West pecking order snapped under the strain.

No flags and no Soriano, either. After the game the previous night, Eric Patterson, who was playing in New Orleans with the Cubs' Triple A club, received a text message from his brother, Corey, of the Reds. It read: "Sori went down, just be ready." That night, both Pattersons would be in uniform on a big-league field for the first time.

I stopped in Dusty's office before the game to say hello. I'd heard he was out at Wrigley during Monday's day off. He visited with the ground crew, some front-office folks, and checked out Ernie's statue.

"I wanted to prepare myself for what was coming," he said.

Dusty didn't have much to say about the boos. But Piniella has heard them before. "When I was with Seattle, they booed me in Yankee Stadium," he said. "They had 'Lou Sucks!' things all over. And, look, what can you do? Did the fans dislike me any more? No, I don't think so. That's part of the culture. When they come to the ballpark, they want to get their money's worth, and sometimes they get their money's worth by booing."

Jeers came after Adam Dunn hit a towering shot onto Sheffield Avenue in the eighth inning. Wrigley's tradition of "throw it back" on an opposing team's homer turned into "throw them back." A delay was caused when more than a dozen baseballs were littered onto the field.

Veteran announcer Marty Brennaman fumed on Cincinnati's WLW-AM: "This is the kind of thing that makes you want to see the Chicago Cubs lose...far and away the most obnoxious fans in baseball."

The vile Chicagoans callously cheered their team's four-run first, six-run third, and 12–3 laugher. Big Z got the win and proved once again it's better to be the hammer than the nail by pretending to pound the diminutive Fontenot into the ground during a pregame handshake the two had started in 2007.

The next morning, talk radio raged about Cubs fans' behavior and Brennaman's comments. Piniella had his own take. "They beat each other up trying to get these balls during batting practice," he said with a chuckle. "They scrape up their knees and elbows. I've seen some fistfights out there. Then all of a sudden they gave them up rather easily."

He groused more about the arms on his own team, specifically southpaws Lilly and Hill. Lilly was better in the series finale if anyone not named Joey Votto was asked. The Reds first baseman had a three-run double and a two-run homer.

With Lieber relieving in the seventh down 5–2, Santo whined, "Gee whiz!" on WGN Radio after Fontenot failed to cover first on a bunt. Griffey followed with his 596th career homer, and the Reds and Baker averted a sweep.

That night I ran into Pirate Matt at Toons, my favorite off-the-beaten-path watering hole, on Southport near Irving Park Road. His beard had grown scruffier, meaning one thing: the Pirates were in town. Arrrhh!

· · · ·

HEADLINES IN THE NEXT MORNING'S papers concerned a 5.2 magnitude earthquake that had an epicenter near the Illinois-Indiana border and was felt as far away as the Florida panhandle. Considering it struck at 4:30 AM, it wasn't a surprise that not many felt it. David Hersey was on security duty at Wrigley at the time and reported nothing. He left at 6:00, still unaware there had been a quake. "We checked around," said Mike Hill, the Cubs' manager of event operations and security. "Everything's fine. When fans jump up and cheer, it probably has more of an effect on the place than that did."

Most Cubs players slept through the seismic episode, but while fetching fly balls during batting practice, relief pitcher Michael Wuertz was telling Marquis and Lieber about being shaken awake. "My uncle was here from Cincinnati, and he felt it, too," Wuertz said. "He got a text message from his wife. She's in Lawrenceburg, Indiana. She said, 'Did you feel that?'"

One woman who might've felt it later reported to work. She had woken up in wet sheets that morning and was having contractions. But she had hoped to get through one more day of work at her upper-deck concessions stand. By 11:00, however, she was taken down the ramps in a wheelchair—her contractions were four minutes apart, and she was gripping Russell Johnson's forearm like a baseball bat. Johnson, a longtime stadium ops employee and former military medic, helped load her into Ambulance 6, narrowly averting the first known childbirth in Wrigley history. The baby was born early the next morning at Illinois Masonic Hospital. "She's lucky the ambulance was right across the street. We couldn't have waited much longer," Johnson said. "At a certain point, they won't move her."

Hill felt reborn, too. The pitcher notched a 3–2 victory, the team's first by a left-hander.

The next morning, overcast and cool, Crankshaft and I watched from the sun porch as Big Joe, Peanut Tom, and other bleachers season-ticket holders took advantage of the "five-minute rule." They enter the same gate employees line up at under the left-field foul pole. Five minutes before the regular gates open, they go in and reserve their customary seats.

After Joe and Tom settled in, about 50 guys and girls in their twenties and thirties gathered at their interpretation of a starter's tee a few rows below. The girls wore white caddie caps and green aprons with the words "Sophisticated Masters Party" scripted across the front. The guys, many dressed in knickers, argyle socks, and stylish hats, looked ready to play 18. "We do this every year. We each are paired up with a golfer. I'm with Greg Norman. See," said Katie, of suburban Park Ridge, as she spun around a guy standing two rows up. "It's random if you don't have a boyfriend."

Crankshaft, who picked up a late extra bleachers ticket, walked up, scanned the caddies, and proclaimed Ian Poulter as "the leader in the clubhouse." He was speaking of the caddie, of course.

I left to spend game day across the street with Derek, fine third baseman on my softball team. "Big D" had gotten drilled in the side of the head by a throw while running the bases two days earlier in our opener. He went down in a heap and had to have incisions made into his ear to bleed the inflammation and prevent cartilage damage. He greeted me with two ugly gauze pads and dried blood on both sides of a mostly blue ear. Laces from the ball had left an imprint on his neck.

A stocky guy with a shaved head, Big D lives in a third-floor corner apartment of the building where the roof-raiser for the fallen policeman was held two weeks earlier. His roommates include Mike, whose spindly build lends itself to the nickname "Tree," and Lucas, the "fifth third roommate" in the six years Big D and Tree have lived there. All three are around 30 years old.

Big D's bedroom was previously occupied by Bobby, captain of our softball team, and actor John Candy. To tell a long story short in a small world, Bobby lived in the same apartment before interviewing Big D for a job and noticing the address on his résumé. Back in the late 1980s, Universal Studios paid Bobby $500 to vacate the premises so they could film scenes for *Uncle Buck*. It was in Big D's closet where Candy's bowling ball fell on his head, the only fate worse than a softball to the ear.

Big D and I stepped out onto their brick outdoor balcony to survey the main bleachers gate at the intersection of Waveland and Sheffield below. "This is where we are most of the time. This is the best room in the house," he said.

These guys had two parrots for a party when Jimmy Buffett played Wrigley and a monkey for a Cubs-Sox Saturday game—to get the monkey off the Cubs' back. So I shouldn't have been surprised when their friend dropped off a Yorkshire terrier named Addison that the boys had promised to watch for the night. Little Addison shot all over the apartment as Big D and I watched the game on his 52-inch flat screen. D-Lee hit his seventh homer, the Cubs built an early 7–0 lead, and Marquis worked six innings in a

13–1 win. We celebrated by walking to a souvenir shop to pick up a little Cubs cap for Addison.

The next morning, the Cubs were stretching on the grass in front of their dugout. Piniella bent over to talk to Fukudome, who had a cyst over his right eye swell up after being cleaned out. Piniella walked over to new recall Matt Murton and barked: "You're playing left field. Where's DeRosa?" DeRo perked his head up. "You're playing right," Piniella directed.

Actress Bonnie Hunt was wandering the grandstands with a camera crew. She was the day's seventh-inning stretch conductor and was filming spots for a half-hour show promoting her syndicated talk show scheduled for a fall debut. I'd heard she was one of us—a Cubs diehard—and wanted to get her story. But she was getting stories of her own. So there we were, simultaneously interviewing each other. When questions finally turned to answers, I discovered she has been to every home opener since 1977 and grew up west down Addison in the same neighborhood in which my father was raised. "I was one of seven kids," she said. "We'd all pile in the station wagon and come down to Wrigley. This really was my backyard."

The yard has grown since those days. At Wrigley Done Right, the rooftop business on Willie B's building, metal bleachers span across a wide six-flat brownstone. A TV was mounted in the corner, and WGN Radio's broadcast was piped over loudspeakers.

A cool breeze off the lake waved the ballpark's flags toward home plate. That didn't stop the Cubs' bats. From here, we could see Ramirez's liner was going to elude two outfielders into the gap for a third-inning double. It was one of four hits for Rammy, who drove in four runs. Theriot had a four-hit game, too. The Cubs had 18 total and scored 13 for the second straight day. Paired with a Cardinals loss, the Cubs moved into first place for the first time in 2008. "Oh, St. Louis lost today?" Rammy said, unaware. "It's fun to be in first place, but we've still got a ways to go."

After the game, employees of WGN-TV and the Cubs gathered upstairs at Rebel's, a new Clark Street bar, to watch a two-hour show celebrating the 60-year marriage between the Cubs and the Chicago superstation.

For Lisa Bates, whose husband, Terry, edited the show, it was her first time out since having their first baby, Abby, three weeks earlier. Lisa is from Philadelphia. She's still faithful to the Eagles but has converted to the Cubs.

Jimmy Farrell, recently retired umpire's room attendant at Wrigley, was there. So was Scoreboard Rick. Someone asked them both to autograph a book published in conjunction with the TV show. Fuhs' teenage daughter, Lindsay, watched in amazement as her father obliged.

Wrigleyville was beaming.

•　•　•　•

DEMPSTER RUNS FOUR MILES the day after a start to flush lactic acids from his body. With Chicago's lakefront path providing the perfect course on a beautiful, crisp spring day, Demp passed a handful of fans waiting outside the bleachers gate as he headed east down Waveland wearing blue shorts with a "C" emblem and a Cubs cap turned backward. "Some recognize me. Others are probably saying, 'Man, that guy really likes the Cubs!'" he said.

The Mets were in town for their second straight ESPN night telecast, which means sleepless nights for the visiting clubhouse staff. The Mets played in Philadelphia the previous evening. Justin, one of the visiting "clubbies," grimaced when he saw David Wright make an unnecessary slide. Those same unwashed uniforms arrived with the equipment truck at 2:15 AM. Justin didn't get to sleep until 7:00. Coaches started arriving four and a half hours later.

I found Santo sitting on the Cubs bench and teased him that his "favorite team" was in town. "You'd think I'd be over that," said the chuckling Mets hater, who obviously was not.

We talked about some of the younger Cubs, like Soto, Pie, and Ronny Cedeno. Pie was struggling of late and had been given several days off. Piniella was working with Pie personally. Youthful anxiousness, Santo said, was getting the young Dominican into pitcher's counts. David Keller, the club's minor league hitting coordinator, was called in. "I know what he does when he gets into a funk," Keller said. "Today, Felix and I watched video from [when

Ryan Dempster jogging around Wrigleyville on the day after he starts is a regular occurrence. *Photo by Will Byington / www.willbyington.com*

he played at Class A] Daytona; we watched video from Iowa. We watched how far his whole mechanics have evolved."

Keller's tutoring paid off in an eighth inning that broke a tension-filled 2–1 lead open. Fukudome and Cedeno singled after working deep counts, and Pie followed with a three-run homer on a 2–0 pitch, making Santo a prophet—and a happy one—in a 7–1 win.

The next morning, tall and slender 27-year-old intern John Morrison stood his post in front of Theriot's locker. Morrison had earned a law degree and passed the New York bar but forewent starting a career as an attorney. Instead, he accepted a job as a marketing schlep for his favorite team, which meant following the orders of Demp and Woody for the time being. "They said Theriot never turned down a camera, so now they're saying everything has to come through this kid," said marketing staffer Jim Oboikowitch. "They wanted him to stand next to [Theriot] out by the cage. Thank God we're not having batting practice today." Attached to a lanyard, Morrison wore a badge that had his headshot and an action photograph of Theriot. It read "The Riot Enterprises—Public Relations—Sports Movies—Broadcasting."

Fontenot, Theriot's teammate at LSU and in the minors, came over saying, "You want to talk to him?" into the cell phone at his ear. He stopped himself. "Can I talk to Ryan for a second?" he asked Morrison. "Ryan, Mike would like to talk to you," Morrison said. The Riot giggled, nodded, and took the phone.

Indeed, the mood was relaxed since the Cubs had gone 6–1 and arrived in first place with their highest-paid player injured. That afternoon, Lilly retired the first 10 Mets and had a quality start in an 8–1 rout. Cedeno started for the second straight game in place of Theriot, whose back spasms were putting Morrison on damage control. Cedeno sliced an RBI double down the right-field line in the fourth inning and yanked a grand slam just inside the left-field foul pole in the eighth. I sent Crankshaft a text: "Cedeno just hit a grand slam into our front yard!"

"Why didn't you catch it?" he queried.

At the time, I was in the press box. The ball skipped over the top of a waiting bus and was corralled on our parkway by a young fan.

Cedeno had said after his clutch at-bat the night before that the Cubs were "thinking about the World Series." He backed off his boast when déjà vu came less than 24 hours later, and he was back in front of the cameras. When he was done talking, Theriot stopped at Cedeno's locker and whispered something in his ear. I asked The Riot if he offered to loan his public relations guy. He smiled and winked. The Cubs were 14–6 for the first time since 1975, and things were going our way. So much so that the Cubs were at 9,999 wins in their history. The following night in Denver would be their first attempt at joining the Giants as the second franchise with 10,000 victories. I called it "clinching practice," a dry run for September.

My cousin Edd and his new wife, Kinga, were in town from England and wanted to watch the game. Willie B, Crankshaft, and

I decided to go to Murphy's, 85 feet below where the W flag flies after a home victory.

On my way down the block, I returned a stray baseball to two girls having a game of catch in the backyard of the building that has the giant red Budweiser ad on its rooftop. I telephoned Big D as I got to Murphy's and looked up to see him in his window. He was staying in to cook dinner with his girlfriend. Worse yet, his cable package didn't carry CLTV, which had the game that night.

Across from Wrigley and can't watch the Cubs. For shame, for shame.

As the game got going, we gave our English guests a cram session on Cubs history. "So they've been around for 132 years?" Edd questioned, "and they haven't won in 100 years?"

Um…yeah. Back to the task at hand, the Cubs took a 6–5 lead in the ninth on Rammy's go-ahead two-run blast, but Woody blew the save, and it went to extras. Jet lag was overcoming Kinga. "In America, you don't have a draw," Edd explained to her. Fortunately, Theriot delivered an RBI single in the tenth, and the bartender rang a bell usually reserved for Cubs home runs and good tips.

The front office had a white flag embroidered with the number 10,000 but couldn't fly it on the scoreboard the next morning. A commercial was being filmed on Waveland Avenue, and Wrigley was made to look like it does on a game day. The scoreboard flags were raised, and the giant clock was frozen at 3:30. The Bucket Boys were drumming on their pails at 9:00 AM. Crowds chanted, "Here we go, Cubbies, here we go!" Take after take was filmed of a scrum for a would-be homer landing on the street two doors down. This went on until 2:00 PM, at which time the 10,000 and W flags were raised, concluding the ground crew's work for the day.

Four of the crew's veterans came over to barbecue and watch Cubs baseball. It was Scoreboard Rick, Mike Conoboy, and Roger Baird, who first became friends at Taft High School on the city's northwest side, and Dale Wheeler, whose father, Lenny, was a long-time crewman.

The Swank II has two choices for television viewing—in the living room on a 32-inch screen with Wrigley as a backdrop and an L-shaped couch on which to relax, or in the dining room on a stool at an eight-foot hunk of bar we commandeered from Toons. Naturally, these guys chose outside, on the back porch. I spun the 19-inch TV in the bar around so we could watch through a window, and we listened to Santo and Pat Hughes on WGN Radio, the "Pat & Ron Show."

The guys told stories of their 20-plus years on the crew, and we talked about the announcement the previous day that Crane Kenney had stepped down as general counsel of Tribune Co. to become full-time chairman of the Cubs. "We gotta get him a locker now," Dale joked.

Meanwhile, the Cubs and Rockies battled to a 1–1 tie through six before Chris Iannetta's homer over DeRosa's leaping reach in left field made it 2–1. All the while, Yosh Kawano was "on his way."

Kawano, who first came aboard as a clubhouse man at Wrigley in the 1940s, recently had retired. Still, the Cubs and the ballpark are his life, so he'd been attending games and hanging around the ground crew clubhouse. Yosh is an octogenarian, and how he could work a cell phone was beyond me. But Scoreboard Rick kept checking in with him while Yosh ran errands. "I'm at Armitage," he said one time. "I'm at Belmont and Clark," he said another. Finally, from the sun porch we saw Yosh's trademark white floppy hat as he got off the No. 22 bus at Waveland—just after the last out was recorded in a 4–2 loss. Rain arrived at the same time. I asked the guys if they could drag the tarp across the street and cover the deck.

A wee little man with tall baseball tales, Yosh spun some considerable postgame yarn, including the story about how he was toting towels in the clubhouse and trying to get past a group of infielders crowded around a card game. "I'll bet if I was a ball I could get through," he told them. For a change, the ground crew enjoyed the rain.

The next night, with the Cubs playing their first game at new Nationals Park in Washington, D.C., bars around Wrigley erupted when Reed Johnson dove onto the warning track and slid into the wall, coming up with the ball in his glove and the bill of his cap bent. "Everyone said [the flipped cap] was the best part," Johnson said.

"I stared at the bullpen guys, and they were staring at me. We couldn't believe it," said left fielder DeRosa. "When I knew I couldn't get to it, I was going to play it off the wall. Then I saw this gray streak flying by."

It was in a losing effort. Wil Nieves, the rookie with the missing *l* in his first name, hung it on the Cubs with a walk-off homer in the ninth.

Zambrano pitched seven innings of a 7–0 shutout the following day, but the club completed a 2–3 road trip after getting shut out in the series finale. The Cardinals were only a half game back, and behind them were the Brewers, who were coming back to town.

. . . .

NEWSPAPERS TALKED of the 25th anniversary of Elia's infamous rant against Cubs fans in 1983 and the $23 billion sale of the Wrigley Company to candy giant Mars Inc. Could something like that have an effect on naming rights, people wondered?

With the Cardinals' loss the night before, the Cubs' maintained sole possession of first place, but that was about to change. In the clubhouse, a dozen writers surrounded Fukudome and his interpreter. News of his appearance on the upcoming *Sports Illustrated* cover had spread, and he was being asked about the famous *SI* curse. "The jinx is something other people are saying," he said. "I'm doing my best not to follow the footsteps of the other people who were on the cover."

D-Lee tied a franchise record with his eighth homer of April, but the Cubs lost the series opener 10–7. Soto clubbed two three-run homers, as they pounded Milwaukee 19–5 the next day. During their six-run first, Mark Cuban was caught on camera sitting in the first row, two seats from the home dugout. Cuban, the notorious owner of the NBA's Dallas Mavericks, was not hiding his interest in becoming the Cubs' next owner.

When somebody named Mike Rivera clubbed a blast onto the sidewalk in front of our apartment, Crankshaft watched a guy snag it away from his dog and chuck it back near the Cubs bullpen. The guy looked up, and they exchanged fist pumps.

Salsa music was going in the clubhouse the following day, which meant Big Z would be taking the mound because the starting pitcher selects the pregame tunes.

Theriot, without his "intern" from a week earlier, was being asked another favor. "News flash!" DeRosa screamed to the other side of the clubhouse as Theriot fought back a sheepish grin. "Kerry! He just turned down a request!"

"Is the doctor here yet?" Woody shouted back. "What's wrong with him?"

Soriano was activated and back in his usual spots in left field and at the top of the order. This would be the Cubs' last meeting with Milwaukee for almost three months. Z's solo homer in the third stood until Ryan Braun matched it in the sixth. Then a sacrifice fly and Soto double in the sixth made it 3–1. The Cubs were three outs away from taking the series and evening their record against Milwaukee. "Welcome to the Jungle" blared as Woody strolled in from the bullpen. But he hit the first batter, reminiscent of Opening Day. Soriano was an elbow's reach from a liner, but it one-hopped the wall. A base hit and double gave Milwaukee a 4–3 win.

Afterward, a curt Piniella met the press. He had inserted Pie as a late defensive replacement, removing Johnson from center and leaving Soriano in left. He snapped when asked if he second-guessed that decision. "You're damn right I thought about it! Do you think I'm stupid or something? God darn it!" he said. The stifled press conference ended there, with Piniella muttering as he stormed out of the dungeon.

Forlorn, Woody sat at his locker at the far end of the clubhouse in his undergarments, staring into nowhere. St. Louis won that night and moved back into first. The Cubs were headed there that evening for a showdown between two of sports' oldest rivals.

C4

MAY

THERE'S A SPANISH WORD they use in New Orleans called "lagniappe." Pronounced *lan-yap*, it means "something extra," like the 13th beignet when buying a dozen.

That said, as our story's heroes headed to St. Louis, I ventured further down the Mississippi River for a little lagniappe—the New Orleans Jazz & Heritage Festival. Louisiana boy Ryan Theriot has been to it, and it's an annual rite of spring for me. It's not without reminders of Cubs baseball, either.

For one thing, flags flying on poles above tarps and lawn chairs help festgoers find each other, and no team in sports is better represented at Jazzfest than the Cubs. We flew a blue nylon pennant with "CUBS" scrawled in red, a farewell gift from my friends in the front office. It flew on the scoreboard in 2007, so it was a division winner!

I was the flag bearer as we walked into the fairgrounds one day. A guy ran up, huffing and puffing, saying something about a daughter named Grace and a son named Wrigley. About an hour later a woman started telling me about her daughter, Grace.

"And you have a son named Wrigley!" I interrupted.

"How'd you know?" she asked.

After telling her I'd run across her husband, she quizzed, "Well where *is* he?"

Then there's the Milan Lounge. After the Cubs lost two of three in St. Louis and the opener of a three-game set in Cincinnati, I went with Dude, my old roommate, and friends to a place in Uptown known as Wrigley Field South.

With a speakeasy feel, patrons are buzzed in at the door. Cubs memorabilia is all over, including a sign at the exit listing the team's upcoming schedule. Peanut shells? Throw 'em on the floor. Cracker Jack? They pass it out after the seventh inning stretch of home games.

Still, it's not perfect. A blue wooden L pennant had been hanging from the ceiling since the previous evening's loss. It triggered my rant over why the Cubs even fly an L flag on Wrigley's scoreboard. Why take the effort to hoist something to declare your failure? Why fly anything? People will figure it out.

"You mean like black smoke, no pope?" one friend said.

"Yeah, yeah, white smoke, Cubs win!" I said.

Moments later, Kerry Wood followed Carlos Zambrano's eight shutout innings with a scoreless ninth to preserve a 3–0 shutout, and I was given the honor of putting up the W pennant.

Thankfully, I didn't return the next day, when the Reds won 9–0 on seven homers, including a club-record-tying four given up by Jon Lieber. The Cubs were two and a half back and headed home.

Arizona was in Chicago two days later—the baseball team, not the weather. It was only 46 degrees, but the Diamondbacks were plenty hot. They had the best record in baseball and bragging rights over the Cubs with 2007's playoff sweep. "We need a good home-stand," manager Lou Piniella said. "I think we're 4–9 in our last 13 games. It's time to turn it around."

During the Thursday off day, I watched from my front window as Ted Lilly threw in the Cubs bullpen. When finished, he proclaimed, "I'm back!" Facing the team that had destroyed him in Game 2 of the NLCS the previous October, the timing couldn't have been better. Until the third batter of the game, Chris Young. Lilly tried to throw a full-count fastball past Young the last time the two faced each other. Young blasted it for a game-changing home run, and Lilly whipped his glove down in a childlike tantrum. A little hardheaded, Lilly tried a first-pitch fastball this time, which Young hit into the bleachers for a 1–0 lead. Fortunately, Lilly was solid the rest of the day and even hacked an RBI single. "You wouldn't sell many hitting tapes if he were the instructor," Piniella said later. "But it was productive."

Next to the Ernie Banks statue, Ronnie Woo was posing for photos with a group of twentysomethings as "Welcome to the Jungle" was cued up inside. Wood was back on Wrigley's mound for the first time since blowing a save against the Brewers. But this was a different Woody. He retired the side on nine pitches, all strikes, to nail down the 3–1 win. Since tweaking his slider during the road trip, he had retired nine of 10 batters. "I've just been watching [teammate Carlos] Marmol. I said, 'I want one of those,'" he joked. "It was just a real small turn of a seam that I was throwing it off of. It's probably a little bit slower than the one I was throwing earlier this year, maybe a couple, few more miles an hour, and for me I thought I could control it better."

Kosuke Fukudome was on the cover of *Sports Illustrated*. Rookie catcher Geovany Soto, who had hit .341 with five homers and 20 RBIs in April, got a little recognition on the center-field message board during the game, too.

"I noticed when I went up to hit, it said, 'NL Rookie of the Month,'" Soto said. "That's pretty good, pretty satisfying."

The next day, Ryan Dempster, coming off his first loss of the season, took a 1–0 lead into the sixth. There, he limited the damage to two runs by leaning on his closer's mentality and a nice play on a high hop in the hole by shortstop Ryan Theriot. "Sometimes we'll be like, 'Nice tackle on that ball.' We joke around with him," Demp said. "But I tell you what, he makes plays."

The Cubs broke out in the seventh with six runs, two coming on Fukudome's first homer since Opening Day. Marmol entered in the ninth to the Spinner's "Rubberband Man," an appropriate choice given his herky-jerky pitching motion. He locked down the 7–2 win, as the Cubs clinched their first series win since sweeping the Mets in April.

From the sun porch that evening, I noticed that the tarp had been put down by the late-night crew. Nasty, cold weather was on the way. The torrent came early and with heavy winds. At 10:30 AM, I peeked in the home dugout and found two lonely souls. Anton, the guy who shuttles new baseballs to the plate umpire, sat on the soggy bench wearing a clear plastic poncho. The other was barely recognizable, looking like a longshoreman in his hooded yellow raincoat.

But he was scooping up debris in front of the dugout, the only clue I needed.

Head groundsman Roger Baird came over and said hello. We chatted about what everyone else chats about with Roger on days like this. Rain was supposed to continue into the mid-afternoon, he reported. There isn't anybody who knows the weather around Wrigley better than Rog. "Nobody can complain, though. We've been lucky so far this spring," said the always-optimistic grounds-keeper with the snappy new field.

On a day when the auction closed on the 10,000-win flag signed by the team (a woman from Lemont, Illinois, spent $16,400 on it for her nephew's 21st birthday), a group of military families huddled in the windy but dry grandstands underneath the upper deck. Dempster and his wife had provided tickets to military groups the previous three years on Father's Day. This year, they moved it to Mother's Day. Rookie pitcher Sean Gallagher joined Demp, and the two signed autographs, took pictures, passed out baseball caps, and warmed the day. Demp told the group if the game ended up rained out he'd get them to another one. "Can we make it in the middle of the summer?" one woman joked.

Many had husbands or wives deployed in Iraq or Afghanistan, or had been there themselves. Brock Zimmerman, 31, of Hoopeston, Illinois, returned in December to be reunited with his mother at the end of a year in which his brother had been fighting a brain tumor.

Major Amy Hess and her husband, Craig, brought their seven-year-old twins and infant daughter. Both longtime military reservists, they'd married in 1996, divorced in 2002 when she was deployed to Saudi Arabia, reconciled in 2005 before Craig went to Iraq, and remarried 10 years to the day of their first wedding.

No amount of rain could wash out this day for them. "Mother's Day is a big deal when you're deployed away from your kids. That's hard," Amy said, her eyes welling up. "This is a gift of time together."

While peanut vendors outside the stadium added ponchos to their trays, the ground crew squeegeed the tarp as the rain slowed. Both teams scratched their starting pitchers—a highly anticipated matchup of Big Z versus the Big Unit. Finally, the delayed start time was announced for 2:15 PM.

Sandra and I ventured out to Peanut Tom and Big Joe's bleachers area but found no familiar faces. Granted, I was wearing long johns and a knit hat, but I called Tom to bust his chops, and he whined he wouldn't even go to a Bears game in weather like this. "Who's wearing the pink hat now?!" I blurted, quickly realizing everyone was. The Cubs had given away 10,000 of them at the gates.

Our story's heroes trailed entering the seventh, but Reed Johnson tied it 4–4 with a two-run homer. An inning later, Daryle Ward came up with the bases loaded, doubled to the wall below us, and left the field for a pinch runner, doffing his helmet to a standing ovation. "It was so quick. I got up there and swung at the first pitch. Then they ran for me. I was probably on the field for, like, two minutes," Ward said. "It was a big [series] because we got a chance to pay them back a little bit for sweeping us in the playoffs." The 6–4 victory bumped the D'backs out of the top spot in the NL. With St. Louis' loss to the Brewers, the Cubs moved percentage points back into first place.

· · · ·

THERE ARE SEASON-TICKET holders, and then there's Don Dando. Having grown up in suburban Western Springs, Illinois, Dando has lived in the Gold Coast since the 1960s.

A semi-retired, self-employed salesman, "Dandy Don" is a creature of habit. He rises every day around 4:30 AM and walks to the health club. He attends most games with his wife, Pat, of 39 years. They take the CTA No. 22 bus up Clark Street or ride the El— always in the first car, looking out the front window as it rises out of the subway tunnel before the Fullerton stop. He calls it his "Six Flags." They arrive two hours before game time and go to Tuscany, an upscale restaurant across from Bernie's. "I used to go to the bars," he said. "But it's kind of nice to sit down at a table with a tablecloth and have someone wait on you."

Don drinks iced tea and sits at the same table inside. When the weather is nice, he sits outside at the front patio table so he can watch the bustle at the corner of Waveland and Clark. He enters the stadium at Gate K and plops down $2 for an official scorecard. His seats—in Section 15, Row 1, Seat 1—may be the very best in the house. He's right at the stairs where the Cubs enter and exit the dugout. He rests his scorecard between a field-access door and the brick wall. "There's even a pen holder," he said, resting his pen on the doorstop. Dusty Baker used to give him a knuckle wrap after the national anthem, and when reliever Rawly Eastwick was on the disabled list in 1981, he sat with Don a few times.

Dandy Don originally purchased season tickets in 1968, moving to these seats in 1973. He won't reveal his age but gives little hints, such as listening to the 1945 World Series radio broadcast in his grammar school gymnasium. "Except for the rooftops and the lights, it's still very much the same," he said of Wrigley. "I still get excited every time I come here."

I joined Dandy Don for the opener of the San Diego series. We were greeted by Jim Carrow and his friend in the seats next to Don's. Jim's dad, Leon, is a retired doctor who delivered many former Cubs' children, including Ron Santo's daughter, Linda, and Todd Hundley. They've had their tickets for nearly 45 years.

With Theriot on first in the opening inning, Derrek Lee doubled down the right-field line. The Riot came racing to third, with coach Mike Quade waiving him on. "He's gonna score!" Dandy Don shrieked. He should know. Cubs up 1–0. Down 2–1 in the fifth, the Cubs mounted a six-run rally started by Alfonso Soriano's wind-blown homer. A teenager in front of us high-fived Sori as he returned to the dugout.

Dave, the usher in Aisle 15, chatted with us between innings from his guard post at the wall. Dandy Don attended funeral services of Ole and Andy, the two ushers who preceded Dave. "You get attached to these people," he said. "Dave's only been here two years, but he's become a friend already."

Don has seen Mr. Cub's 500th homer, Wood's 20K game, the Sandberg Game, and 1972 no-hitters by Milt Pappas and Burt Hooton. In many of his seasons, he had perfect attendance. I wondered how many games he'd seen. Estimating 75 games a year for 40 years, he came up with 3,000. That's not counting spring training, where he and Pat have had season tickets at HoHoKam Park since 1979.

Add one more to Dandy Don's win column. The Cubs batted around again in the sixth inning for five more runs in a 12–3 thrashing.

The next afternoon, the fans were on the field, and the players were in the grandstands for a change. Before a night game against the Padres, the organization held its annual "Meet the Team, Have a Ball" event for 300-plus fans. Fans walked the outfield grass, played catch, and took photographs and videos. Then the Cubs came out and sat in the first row of the terrace box seats from third base around to home plate. Fans lined up with a baseball to be signed by the entire team. It was a pricey event at $300 apiece, but proceeds went to charity, and the memories became treasures.

One couple came from West Palm Beach, Florida, to celebrate their 25th wedding anniversary. Another engaged couple from Columbus, Ohio, gave it to each other as a gift 11 days before their nuptials. The woman even wore her veil.

For Alice Morrow and her nine-year-old son, Nicholas, of Rockford, Illinois, it was bittersweet. Nicholas' father died of cancer the previous September, and the chance to take a photograph with D-Lee helped him cope. "His dream is to play pro ball," Alice said.

Then there was Kathleen Clesen and her two sons, Brandon, seven, and Patrick, four, and their friend, nine-year-old Neil Udelhofen. "I pulled them out of school today and told them we were going to the dentist," Clesen said with a devilish smile. Clesen's sons, adopted from Guatemala, spoke Spanish with Marmol and Zambrano.

In English, the day's headline on the *Chicago Sun-Times* screamed, "ZELL NO." The article reported that Tribune Co. chairman Sam Zell rejected a $400 million offer for Wrigley Field from the Illinois Sports Facilities Authority and had decided to package the team and ballpark together. Curiously, on this same night, John Canning, front man for a group contending to purchase the team, was on the rooftop against which the Cubs had been litigating only weeks earlier for failure to pay the team its share of 2007 profits.

It was my night to be a squatter, starting in Aisle 224. When the rightful ticket holders arrived, I moved to 222, three rows behind a post. Curses! This had to be the worst seat in the house. Then I realized there was a guy sitting two rows in front of me.

When the drizzly rain came, that same post was holding up the world's largest umbrella—the upper deck. Another advantage to this section is backstage passes to live music. As the top of the fifth unfolds every game, a mike is set up in the aisle in front of us. When the last out is recorded, the public-address announcer introduces Ted Butterman's Dixieland Band and their selection for the evening. On this night, they played Bob Carleton's "Ja-Da."

Butterman's band has been playing Wrigley since the mid-1980s. They jam inside and outside the ballpark before and during games, but the fifth inning is their one chance to play for everybody. "It's the highlight of our day, no doubt about it," Butterman said. "To play in front of 40,000 people is quite a thrill."

The Cubs built a 3–0 lead, but Jason Marquis gave up two singles and a game-tying homer that Khalil Greene clubbed onto Waveland. A Jody Gerut RBI double completed the four-run inning. The misty rain never stopped, and Trevor Hoffman recorded his 531st career save in a 4–3 Padres win that snapped the Cubs' four-game winning streak.

The media was out in full force before batting practice the next day with rumors circulating about the Cubs signing former Cardinals All-Star Jim Edmonds. Marquis, a former teammate, was being interviewed in the clubhouse. Mark DeRosa was caught as he came in from the dugout tunnel. Ironically, the team that had released Edmonds was in the clubhouse across the diamond. "I talked to Phil Nevin today, and he said he thought Jim Edmonds was about to turn it on when they pulled the plug," DeRo said, his face illuminated by camera lights.

Lilly, the day's starting pitcher, was trying to pass through this clogged scene and nervously looked over his shoulder at a wall clock. "I have like a minute to get out there. Good call on the interview right here," he said as it broke up.

The Cubs were doing pretty good without Edmonds. Soriano homered in the first and singled home two runs an inning later. Soto drove in a run in the third and belted his seventh homer with a man on in the fifth.

After the 8–5 victory, Piniella and Lilly were expected visitors to the dungeon. Then came surprise guest Jim Hendry. The general manager announced that Edmonds would be in pinstripes the following day, and Felix Pie was bound for Round Rock, Texas, to join Triple A Iowa. "We're not down on Felix. He is a tremendous defender with a lot of athletic ability," Hendry said. "My job is to manage the roster on a daily basis, and we're going to give this a shot."

By 10:00 the next morning, Pie's locker was empty, and veteran clubbie Gary Stark was setting up a locker next to Aramis Ramirez's. The last thing to go on was the nameplate, EDMONDS #15, which Stark slid into its metal groove.

A collection of media members were waiting for Edmonds' arrival, and Zambrano joked that he'd be having a press conference about his new teammate. Big Z and Edmonds have a history that dates back to July 2004, when the young Cubs pitcher was ejected from a game after plunking then-Cardinal Edmonds, whom angered Zambrano by admiring a home run earlier in that game.

Edmonds came in wearing jeans and a blue hoodie, and clubbie Tim Hellmann helped him unpack. When Z shook hands and hugged Edmonds, it happened so fast that many media types missed it. So they reenacted the gesture.

"There! You happy?" Z said to the newshounds.

"Teammates, right?" Edmonds affirmed.

Edmonds used all the usual baseball clichés about just trying to do his small part for the winning effort. "The tradition in which I've played for the last eight years was unbelievable," he said. "Now I'm a Cub." He sat at his locker, putting on pieces of blue clothing one by one, looking like Larry Bird trying on Lakers gold.

Big Z stopped joking and explained that the two All-Stars had made nice-nice the night before. "You may hate him when he plays on the opposing team, but you love him when he's playing for your team," Zambrano said.

Would fans be as quick to accept Edmonds? I headed out to the bleachers to witness firsthand as he ran out to center field to a medley of boos and cheers. I sat with Al Yellon and his band of regulars in the left-field corner, basically about 75 feet across from our sun porch. Come to think of it, I was closer to my refrigerator than the concessions stand.

Yellon, 51, directs the morning news for the local ABC affiliate. He grew up in Highland Park, and his dad took him to his first Cubs game as a seven-year-old during the Santo/Banks era, a familiar story to me. Al started coming to Cubs games regularly in 1978. A few years back, he started blogging about his game-day experiences. In February 2005 he joined SB Nation, which has grown to include well over 100 blogs from fans of teams in MLB, the NFL, NBA, and NHL. Yellon's blog, called "BleedCubbieBlue," ranks among the most popular, averaging 7,000 hits a day.

Less than 300 of the Cubs' season tickets issued are in the bleachers. "BleedCubbieBlue Al" has two of them, and has congregated with other such season-ticket holders. Al has a thick goatee and wears a ballcap over his shaved head. He sits on the top row with his girlfriend, Miriam Romain.

With a goatee and wavy brown hair sticking out from under a cap, and wearing his usual button-down Hawaiian shirt, Jeff sits on the aisle one row down. His 24 years as a flight attendant for Continental gives him seniority to bid on a schedule befitting a guy who's been spending most of his summers in Wrigley's bleachers since 1979. Next to "Hawaii Jeff" were Jon and Jon's father, Howard. A ponytail-wearing bassist in a bluegrass band, Jon attached his scorecard to a worn Kellogg's clipboard that was a Wrigley promotional giveaway in 1987. Al, Jeff, and Howard also kept score. Harry Gibson, the newcomer who had moved from Arizona just five days prior, sat one row down. "There seems to be a seniority thing with getting up to the back row," said "Bluegrass Jon" with a smile.

Two young girls who settled in next to "Harry the Rookie" started chatting up the group as Ronny Cedeno began a four-run rally in the fifth inning with a single. Wondering who the imposter was wearing Cedeno's No. 5 jersey, Yellon handed the girls a business card for his blog. "Wow! You're hardcore. Do I get to keep this?" the girl wearing a Jacque Jones T-shirt said.

Shortstop Ryan "The Riot" Theriot provided a spark hitting in the number-two spot and ended up leading the team in batting average in 2008.
Steve Green photo courtesy Chicago Cubs

Al knows his baseball, and his site reflects it in a Web world in which blogs have free rein to curse and rant. "If you read a lot of other sites, there's a lot of profanity," he said. "I try to be the voice of reason. Do I get as pissed off as others? Sure I do. But I try to be mature about it. You can sound off without [profanity]."

Edmonds, who singled in his first at-bat, grounded into an inning-ending double play in the fourth and came up with the bases loaded in the seventh. We polled each other on what former nemeses looked as odd in Cubs pinstripes. Howard said Dave Magadan; Al went with Howard Johnson. I suggested that Lenny Dykstra, had he become a Cub, would have been the only one comparably as odd as Edmonds in blue pinstripes. The new guy struck out, and the boos began droning out the cheers.

Fortunately, Dempster was working on a shutout. When he came to bat in the bottom of the eighth, we stood and applauded.

HOME OF THE BRAVE

Engine Co. 78 has been located at 1052 Waveland Avenue since 1884. Lieutenant Steve Bezazian grew up in Uptown and used to walk to Wrigley with a buddy, saving their bus money for a soda to wash down the bologna-and-mustard sandwiches they packed. "Who knew that I'd become the protector of the Holy Grail?" he said, gesturing at the ballpark. "Lieutenant Steve" has a tattoo on his left arm with a Cubs logo and the words "World Series Champions" followed by the years 1907, 1908, and 2007. He's got a date with the tattoo artist after the season is done, hopefully to change the *2007* to an *2008*.

He's been in the Chicago Fire Department 23 years and in this house for four. On the day we met, he was covering the shift of another lieutenant, who was taking the captain's test. Bezazian could have taken it, too. "If I'd make captain, I'd have to leave. I'm actually passing up a promotion to stay here," he said. "When you're happy, you're happy."

Ryan Dempster, whose father and brother are firemen back in the Vancouver area, has come by to play catch with the guys. Harry Caray, Yosh Kawano, and Mark Grace all have been frequent visitors.

Managers are a different story. Tom Trebelhorn had a famous "firehouse chat" with fans out front during a struggling 1994 season and was fired a short time later. Jim Riggleman came over in 1999. Gone. Dusty Baker filmed a commercial there in 2006. Bye-bye. I said I'd advise Piniella to steer clear. "Just as long as he doesn't step in. He can stand outside, but he shouldn't actually come in," said Bill "Murph" Murphy, another firefighter at the house.

Firefighter Mike, a White Sox fan who lives just blocks west from the firehouse, explained how they sell T-shirts for $15 and use the slush fund to pay for such extras as cable. They donate whatever's left to charity. Their cars are parked in the neighborhood so they can save spots in back for CFD brethren.

Jimmy Buffett played Wrigley on Labor Day weekend 2005, a week after Hurricane Katrina hit the Gulf Coast. While the massive stage was being assembled in center field, Buffett road a bicycle incognito around the city and stopped by the firehouse. Lieutenant Steve was talking on the phone to his wife. Buffett grabbed the phone and started chatting her up. The firemen raised about $35,000 for the ⸱⸱⸱⸱⸱⟩

Katrina relief effort, and Buffett expressed his gratitude by posing for a photo with the guys that's now on the firehouse wall.

Lee is one of the guys in the photo. The engineer who drives the fire truck, he is careful not to blow the horn or run the sirens when the Cubs aren't playing. He'll wait until he's out of the residential area. But if there's a game going, it's a different story. "My mom watches Cubs games on TV, and she's in a nursing home. She knows it's me if I ring it three times," Lee said. "That's our little code."

A three-legged dog walked up the driveway and looked up at another fireman named Jim, who dutifully retrieved a treat from a large box of doggie snacks. "We must get 200 dogs," Lieutenant Steve said. "They pull their masters over here. It's disheartening in the winter because the dogs scrape at the door."

Murph, who's from the Sauganash neighborhood, shares a partial season ticket package in Section 204 with three other guys. He's in his early thirties and has been at this firehouse 12 years. He has the distinction of having the largest head of any fireman in the continental United States. He grumbles about a Samoan in Hawaii who forces the qualifier of "continental." "It's 26-and-a-half inches around," Murph said proudly. "Most women have smaller waists."

Members of Engine Co. 78 include Lee (far right) and Murph (middle).
Photo by Will Byington / www.willbyington.com

"How many times do you get a chance to do this anymore?" Al asked. "The last complete game by a Cubs pitcher was in 2006 by Rich Hill. It was almost the first time ever that a team went a whole season without one. Last year three teams did it." A double and a single prevented Demp from finishing, but Woody closed down the 4–0 shutout with two strikeouts. I bid farewell, walked down a flight of stairs and out Gate L. Thirty-six steps later, I was at my front door.

• • • •

FOR THE UPCOMING weekend series against Pittsburgh, Wrigley Field surpassed the 1 million mark in attendance at the earliest point ever. The Pirates tabbed three southpaws to start against the Cubs, so Piniella stacked his lineup with right-handed bats.

All he needed was one. Soriano stayed hot, hitting Tom Gorzelanny's first pitch a few rows below BleedCubbieBlue Al's group. It was the third time in four games that he'd led off the game with a home run. Soto hit a solo shot later in the inning, and Sori's three-run blast in the second spotted Gallagher to a 6–0 lead. "I have my confidence back right now," Soriano said. "I'm controlling my hands and staying back on the ball."

"When Sori is going good, he's charismatic; he keeps us loose," added DeRosa, who capped the Cubs' scoring in the 7–4 victory with a solo homer in the sixth. "He's one of the best ballplayers in the game for a reason. When you go that bad [as Soriano had been in April] it means you're going to go that good at some point."

Dating back to 2007, the Cubs had beaten Pittsburgh a franchise-record-tying 10 straight games. But Pirate Matt was coming to Saturday's game, a ruffian's curse if there ever was one.

Late that morning, as I walked up Waveland to the firehouse four buildings to the west, Wrigley organist Gary Pressy was playing "The Girl From Ipanema." It wasn't "15 Men on a Deadman's Chest," but very tropical.

Across the street, our story's heroes took a 3–1 lead in the third. Soto was thrown out at home plate on a close play, and Piniella argued. "He should be arguing. He was safe," Lieutenant Steve said, watching the replay on the firehouse television set. "Well, it was interference. The catcher is allowed to block the plate, but nobody is allowed to block the base path. He was way up there."

A little boy in a Cubs jersey and cap was walking by. "Fire truck!" he exclaimed.

Lee asked, "Wanna come in and see it?"

"Wanna drive?" Murph chimed.

The boy took a photo in Lee's driver's seat. While walking away, he noticed the familiar red and blue logo on the front of Engine No. 78. "Cubs!" he howled.

The guys kill a lot of time this way. They play catch and keep tabs on the game by watching and listening. Soriano hit a solo homer in the seventh inning to tie it, and Jim came running in from the bench out front to see the replay.

At the end of the eighth inning, a call came in for a stalled car on Lake Shore Drive. Lee roared on the horn, "Honk! Honk! Honk!" as the engine sped off. While they were gone, Nate McLouth hit a two-run homer into the right-field basket to give the Pirates the lead again. As Lee backed the rig in, Theriot lined an RBI single to make it 7–6. But arriving at the same time as a gang of eight girls in a bachelorette party was D-Lee's game-ending fly-out. Firefighter Jim finished snapping a picture with the girls, turned to me, and asked, "Did we win?"

Fortunately, the Cubs had one more shot at logging an eighth victory on a homestand for the first time since 1978. Piniella considered the fact that his club had lost nine of 13 coming into the season-high 10-game house party.

"We needed to turn ourselves around, and, basically, we have," he said. "If you win seven out of nine you're always happy. Now, there's nothing wrong with getting a little greedy, and hopefully today we will."

Already, a third of their home games were off the docket, and the temperature in Chicago had barely touched 70. For the series finale with the Pirates, it dipped into the 30s by the final out. But the Cubs had heated up. In a 10-game stretch in which they outscored their visitors 60–33 and batted .303, Soriano hit .512 with seven homers, en route to NL Player of the Week honors.

And Dorothy Farrell conducted the "Y.M.C.A." every day.

The 1978 disco hit by Village People is played routinely at Wrigley during the opponent's first pitching change. Dorothy, a white-haired, 82-year-old great-grandmother of six, inherited a single season ticket on the visitor's dugout wall 22 years ago, once her own five kids left the nest.

She has two high-profile traditions. One is when the "Y.M.C.A." is played. From her seat in row 1 of aisle 31, she becomes a focal point by turning around, facing the crowd, and choreographing the song's famous dance with her outstretched arms. "I just got up one day and did it. Everyone expects me to get up now," she said. "The other night when it was raining, I peeled off my raincoat and did it anyway." Those not attending the game are likely to see her on television during the singing of "Take Me Out to the Ball Game" in the seventh inning. The cameraman stationed at the end of the visitor's dugout whirls around, and there she is, almost every day since 1985.

"YMCA Dorothy" is a regular at the Cubs Convention and has gotten to know some of the players. Mark Grace is her favorite, even though she used to chastise him when he played first base just a few feet away. Grace had just been in town as color man for Arizona's broadcast team. "The cameraman told me to turn around and wave to him, so I did. There he was up in the press box, waving back," Dorothy said.

Dorothy spelled out the letters in the fifth inning, when the Cubs chased Pittsburgh starter Phil Dumatrait, who gave up only four hits but walked seven. With the 4–3 victory, they headed out of town with a two-game lead on the Cardinals. Marquis had his first quality start in almost a month, as all five starters registered a win during the stretch at home. "When you get good pitching, you don't need to hit nearly as much," Piniella said. "That was a wonderful homestand." The only negative was Ward being put on the disabled list after days of deliberation about a bulging disc in his lower back. Micah Hoffpauir was brought up from Iowa. The 28-year-old left-handed first baseman/outfielder batted a collective .385 over the past two spring trainings to get into Piniella's good graces.

. . . .

IN 1941 PAT KELLY'S grandfather purchased the building at 3701 North Kenmore Avenue (commonly referred to as the Bud Building). Advertising always has been on the rooftop. Before Budweiser went up in 1990, there was Sapporo beer for a year, and WGN Radio for almost 30. A restaurant that was south down Clark Street called Ricketts advertised as far back as the 1930s.

Kelly himself negotiated the last deal with Bud, which paid $346,000 in 2008. The last 20 years, however, has uncovered a more profitable use for rooftop space. Alas, the May 21 closing date for the sale of the property to rooftop mogul Tom Gramatis was delayed into June. On May 19 Pat visited for what he thought would be the last time. Ken Yohanna, his childhood friend from the neighborhood, carried out two large boards that used to comprise the back two rows of the attic bleachers. Kelly was leaving the rest behind. "They're probably part of the building, but I gotta have something, you know what I mean? Wednesday could be the end," he said plaintively. "It's kind of an emotional time for me." Kelly, a retired engineer in the city's water department, is 55 and walks with a cane, the result of a 1972 automobile accident and subsequent back surgeries. But nothing could keep him from a last nostalgic peek out the loft windows.

The bleachers were there when his family bought the building. Pat grew up with his siblings in the first-floor apartment, and cousins lived upstairs. His oldest brother, Jim, sold beer at the ballpark. His sister, Beth, was still living in the garden apartment. He has fond memories of watching games from the attic. In the late 1960s, he caught a football that had been booted out during a Bears-Cowboys game. Bored one day when he was about 10, Pat picked up a stick full of gooey tar from a construction site and drew a smiley face on the outer wall of the bleachers. It remained there, faint, until the wall was torn down in 2005. "You grew up with a glove on your hand here or strapped to your belt all the time," he said. "I never knew how much I loved this building until it's coming to the end."

Pat Kelly (leaning on window sill) and his friend Ken Yohanna enjoy the view from the attic of the "Bud Building" one last time.

Photo by Will Byington / www.willbyington.com

The Cubs were running into delays, too. They're called road trips. Soto hit a three-run inside-the-park homer to help make Lilly a 7–2 winner in the opener of the series in Houston, but Dempster gave up a grand slam in one loss, and Gallagher was pounded for five runs in another.

They won the series opener again in Pittsburgh, only to suffer two gut-wrenching losses. First, after a three-run rally in the eighth gave them a 4–3 lead, Woody hit the first batter of the ninth—which was becoming a harbinger of disaster for him. The Bucs tied it and went on to win in the fourteenth.

The next day was even worse. Soriano camped under the last out of the game. *The last out!* He lost the pop fly in the sun, allowing the tying run to score. Jason Bay collected his second game-winning extra-inning single in as many days.

"ARGH!!!!" read my text to Pirate Matt.

The good news of the day? She said, "yes." While conducting tours at Wrigley that afternoon, I was handed a note: *I am planning on proposing to my girlfriend today. Can we hang back from the tour and spend time alone on the field? Don't answer this to me, just nod!*

Nonverbally, I gave Eric the green light. He took a knee in the gravel in front of the visitors' dugout, and they took the field of marital life.

I also met a woman who worked directly with William Wrigley Jr. of the Wrigley Company. So I asked if she ever spoke to him about this thorny naming rights issue? She explained that Wrigley's isn't the company's most popular brand anymore. I offered up the irony of if the company ever agreed to pay for naming rights—and then renamed the ballpark Orbitz Field!

· · · ·

THE CUBS WERE BACK in town on Monday. So were the guys at the firehouse, for the time being. Displaced while their spiffy new floor was laid, Engine 78 sat outside on the driveway. "We can't have the rig on the floor yet," Lee said.

They'd move back in the next day and were just there in the afternoon for appearance's sake. Speaking of shows, 30 members of the cast and crew of *Jersey Boys* were up on Skybox on Sheffield, my old building.

It was Memorial Day, and the Cubs had a moment of silence for former pitcher Geremi Gonzalez, who had been killed by lightning in his native Venezuela. American flags were taped to the front corner posts of Skybox's raised top deck. As a bald eagle circled the field during the national anthem, I met *Jersey Boys* stage manager Larry Baker, who organized their day in the Wrigley skyline. He called it "the ultimate company field trip."

Bryan McElroy was one of the first to sign up for the outing. A native of northwest-suburban Elk Grove, Illinois, McElroy, 30, plays guitar as one of the Four Seasons in the production. His name was printed on the back of a Cubs jersey he wore when they were seventh-inning-stretch guest conductors at Wrigley a couple weeks earlier. McElroy proudly showed off the grime on his Cubs cap. "I've been going to Cubs games my whole life," he said. "I remember when they put lights in here. My brother and I came to, like, the second or third night game."

D-Lee's 250th career homer gave the Cubs a 2–0 lead in the first. On the very top of the upper deck, Jon Smith snapped a cell phone photo of a train stopping behind us at the Addison station. Smith, the conductor for *Jersey Boys*, likened it to the Lexington Avenue Express line outside Yankee Stadium. "In the new [Yankee] Stadium, they left an intentional gap so you can see in from the train. Just a little teaser," he said.

He became a baseball fan during college in Boston, where he lived near Fenway Park during the Red Sox's 1986 Series run. I asked if there were similarities in his job to what the players across the street do. "They call it 'the Show,' and there's a reason for that, because it is a show," he said. "But what we do is infinitely more predictable."

With a pair of binoculars, Jon was watching Joe Torre in the Dodgers dugout. His kids cried when Torre and the Yankees parted ways, just like they did when Soriano was traded away in 2004. Spying with the binoculars, Smith detected backspin on a fifth-inning ball Juan Pierre nubbed for a soft infield single to break Demp's shutout bid.

The cast and crew of *Jersey Boys* pose during a Cubs win with Wrigley as a prop.
Photo by John "Nunu" Zomot

Across the street, Dude, my old roommate, handed his infant daughter outside Gate K to his au pair. He and his wife had come up from New Orleans over the holiday weekend and brought little Irene to her first Cubs game. They returned to their seats; she slept through the end at my apartment. "But she made it through five innings," he noted, "and qualifies for the win."

Atop Skybox, McElroy was leaning on a counter to give his knee a break. He'd had surgery on it not long before and gets physical therapy at the same place some Cubs have gone. Just like them, he has to arrive early for a performance to prepare his body. "It's a lot like performing on an athletic field," he said. "You're turning, stopping, jumping, running."

When Chin-lung Hu pinch ran after Jeff Kent singled to open the eighth, WGN Radio's Pat Hughes deadpanned over the speakers in the corner, "The 'Hu's on First' reference would be too easy right now, Ron, so we won't use it."

Humor turned to tension when L.A. loaded the bases with one out, and James Loney clubbed a would-be grand slam just foul of the yellow post in front of us. But Bob Howry struck out Loney and got a pop-out to wiggle out of it. Ramirez hit a solo homer to make it 3-1 in the bottom of the inning, and John Dias, aka Frankie Valli twice a week as an understudy, gathered the cast for a photo in the aisle up top.

Everyone rose to their feet with the crowd across the street after Woody recorded the second out in the ninth, and Smith was digging Steve Goodman's "Go Cubs Go" as the Cubs shook hands on the mound moments later. "This is better than Frank Sinatra's 'New York, New York,'" he said of the Yankees' victory dance.

Later that evening, as I joined Peanut Tom, Big Joe, Crankshaft, and the gang over at Bernie's, we cheered Demp as he walked by with his wife pushing a stroller, headed home to celebrate Brady's first birthday and Daddy's sixth victory.

June was less than a week away, but the game-time temperature the next evening—35 degrees with the wind chill—was 30 degrees colder than the previous day. An extra undershirt seemed like a good idea. When a box arrived from the organization's Triple A affiliate addressed to Gallagher, he tore it open and pulled out one of the many blue T-shirts with his name and No. 36 in red silkscreen on the back. Edmonds, in the next locker, sized it up. "I guess it was a giveaway they had down in Des Moines," Gallagher said. "They probably put the order in before I got called back up....Jimmy saw them and goes, 'I want one.' It just went from there. Everyone just kept picking one."

Fans settled for Fukudome bobblehead giveaway night. The real Fukudome batted against his first familiar face of the season in Dodgers starter Hiroki Kuroda. Eighteen Japanese media outlets covered the game. One of them was Takako Nakamichi, a producer/director for Japanese TV who goes by "T." She had covered Fukudome daily since spring training. "[Fukudome] is very popular in

Japan, because they follow major league baseball. But Ichiro [Suzuki] and Dice K [Boston's Daisuke Matsuzaka] are bigger," T said. "But he's a Japanese player, and they want to see him do well."

Newspapers were filled with stories about Soriano, whose sore legs and poor defense were a topic of discussion over the weekend on television broadcasts. Commentator Bob Brenly remarked that one could throw a dart into the Cubs dugout and hit someone who could play a better left field. Reports the Cubs later denied said a team official had visited the left-field bleachers before Monday's game, warning that profanity and inappropriate comments directed at Soriano would not be tolerated.

Sori continued to keep the confines friendly with his offense. His second hit of the night put runners on the corners in the seventh. After an error allowed the Cubs to tie it, Ramirez worked a full count before grounding an RBI single up the middle. Fukudome then sliced a double down the left-field line to make it 3–1 and secured that as the final score with a running catch in the gap of a would-be extra-base hit in the eighth.

Gallagher picked up his second career win despite sporting short sleeves and a new short haircut on a frigid night. Wind at his back will give a pitcher confidence, but he talked after the game of feeling a sense of belonging. "He's still got a couple things to work on," Piniella pointed out, "but he's telling us he wants to stay in the rotation."

. . . .

THE PHONE CALL CAME at 3:30 AM. My longtime friend Kathleen T. Knorr was going into labor. It had been an unplanned pregnancy, and she and the father were no longer dating. But at 40, "KT" wanted to be a mom. I'd volunteered to be her coach. The rest of her "birthing team" included friends Nicole and Sarah, and KT's sister Mary and niece Chrissy. The W flag was still flying on the scoreboard, and Ambulance 6 sped down the block with its lights flashing just before Nicole picked me up on her way to KT's three-flat a few blocks away on Irving Park Road. When we got to Northwestern Memorial Hospital, the contractions were five minutes apart. I was thinking this was a Greg Maddux outing.

Instead, we got Steve Trachsel. It wasn't until almost 4:30 PM that KT was dilated enough to start pushing.

We made a game out of challenging something called intrauterine pressure, which gauged how hard she pushed. She reached the 120s and 130s on the IUP monitor next to her bed before setting what the nurse said was a record at 141. KT, the poor thing, had slept only two hours in each of the previous two nights and was calling for the bullpen two hours later. But she had to complete this game. Finally, the doctors had to use one of those suction cup doohickeys to pull the baby out by its head.

At 6:46 PM on May 28, after her mommy had endured nearly 18 hours of labor, Peyton Ella Knorr came into this world weighing 6 pounds, 7 ounces and measuring 20 inches long. Exhausted, tears of joy streamed down our cheeks after witnessing the miracle.

"Hey Jimmy," Nicole said as I threw my arm around Sarah's shoulders, "you can still make first pitch!" Indeed, I probably could have. But I stuck around for the champagne celebration of this victory. We got mother and child settled into their overnight room and realized we hadn't eaten in 12 hours.

After texting Crankshaft a photograph of Peyton, I got a response that the Cubs were trailing 1–0 in the ninth. We were eating in a hospital cafeteria that didn't have any televisions, so I replied, "They must rally for the munchkin!" and asked for updates. The following text exchange transpired:

CRANKSHAFT: riot on 1st. lee at plate
      ME: Hee hee!!
CRANKSHAFT: lee foul ball homer. then pops out....1st and 2nd. fukie dukie up. 1 out....inf hit. bases loaded....geo sac fly to right, 1–1.
      ME: Hooray team!
CRANKSHAFT: 1st and 3rd. dero up
      ME: Dero is KT's favorite
CRANKSHAFT: dero flies 2 rt. surprise. extra innings
      ME: I've already been thru extras. Why not a few more?
CRANKSHAFT: you've played 2, ernie

In the bottom of the tenth, it continued, and we were back in KT's room, saying good night as she nursed her newborn daughter:

CRANKSHAFT: fontenot ph 2b w/1 out
ME: rally cap on...
CRANKSHAFT: go cubs go! fonz gw hit!
ME: Hey Chicago, waddaya say? We made a baby today!

It would be hard to top that day, so I was primed for a letdown. So were the Cubs after sweeping L.A. The Rockies were in town, however, and they were hurtin' right smart. With stars Matt Holliday, Brad Hawpe, and Troy Tulowitzki on the disabled list, the defending NL champions had lost 12 of their last 17. Nevertheless, three sixth-inning singles and an Ian Stewart RBI double in the seventh turned a 3–1 Cubs lead into a 4–3 deficit. Sloppy play by Colorado helped the Cubs scratch out two runs in the seventh and add three more in the eighth. Marmol and Woody got the last five outs on strikeouts for an 8–4 win. "If we get down, we have the attitude we can come from behind," said Marquis, happy with the victory, if not the no-decision. "When we get ahead, we're relentless."

With an assist begrudgingly given to the White Sox, who beat the Rays in Tampa, the Cubs had the majors' best record this deep in the season for the first time since 1977. "If you told me that with a week to go in the season, it means a heck of a lot," Piniella warned. "Right now, we're just jockeying for position."

I've been snookered by Chicago weather before, so it was no surprise that I showed up for the grand reopening of 3639 Wrigley Rooftop the next afternoon with a raincoat and without sunglasses for a game played in 70-degree, sunny weather. They didn't have the old sprinkler that shoots across the front façade of the building installed yet, but the rest of the place was ready to go. Jim Lourgos, one of the building's three owners, was somewhat astounded. Back in March, their steel order was three months late. "I thought we might lose the whole season," he said. "But every day you came here we had 65 guys working. You could not believe what happened in one day."

Steve Woodruff, another owner of the place they've come to simply call "3639" (the building's Sheffield address), flew in from Colorado. What he found the previous day was 40 workers trying to stay out of each other's way while making final preparations. Lourgos added the finishing touches with six crab apple trees and some bushes in large pots placed around the perimeter of the top deck. "I picked them up this morning at Home Depot. I could have used your help earlier getting them up here," he quipped. "We're going to give it a different look, put a lot of shrubbery up here, put lights up, make it kind of gardeny." The place had three service bars, ice cream freezers, and all kinds of food. In the third-floor lounge, Lourgos showed off a large wall frame displaying 30 photographs from 1978, the first year they owned the building.

As I continued my exploration, the Rockies scored four runs in the first inning, three more in the third, and another in the fourth. Down 9–1 in the sixth, Piniella conceded and pulled D-Lee and Soto. Theriot and Ramirez had gotten the day off. Uninterested, not many among the crowd of 80 for 3639's big day sat in the 116 stadium-style seats on the top deck.

Fukudome and Edmonds hit back-to-back jacks in the sixth. In the seventh, as operations manager Steve Alexander walked around with trays of baseball-themed cupcakes and cookies, Blanco blasted a two-run smash to make it 9–6. I spotted Peanut Tom, Big Joe, and Christie in their usual back-row bleachers spot and shot them a text. Edmonds doubled home two runs moments later, and there we were, locking eyes across the Sheffield Avenue chasm while jumping up and down amid a heightening Wrigleyville frenzy.

Lourgos and Woodruff also are part owners of Jackson's Brewery in Denver, across the street from Coors Field. With the Rockies in town, they flew out some of the staff. I found Jackson's manager, Scott Minshall, in the back row with the covers metaphorically pulled to his eyes. DeRosa's two-run blast completed the inconceivable comeback and gave the Cubs the lead. When Marmol struck out the side on 10 pitches in the eighth, Scott stammered. "This is about as gut-wrenching a game as I've ever seen," he said. "The Rockies have done a complete 180 this year. But this is a great environment, so it's tough to be mad."

Across the street in the clubhouse, the Cubs rejoiced over the benchmark 10–9 victory. DeRosa compared the noise level to the fifth inning of Game 3 of the 2007 playoffs—before he grounded into a rally-stopping double play. "I've been part of a few special comebacks, but this is right up there because of the guys who did it. D-Lee was out of the game; Soto was out of the game. Hoffpauir goes 2-for-3. Henry Blanco hits a home run. Jim Edmonds, who the fans have been riding pretty hard, comes through," DeRosa said. "It was one of those special moments I'll remember personally for a long time."

It was Friday evening, and Wrigleyville was giddy. But the ballpark was chipper the next morning as I stepped out my front entryway to a familiar song on the loudspeakers: *Let's go...batter up...we're take-ing the af-ter-noon off!* It's been a Wrigley staple for years, Harry Simeone Chorale's "It's a Beautiful Day for a Ball Game." And it was.

My Saturday work site wasn't far. Two buildings east, I found Ken Vangeloff wearing a tattered yellow T-shirt, an old green Devil Rays cap, and a five o'clock shadow. Oh, and a baseball glove on his right hand. "Ballhawk Kenny" stared stoically over the bleachers from the west side of the Kenmore Avenue crosswalk. Shortly after moving to Chicago from Ohio in 1990, he became a ballhawk, joining the likes of "Cincinnati Johnny" Rosenstein, Gary "Moe" Mullins, Andy Mielke, and Rich Buhrke.

Dave Davison came onto the scene a short time later. He has his own website, with lots of homemade film clips and the fitting URL of www.ballhawk.net. Davison claims to have caught more than 4,000 baseballs (most of them coming from batting practice).

Buhrke counts Santo's 300th home run among his 3,000-plus balls, although he returned it to its rightful owner years ago. Mullins, the dean of them all, grew up on Kenmore and started hawking in 1958. He opened the season with a count of 5,215 balls. Moe gained notoriety in 1998 after getting roughed up in the scrum for Sammy Sosa's 62nd homer. Ownership of the ball was settled in court (Moe didn't get it).

Ballhawk Kenny caught two during that race: Sosa's 14th and Mark McGwire's 48th (he turned down a $1,500 offer to sell). He also has nabbed two Ryne Sandberg homers, a 537-foot blast Sosa hit four car lengths down Kenmore, and ex-Marlin Mitch Lyden's only major league home run, which he traded for a Jeff Conine signed bat. "They're like currency for me. I don't sell any of them, but if I can't get a ticket and it's a cool giveaway, I'll give someone a ball for a ticket," he said. Ballhawk Kenny collected his 3,000th ball in 2007. "I'm a shoo-in for the ballhawk Hall of Fame," he cracked.

Moe, wearing a blue T-shirt with the *K* logo seen on Woody's famous placards, walked up. Without saying a word, he opened up his hand, revealing two dimes. Vangeloff grinned and shook his head. "We have a running contest to see who can find the most money out here," he said. "I'm kicking his ass right now. I'm at $2.94; he's at, like, 89 cents. But with that luck of the Irish, he'll probably find 20 bucks."

Soriano gave the Cubs a 3–2 lead with a two-run homer—into the right-field bleachers, not "out" to us. Unfortunately, this is more common since the 2005–2006 bleachers expansion project. Where an average of 1,000 batting-practice and game-action balls used to be hit out of the stadium in a season, 400 is now the norm.

Tracking balls also has become more difficult. 'Hawks used to pick up the white balls against the dark backdrop of the upper deck rooftop. That's no longer visible. On the other hand, without the high chain-link fence in the back of the bleachers, there are more "bounce outs." "You can't track them until they're right on you," Kenny said. "There were a few balls the last couple years where they caught me; I didn't catch them. It was self-defense." Kenny, 47, lives nearby on Newport and scheduled his wedding reception at Wrigley's Stadium Club in September. He was a consultant for Accenture until being laid off recently.

With an earpiece in his left ear piping in the Pat & Ron Show, he stayed keenly aware of the situation. He wrote the lineups on the back of a business card and updated substitutions. One of the others came up and asked, "Ian Stewart, righty or lefty?" "Lefty," Kenny responded, and the ballhawk started jogging toward Sheffield Avenue.

If an opponent comes up looking for his first big-league homer or a milestone such as No. 100, these guys know it. Ballhawk Kenny took a ball out of his pocket with a "Rockies" logo imprinted on it. This was the decoy should he catch a Colorado homer and be compelled to throw it back.

As the afternoon wore on, a simulated game started on Waveland, with Moe pitching, Davison catching, and a hawk named Bruce standing at the plate, er, glove, with an imaginary bat. A couple of high school–age kids, the "next generation," also participated, one calling balls and strikes, the other taking throws from Davison at a make-believe second base. The game stopped when D-Lee came up with the bases full in the eighth. He was called out on strikes, but the Cubs held on for a 5–4 win.

"Not a lot of home runs today," I said to Kenny.

"Same thing yesterday," he said. "There were four of them; none came out. Very disappointing."

The next morning as I left the Swank and walked out the front gate, I saw Ballhawk Kenny back at his post, staring at the sky. I ran into Big Joe near the players' parking lot wearing his unbuttoned new pinstriped Cubs jersey. We talked about the possibility of sweeping a homestand of seven or more games for the first time since 1970.

It was June 1, and Elias Sports Bureau was reporting that the Cubs entered the month with the majors' best record for the first time since 1908. The ushers and security staff, waiting for their daily briefing in the left-field grandstands, sang "Happy Birthday" to Big Z, who was stretching out nearby.

I joined BleedCubbieBlue Al and his gang at the top of bleachers Section 301. Al had missed the last couple of games to attend his college reunion. "I go every five years, and every five years the Cubs make the playoffs," he said. "It happened in 1998 and 2003."

"You gotta go to more reunions," I told him. "Have one every year."

A sturdy, bald man named Dave Ciarrachi sat next to me and picked the right day to wear orange. University of Illinois alums had purchased blocks of tickets, and football coach Ron Zook sang the stretch. Dave is part owner of the independent league Rockford RiverHawks. Between the Cubs and Sox, he attends about 50 games a year. His son, Jake, works in the Cubs' baseball operations department, and another son played minor league ball in the Cubs' system.

Dave became a bleachers regular in the 1970s, when he met Al. "I still don't think [former manager Leo] Durocher gets enough credit in Cubs history," he said. "This was a Sox town until the 1960s. Go look at the attendance figures."

I did. From 1951 until 1968, Durocher's third season at the helm, the Sox outdrew the Cubs in every season but one. In 40 seasons since that time, the South Siders led in city attendance only eight times, the last being 1992.

In front of another sellout, the Cubs took an early lead but fell behind 2–1 in the fourth. Al remarked how they had led in 23 straight games—and trailed in every game of the homestand with the exception of the opener. Then Edmonds cracked a ball deep our way. "It's over his head! It's over his head!" Phil shouted from the back row. A run scored on the double, and Edmonds scored on an error to retake the lead.

Harry the Rookie had his Wilson A2000 mitt, and Soriano belted a homer toward us in the sixth. But it landed across the aisle, skipping off some hands into the back walkway, where a guy got a nice reward for enduring standing-room seats. Howry, who'd turned his season around by posting a 1.76 ERA in May, and Wood finished off the 5–3 victory.

Even in the concrete dungeon, the euphoria of exiting fans in the concourse could be heard faintly. Piniella talked like a proud papa: "The homestand couldn't have been better. Everyone on the roster contributed. It's a nice brand of baseball that we're playing." Between the extra media on hand and duffle bags laid out as players packed for a West Coast road trip, navigating through the clubhouse was full of pitfalls. Rookie Hoffpauir sped around a corner wearing a towel, but The Riot and DeRo were entertaining interviewers concurrently between Hoffpauir and his locker.

"Whoa!" Hoffpauir exclaimed.

Ward was talking out loud as Gallagher, the day's winning pitcher, packed his things. "The more you win, the more of them show up," Ward said. "It's better than the alternative. In the beginning of last year, it was empty in here."

A herd of media camped out at Edmonds' locker. "Who are you guys talking to?" the smirking outfielder asked as he walked up wearing his Gallagher T-shirt. "We have a talented team, and when you're talented and everybody's pitching in, things just kind of go your way," Edmonds said. "We just can't get too cocky or too crazy. I think everybody's keeping a pretty level head."

Back home, I watched from the sun porch as a couple dozen fans crowded around the front of the team bus. Piniella climbed down to sign a few autographs. They chanted, "Lou! Lou! Lou!" as the best team in baseball pulled away into a stretch of 23 road games over its next 32 contests.

5

JUNE

IN DON EVANS' OPENING COMMENTS of the third gathering of the Lovable Losers Literary Revue, he gave an abridged synopsis of the season's first two months.

The Cubs just had opened a West Coast trip by extending their streak of comeback wins to eight with 7–6 and 9–6 wins over the Padres. With the rubber game starting later that night, they were assured of their first road series victory since early April. But being a Cubs fan is a forbearing sentence. "We're not quite ready to change the name of our group to the Lovable Powerhouse Literary Revue," Evans told his audience at El Jardin.

Actors Joe Tokarz and John Leen examined the presidential candidates, pointing out that Barack Obama is a White Sox fan from Chicago's South Side, and Arizonan John McCain is a Diamondbacks fan, which Leen likened to "being a fan of rocks and black jujubes." They questioned why Hillary Clinton, a lifelong Cubs fan, had been seen in a Yankees cap. A confusing election year, indeed.

Jonathan Eig, author of *Luckiest Man: The Life and Death of Lou Gehrig*, divulged that the Iron Horse hit his first homer in a big-league ballpark at Wrigley (while he was a high schooler), and that Gehrig met his wife at a party in Chicago during the 1932 World Series.

In the spirit of literary drama, all streaks ended that night. Our story's heroes never had the lead and lost for the first time in 10 games.

Up I-5 the next evening at Chavez Ravine, the Cubs got back on the winning track behind Kosuke Fukudome, who hit his first road home run and added a tie-breaking ninth-inning single with his newly arrived wife watching in the stands with their infant son. Still, it wasn't without theatrics, as closer Kerry Wood loaded the bases, and went 2–0 on the Dodgers' Matt Kemp before fanning him on a 95-mph fastball to end the game. "I've had all the fun I want for one evening," said manager Lou Piniella.

The following night was no fun at all, as Hiroki Kuroda pitched a four-hit shutout. On Saturday, Carlos Zambrano had a melt-down after exiting a 7–3 loss, just his second of the season. Big Z went WWE on a couple of Gatorade coolers, chucked his hat, and stormed down a clubhouse tunnel. Piniella missed the show while he was on the mound making a pitching change, and his only con-cern later was his pitcher injuring himself. "I have one scratch here on my hand, maybe two, three," Zambrano said, showing his self-inflicted war wounds. "But this is my left hand."

The next night, Jason Marquis' second win on the trip, by a 3–1 final, completed the team's first winning road trip in almost two months. Woody, who notched his league-leading 18th save, com-pared this team to Cubs playoff teams in 1998, 2003, and 2007. "It's a different feeling here," he said. "We all know we have some-thing special."

· · · ·

WITH ANOTHER WEEK-LONG trip looming, the Cubs stopped home for three games against Atlanta. The Braves missed the play-offs a year earlier for the first time in 15 years, but their dynasty of the 1990s and 2000s set the bar all others aspire to reach. "Those guys are my buddies," former Brave and current Atlanta native Mark DeRosa said. "Those are the guys I work out with in the off-season, but for three days I'm hoping to take it to them and get bragging rights."

The looseness of the club was evident in pitcher Ryan Dempster, who was asked about the confusing differences in his numbers at home (7–0, 3.10 ERA) and on the road (0–2, 2.59). "They're just going to keep me back on road trips from now on," he deadpanned.

"I'd miss you too much," said Scott Eyre from his locker next door.

I watched the game with one of the Lakeview Baseball Club's longest-tenured members. Barbara Levine's husband was Bob Racke's attorney when he first bought the building on which the first legally operating speakeasy in the sky was established. The saying "you can't fight city hall" seemed like it was written about Chicago, and Harold Levine had to find legal precedents. Mike Racke said of his father's unique business plan: "He sort of made it like a real business, rather than just kind of friends and family going up on a rooftop. He was kind of a pioneer of going through the legal channels."

After Levine died five years ago, Racke assured Barbara she was still welcome at LBC. A kindly and petite elderly woman with curly salt-and-pepper hair, Barbara lives in Lake Point Tower, the 70-story condominium building at the base of Navy Pier where Sammy Sosa lived. She met her son, Samuel, a Loop attorney, in Wrigleyville and scaled four flights of stairs to LBC's rooftop deck.

Note to self: next time bring a baseball cap to cut the sunset glare above the firehouse to the west. Regrettably, by the time I arrived up top, I still could see the scoreboard on the left-field façade reading Braves 3, Cubs 0. Tracking Derrek Lee's game-tying homer to lead off the third had to be done by watching the outfielders, who stood rooted, and the bleacherites, who rooted wildly.

Barbara recalled going to games with her mother when they lived a few blocks away. Samuel used to take the train from the North Shore. Neither could foresee watching games from across the street one day, but it's been their method for more than 10 years. "I like coming here at night," said the dark-haired and bespectacled 51-year-old Samuel, wearing a blue mesh Cubs button-down jersey. "It's a nice way to end the day."

"It's so lovely," Barbara added. "You get one of the nicest views of the city from the deck behind here."

The Cubs took a 4–3 lead into the fourth, where a beautifully orange twilight sky provided a backdrop to Reed Johnson's running, leaping catch at the left-center-field wall. Carlos Marmol got starter Ted Lilly out of a seventh-inning jam, but Atlanta crept to within 6–5 with four singles in the eighth against Bob Howry. "[Piniella] is going to get criticized for not sticking with Marmol in the eighth," Samuel said. After Eyre came out of the bullpen to end the threat, Samuel pointed out that Eyre had not allowed an earned run in 31 straight appearances, tying a club record.

Woody warmed up in the eighth, but four insurance runs—including a three-run blast by Geovany Soto—gave him the night off, and Jon Lieber mopped up in the 10–5 victory. The Cubs' 27–8 home record was their best since the 1907 squad started with the same record. That was at West Side Grounds; this was at the Disneyland of baseball.

And everybody wanted to be there. "Dandy Don" Dando knew it too well. He's getting soft in his golden years, giving up his golden tickets to friends and family for the first two games of the series. "I've missed more games than usual," he admitted while sipping an iced tea at Tuscany's. "I used to be cold-hearted or hard-nosed, but I've loosened up a bit." Sometimes he'll grab a radio and sit out on Navy Pier, watching the boats and listening to the Pat & Ron Show. Other times, he'll dine at a Rush Street restaurant and watch on television. Then there's the temptation to come north to Wrigleyville's scene and Tuscany's delectable food. Chef Alex came out with a plate of fried calamari, some prosciutto-wrapped cantaloupe appetizers, and a hefty serving of optimism. "If they go to the World Series, I told my son we're going no matter how much the tickets are. I don't care," Alex said.

Alex and every other Cubs fan wanted to be pinched. Were these really *our* Cubbies? I pleaded with Dandy Don for humility. He was there in 1977, right? "Yeah, I remember that team," he said. "Their uniforms weren't that great, their traveling uniforms. Weren't they sort of light blue with white stripes?"

Actually, they switched to those groovy duds in 1978. The '77 team started 47–22 and put Rick Reuschel, Jerry Morales, Manny Trillo, and Bruce Sutter on the NL All-Star squad. They finished in fourth place, 20 games out at 81–81. What happened? Sutter, who had flimflammed hitters with his revolutionary split-fingered fastball, got hurt. We agreed it was the kind of adversity this year's team hadn't faced. We spoke too soon.

I joined friends on Beyond the Ivy's Waveland/Sheffield rooftop. We sat two rows from the top, looking at the back of the scoreboard. This is about as remote from home plate as possible in the whale's ecosystem. But we still could see Jeff Bennett's second-inning pitch as it rode in and hit Alfonso Soriano's hand. While Dempster finished off a 7–2 complete-game victory, Soriano went for X-rays. "He's a tough kid," Piniella said. "When he wanted to come out of the ballgame, that was a pretty good indication something was wrong. So it didn't surprise me when the trainer came up to me in the fifth inning and told me he had a little crack in there."

Johnson contemplated Soriano's absence, which would give him more playing time. "He's always walking around with a smile on his face. He makes it fun to come to work," he said. "It's going to be tough for us to fill the void."

The Cubs had to forge ahead, even if it was turn-back-the-clock day at Wrigley Field for a Thursday matinee. The ballpark's first-ever throwback game was inspired by WGN-TV's 60th year of broadcasting Cubs baseball.

The retro feel was everywhere, from the bunting on the walls and façades to the music, scorecards, $1 smokey links, and 75¢ Pepsi-Colas. Teams wore replica 1948 uniforms, with the Cubs shedding the pinstripes for a day and wearing blue stirrup socks with three horizontal red stripes. In the clubhouse that morning, diminutive Mike Fontenot checked out recent recall Micah Hoffpauir in his retro uni, then gave Ronny Cedeno the once-over in passing. "I'm gonna look like an oompa loompa in those things," Fontenot cracked.

Ushers donned straw hats, and the marketing department got into the act—the guys wearing zoot suits, and the gals wearing dresses with shank sleeves and Lilly Dache–era pancake hats. Some writers even wore fedoras with "press" tags tucked in the band. Across the street at the Lakeview Baseball Club, the "Anno Catuli" sign was altered to circa 1948, as in AC000239.

At the Waveland/Kenmore crosswalk, Ballhawk Kenny got into the spirit, too, breaking out his Sears Roebuck 1947 Alvin Dark model three-fingered mitt for batting practice. Wearing an early 1900s gray Cubs cap with black pinstripes and a black bill, he showed how the padding had worn on the glove. He held a dish

sponge in his palm as he inserted his hand. Kenny had one oppor-
tunity to catch a ball on the fly but tried one-handing it. "Gotta
use two hands with those things," I advised, and he shot me a look
that said, *Tell me something I don't know.*

A ball bounced down the gangway next to my building, but two
other ballhawks beat Kenny down the narrow passage. One hit the
corner building, and he played the rebound perfectly with two
hands. He got outreached for another in the crosswalk. The last of
seven to come out bounced into the backyard of the Bud building,
where Pat Kelly was waiting for his sister to join him at their first
game since closing on the property. His friend Ken Yohanna
scooped up the baseball—one final souvenir for the old guard.

Inside Wrigley, minor league recalls Hoffpauir and Eric Patterson caught fly balls and a lecture by coach Mike Quade in left field.
With their next 15 games against AL teams, the designated hitter
was about to come into play, and the extra bat was needed. "That's
part of proving you're a good organization," GM Jim Hendry said.
"We're trying to give Lou the guys who fit at the time and who are
the hottest."

The first two innings were broadcast in black and white from
camera angles of another era. A simple screen graphic read: "Don't
adjust your set. We know it's black and white. It's 1948 for a few
innings, so relax and enjoy." Jack Rosenberg, the retired WGN
sports editor who helped nurture the station's relationship with the
Cubs, brought his old manual typewriter. "Rosey" used to spend
hours chewing the fat with players and coaches by the hitting cage.
He'd type up these anecdotes for play-by-play man Jack Brickhouse to inject seamlessly. Rosey's protégé, Bob Vorwald, typed
away in the booth, a sound that was constantly emanating behind
Brickhouse's broadcasts in those days.

On a hot day with the wind blowing out, Jeff Francoeur spotted
the Braves a 2–0 lead with a homer in the second. Jim Edmonds got
those back with a sacrifice fly in the seventh and a one-out solo
homer in the ninth to the opposite field. In the eleventh, Edmonds
came up again, this time with the bases loaded and nobody out.
Braves manager Bobby Cox brought in lefty Jeff Ridgway; Piniella
countered with pinch-hitter Reed Johnson. Checkmate! Ridgway's

first pitch was a slider that hit Johnson in the calf. Talk about taking one for the team! "I was trying to get out of the way. If it didn't hit me, I think that ball's going to the backstop," Johnson said. "When you have games like that, it just breeds more confidence."

. . . .

FOR THE SECOND straight day, the Cubs were involved in a game with throwback uniforms. This time, it was the Blue Jays donning circa 1970s unis on "Flashback Friday" in Toronto. The only mystery was why they were wearing their powder-blue roadies.

In my second trip of the season, Big Joe and Christie tapped into their abundance in miles and points from sales jobs to "sponsor" me. Peanut Tom and Ginger met us there, and we immediately recognized some cultural differences, like how they spelled the words "offence," "favourite," and "centre"; and that loons on the backside of dollar coins inspired the nickname "loonies."

When the Jays hit the field, Crankshaft texted from home wondering where I got my time machine. He asked, where were Dave Stieb, Lloyd Moseby, and Jesse Barfield? Onto his game, I replied Garth Iorg was the DH. He countered with Kelly Gruber and John Mayberry. I aced with Doug Ault, who hit the first homer in Jays history.

But it was the modern-day Jays who were getting rookie Sean Gallagher up to speed. A two-run homer by former Cub Matt Stairs followed by a solo shot by ex-Cardinal Scott Rolen spotted Toronto a 3–0 lead in the third. A couple sitting in front of us with their two boys on the first-base line were perplexing. The boys wore Cubs gear, and the wife was a Chicagoan. But the husband, in a gray Jays jersey, taunted his kids mercilessly after those two clouts.

"Did you lose your luggage?" Big Joe teased.

Turns out he was a native of Toronto who'd moved to Chicago in '94. Gotta give him props for loyalty.

Edmonds stayed hot with an RBI double in the fourth, but his sixth-inning hard smash hit second-base umpire Jeff Nelson. Because Nelson was inside the base line and the ball hit him before it could be fielded, it was a dead ball, sending Fukudome back to

Peanut Tom and Ginger celebrate a Cubs win in Toronto on Wayne Gretzky's rooftop beer garden. *Photo by Jim McArdle*

third base and leaving Edmonds at first with a single. Peanut Tom and Ginger debated over the consequences. Was it a rally stopper? They wagered a bet and shook on it. Patterson drove in a run with a single, but the Cubs fell short of tying the game. "You owe me a loonie," he told her. It cost more than that. The scoring ended there in a 3–2 Toronto victory.

The roof was closed all night, and we could hear thunder booming above. So we stayed inside the Rogers Centre after the game, eating at the Hard Rock Café with a nice view of the field. We were surprised to see the grounds crew feverishly working on a synthetic turf field and covering the pitching mound and dirt areas around the bases—under a closed roof!

Fortunately, we barely had to walk outside to get to our rooms at the Renaissance. Big Joe was hell-bent on upgrading to one of their 70 rooms overlooking the playing field, and darned if he didn't get one the next morning. I would've felt right at home in one with a view from behind the left-field foul pole—except they were so high I would've needed an oxygen tank. As we left the hotel near game time, dozens of people, mostly kids, were waiting in line with sleeping bags. Ginger explained she'd read online that it was sleepover night in the outfield.

"D'oh!" Joe wailed. "Why didn't you tell us that before?"

Sunny skies, Marquis, and Johnson tempered Big Joe's lodging discontent. With the roof open for more of a true baseball feel, Marquis yielded just one run on four hits in seven-plus innings. Johnson delivered a three-run homer in a four-run second inning as the Cubs beat former Cy Young winner Roy Halladay 6–2. The night before, Johnson had received a lengthy standing ovation in his return to where he played the previous five years. "There are only two guys I've seen that for, and that's him and [Carlos] Delgado," said Vernon Wells, a longtime Jay. "That's pretty high praise considering what Delgado was able to do in his time here. Obviously, the fans respected and loved the way [Johnson] played." We celebrated the win Canada style, at Wayne Gretzky's rooftop beer garden. Cubs Nation was prevalent, including Bleed-CubbieBlue Al and Miriam.

Lilly, another former Jay, beat his old team in the series finale. Eyre's streak of consecutive scoreless outings ended at 33, but the Cubs clinched the series win with three runs in the third and four in the seventh. It was time to trade in our loonies and head back to Wrigleyville. The Cubs had a pit stop in Cooperstown, New York, on their way to South Florida.

Piniella grew up in West Tampa to parents of Spanish descent and was a legend in athletics at Jesuit High School. The bypass to Cooperstown cost him an off-day at home. What's more, what was to be the final Hall of Fame Game was canceled by thunderstorms and hail. But the Cubs skipper remained gracious.

"I could have had a day off in my hometown today, but Cooperstown means a lot to baseball," he said. "If you had your druthers, you would rather have the day off. It's only one day. It's not going to kill us." Yosh Kawano, the Cubs' 87-year-old longtime clubhouse manager, was honored by the Hall and donated his trademark white floppy hat to the museum. But the day ended abruptly, and the team was off to Albany for their flight to Lou-town.

In Tampa, Piniella visited with his 88-year-old mother, Margaret, in his boyhood home. Across a cobblestone street is the park where he and his brother spent their summers. The ballfield was renamed in his honor. He slept in his own bed and spent mornings on the beach with his wife, Anita, two sons, daughter, and three grandchildren. Countless longtime friends came to the three-game series across the Howard Frankland Bridge at Tropicana Field. Anita handled the ticket requests; Lou managed the pregame schmoozing. But his former team wasn't so welcoming.

Two key mistakes—Johnson breaking a cardinal rule and making the final out at third base in one inning, and pitcher Neal Cotts throwing away a comebacker to let the eventual winning run get to third base—cost the Cubs the opener. Johnson almost made amends with a two-out surprise bunt as the tying run charged home from third in the ninth inning. But rookie third baseman Evan Longoria scooped it bare-handed, and first baseman Willy Aybar dug out the throw to secure the Rays' 3–2 victory.

After another one-run loss the next night (5–4), the series finale witnessed two usually solid members of the bullpen unraveling during a seven-run Tampa Bay seventh inning. Marmol walked two batters, then hit the next two. Eyre was called upon and yielded a grand slam to Carl Crawford. The Rays won 8–3, handing the Cubs their first three-game losing streak of the season. The team bus pulled up to Gate K across the street at about 2:00 AM. In less than 12 hours, they would be playing the cross-town rival White Sox here.

• • • •

THE BUZZ WAS EARLY. I bumped into my scorecard delivery guy at 9:00 AM on my way to the fray. WGN Radio's Kathy and Judy were doing a remote show across from Marquee Plaza. I went to Harry Caray's, where WLUP radio personality Jonathon Brandmeier was live with Mr. Cub and former White Sox slugger Ron Kittle.

When I arrived, two guys were chewing both ends of a beefy six-foot submarine sandwich. Whoever ate the most got tickets for

WEST SIDE ROOTERS

On the evening of June 18, with the Cubs-Rays game on every TV at Harry Caray's Tavern in Wrigleyville, the West Side Rooters Social Club held its first organized meeting. The Cubs fan club was disbanded after the 1908 season by team president Charles W. Murphy, who considered its "organized noisemaking" obnoxious. The club was being resurrected by Grant DePorter. DePorter, a Chicago native and the longtime president and managing general partner of Harry Caray's Restaurant Group, gained national prominence by paying more than $110,000 for the infamous Bartman ball in 2004. He destroyed the ball with explosives on national television in an attempt to end the Billy Goat Curse. When that didn't work, he served the remaining shards in a spaghetti the next year.

"After all this other stuff we tried hadn't worked, like blowing up balls, I started looking for something," DePorter said. "I stumbled on this Rooters thing. I thought this was something unique about '08 that I hadn't seen before." The Rooters were started by Joe Tinker, the shortstop on the last Cubs championship team and the first name in the refrain of Franklin Pierce Adams' famous poem, "Baseball's Sad Lexicon." The Cubs were playing at West Side Grounds back then, hence the fan club's name.

Rooters Chairman Ernie Banks called the meeting to order, and DePorter explained the club's history and culture—how they practiced organized "scientific cheering" and held "tallyho" pep rallies, bellowing the war cry "Oof Wah!" as they paraded to the ballpark for games. Membership was free, and Mr. Cub swore them in by having them repeat an oath DePorter found from the original club:

> I do hereby agree to attend each and every game during
> the season of 2008, providing the laws of health, nature,
> and coinage permit—that I will not allow domestic or busi-
> ness affairs to be sufficient excuse for breaking of this con-
> tract, so help me. Oof Wah!

Fittingly, the Cubs plated the tying run moments later. DePorter announced tentative dates for the club's first tallyho and a ⤑

fund-raising charity ball in September—and the Cubs took a 2–1 lead on The Riot's RBI single.

But curses never die easy. By the time Mr. Cub and Dutchie Caray, wife of the establishment's namesake and the Rooters' treasurer, led the crowd in singing "Take Me Out to the Ball Game," the Rays had retaken the lead. And when the 5–4 loss was complete, reports circulated that Big Z (shoulder) and Edmonds (foot) had left due to injuries.

Oof, indeed!

that day's game. The Sox guy was winning, and his buddy offered encouragement...sort of. "Way to go, Johnnie!" he said, slapping a Cubs sticker on his back.

The media, out in full force, was on hand before most of the Cubs, who were allowed to sleep in. Photographers surrounded Piniella when he walked out to the dugout and was greeted by Sox manager Ozzie Guillen. The two skippers had filmed a Chevy commercial just a couple weeks earlier, depicting them as bosom buddies—walking their dogs, skipping rope, fishing off the North Michigan Avenue Bridge, and bouncing on a trampoline. "It's in fun is all it was. I can see where people in Chicago enjoy these ads," Piniella said. "It's good for the city of Chicago. That's what's important. It gets the fans excited; it gets them into it."

While surveying the neighborhood scene in the morning, I met WXRT morning producer Marc Alghini as he was setting up the station's mini concert at Cubby Bear. Ironically, we were both headed to the same place for the game—on the top two rows of the bleachers to the immediate right-field side of the center-field batter's eye. That's where Stephanie Leathers sits. For the past 18 years, she's published a newspaper called *Bleacher Banter* that circulates to bleachers regulars. At one time there were hundreds like them in baseball, but it's now one of the last of its kind.

"Scoop Steph," 66 and a former South Sider, still has the original photo ID that was her early 1990s season bleachers pass. She became a bleachers mainstay shortly after attending her first Cubs game in 1979. The Phillies beat the Cubs 23–22 that afternoon in one of the wildest games Wrigley ever has seen. She was hooked and started coming by herself. Like the rookie who follows baseball etiquette and is seen and not heard, she sat in front of the old-timers and listened. Before long, they welcomed her in.

"They" included people like the red-headed Elsie; the cigarette-smoking, leather-skinned, and toothless Bernie; and Marv, whose seat she now occupies on the aisle of Section 311. This used to be section 147 before the bleachers were rebuilt in 2005–2006. Her seat was and still is known as "the death seat" because the last four people who sat there died. The right to sit in the death seat gets passed down by tenure.

Others in Scoop Steph's group include Judy Caldow, a retired Chicago public school teacher, and Howard Tucker, a blind man who follows the game by radio. Caldow started coming to games regularly in 1963 and has a collection of 3,000 completed score-cards. She was pregnant when she met Scoop Steph and brought her daughter, Kathy, to her first game when she was three days old. Kathy is now 23 and engaged. Howard, 61, went to his first game in 1956, borrowing a transistor radio so he could listen along. He was late arriving today. Having learned he was married to a blind White Sox fan, I had to restrain myself from making jokes. Judy cut through the restraints: "He's parking the car."

Just as Scoop Steph was once taken under a wing, they do the same with the younger generation. There's 29-year-old Iowa native Jessica Lee, number 23,372 on the waiting list for season tickets. Alghini's family has had season tickets seven rows back of the first-base dugout since he was a kid. These days, the 42-year-old prefers the bleachers.

After rain delayed the start of the series opener, the Cubs fell behind 3–1 early. In the sixth inning, Marc passed out sticks of gum in a seemingly benign act of sharing. We all chewed and drowned out Sox fans with "root, root, root for the CUBBIES" during the seventh-inning stretch. Then Marc proclaimed: "Here's where it all happens."

D-Lee hit the next pitch into the right-field bleachers. Ramirez followed by jacking one into left. Tie game! The bleachers seemed to be one big trampoline of bouncing bodies as Howard wildly

Aramis Ramirez watches his walk-off home run against the White Sox on its flight to the center-field juniper bushes.
Steve Green photo courtesy Chicago Cubs

rang a cowbell he's brought to games since the 1970s. In the ninth, Marc waved his hands around in horizontal circles. Needing as much baseball karma as possible, I was still turning my cap inside out when Rammy hit the second pitch of the inning into the bushes just below us to the right. Jumpin' junipers! Cubs win 4–3! Wrigleyville turned giddy!

"You're Magic Marc!" I told him. Turns out it was magic gum that almost went the way of the beanstalk. Marc had passed it out in the sixth inning of comeback wins against the Rockies and Braves during the previous two weeks but left it at Cubby Bear that morning. Willy B saved the day by bringing it over and passing it through the bleachers gate. The brand? Wrigley's, of course!

That night, they lined up at the day-of-game ticket windows. The Sox series is the one time all year that barricades were put up to keep bleachers lines from flooding onto Waveland and Sheffield avenues. They were filled with people by 9:00 AM. The buzz inside was created by a press release issued by the Cubs. Big Z was headed to the disabled list for just the second time in his career. "He wasn't real pleased with me right away, but we talked through it," Hendry said. "It's our job to look at the calendar at the end of the year and work backward. Let's get it all cleared up. Let's get the inflammation out and have him fresh and ready to go for the next 18 to 20 starts."

Crankshaft and I started the day by bopping down the block to Big D's apartment with a jar of Spanish olives for Bloody Marys. Their friend was dressed in a ridiculous tight pink tank top, ready for his bachelor party in the bleachers. From Big D's brick balcony, we surveyed the scene of mass Chicago baseball fever below. Across the intersection, the sign at Murphy's Bleachers poked fun at White Sox picher Jose Contreras: "Contreras translates into choke artist."

While I was in the press box for my No. 1 duties in the first inning, Scoreboard Rick predicted two doubles, two singles, two runs, and an RBI out of Patterson. Darned if the rookie only fell a double short of that lofty forecast.

Edmonds improved his batting average to .311 as a Cub with a pair of home runs in a nine-run second inning that obliterated a 4–1 deficit. He joined Sammy Sosa and Mark Bellhorn as the only Cubs to homer twice in an inning. Oddly enough, Fontenot, who had followed Edmonds' first homer with one of his own, could have become the fourth. Unaware of the possibility of that particular baseball oddity, Piniella pinch hit for Fontenot the second time around, later joking he had a "senior moment."

Marmol struggled with his control for the second straight outing, and Howry was hit hard in the ninth. Woody rode in from the jungle for his 19th save in the 11–7 victory. I had been watching in the bleachers with Big Joe and Peanut Tom, sitting behind Big D and Tree and their pink-clad friend. On my way out, I shared some revelry with Scoop Steph's group. "Hey, Magic Marc, didn't need the gum today, huh?" I said. He was chewing away. On this day it was victory gum.

The next afternoon at the firehouse on the corner, Lee and Jim wore unbuttoned Cubs pinstripes jerseys over their black fireman's polos. Mike was in his Sox jersey and black Sox Crocs. Jamie, the EMT, was holding a White Sox visor, pointing out the autographs of Jermaine Dye and Jim Thome on the bill.

Many Sox players parked in the lot on the other side of Seminary Avenue from the firehouse. Lee caught Thome trying to sneak back across the street to retrieve something from his car. Jamie and some other autograph seekers pounced. Several brooms were stuck upside down in two giant planters flanking both sides of the firehouse garage door. Up on Southport, guys parking cars at Blaine School waved them in with brooms.

Just like the first two days of the series, showers rained out batting practice. It evolved into a sun shower a half hour before game time, and a rainbow cascaded over the city's picturesque skyline to the south. Indeed, with ESPN's national broadcast of a series finale where two Chicago teams met while holding first place for the first time ever, the Windy City was a pot of gold in the baseball world. The Sox had dissed Cubs fans and their team's ballpark all weekend. Catcher A.J. Pierzynski, the most wanted man on the North Side since John Dillinger was gunned down by the feds outside the Biograph Theatre, seconded Lee Elia's rant, 25 years later, about Cubs fans being "idiots." Pitcher John Danks said Wrigley is a "[bleeping] hole" that reeks of urine. Even general manager Kenny Williams wished fans a "happy [100th] anniversary!"

Guillen wisecracked that the rats were so big they must be lifting weights. He'd made the claim about seeing furry rodents in the past, and the visiting clubbies have fun with it, leaving fake rats and mice in his desk and shower. This time around, they had a remote-controlled rat named Ozzie motoring around the clubhouse. What Guillen overlooked is that 2008 is the year of the rat on the Chinese calendar.

Reporters baited Piniella about all this in the dungeon. He took the high road but defended the old whale. "It's fine. It's small. It's an old park, and you're not going to have as spacious or luxurious accommodations as other stadiums," he said. "Quaintness in a clubhouse keeps a team together. You get too big, you get too modern, you get too spaced out, and you lose that closeness."

Speaking of closeness, I elected to experience the series finale as a standing-room-only patron with Crankshaft, Willy B, and friends. We found a spot next to a portable beer stand on the first-base side, at the base of a ramp leading to the upper deck. Boxes painted onto the concrete walkways designate SRO areas. Being tucked deep behind the main grandstand and under the upper deck has the feel of watching from inside a cave. Fly balls have to be tracked by watching the outfielders. Most of the field is viewable unless the crowd blocks sightlines by getting on its feet, so I had a few *ww*'s on my scorecard (for "wasn't watching," a little trick I learned from Phil Rizzuto).

The Cubs jumped all over the Sox, scoring two in the first and making it 5–0 four innings later with Patterson's first career homer followed by Rammy's fourth long ball of the series.

"Sweep! Sweep! Sweep!" the crowd chanted.

In the seventh, the game was delayed momentarily while fireworks exploded across Addison Street, behind where we were standing. A police squad car sped down the alley, while the Cubs continued to bomb the South Siders in the seventh and eighth. Demp left to a standing ovation in the ninth inning of his ninth victory, this one by a 7–1 count.

The teams had come into the series even in wins (30 apiece) and runs scored (291) against each other, but the Cubs clearly came out on top. "The thing I'm most proud of is our ability to come back after getting swept at Tampa," DeRosa said. "To come off that road trip and our first adversity of the year, I felt [if there was] a time if we were going to question ourselves…but we didn't do it."

The morning after Monday's day off, Piniella picked up the *Chicago Sun-Times* and turned to the back page. The headline blared in bold letters: "SAFE AT HOME." The accompanying art was 32 mini photos of the scoreboard's W and L flags, with scores of the Cubs' first 40 games. Three of the first four were L's; most of the rest were W's.

"It scared me a little bit," Piniella said. "Usually, when everybody catches on, it's time you start cooling off." The Baltimore Orioles were making their first visit to the not-so-friendly confines. Their hosts had won 14 straight at home, the most since 1936, and were a win away from matching their longest home winning streak since 1890. Their home winning percentage of .800, if maintained, would be an NL record in the 162-game era.

Ozzie Guillen and Jim Hendry share a fun-loving moment during the White Sox's visit to Wrigley. *Steve Green photo courtesy Chicago Cubs*

Former Cubs president/CEO Andy MacPhail was returning to Wrigley in the public eye for the first time since unceremoniously stepping down on the final day of the 2006 season. The new man in charge of the O's, his favorite boyhood team, lunched with D-Lee and dined with Hendry during Monday's off day. A man with baseball pedigree (his grandfather, Larry, and father, Lee, are Hall of Fame baseball executives), MacPhail addressed the Cubs' success in the wake of his stewardship. "It's actually better that they get better. You would prefer, I think, that the foundation be in place where at least they could do well," he said. "But you never know, really, what piece is the final piece with what came before."

Kerry Wood was drafted in the first year of the MacPhail administration. "There are people here that he put in place and that he went after who are helping us win, so he's got to get a little credit," Woody said. "The attitude changed while he was here. I think he had a big part to do with that."

Brian Roberts had been rumored to be coming to Chicago in an off-season deal that never got made. In his first visit to Wrigley since attending Game 6 of the 2003 NLCS as a fan, the second baseman contributed three hits as the O's jumped out to a 7–1 lead. Edmonds hit a three-run homer in the seventh. Two innings later, singles by Soto and Theriot, and a walk by DeRosa loaded the bases against Baltimore closer George Sherrill. I started to wonder if Scoop Steph's group was chomping on Magic Marc's sixth-inning gum.

Turns out he and his edible epoxy weren't there. Sherrill struck out Cedeno, Fukudome, and Henry Blanco on 11 pitches. Groundskeeper Brian Helmus, who'd written the date of each win on the W flag during the streak, had to break the L flag out of mothballs. It had been 38 days since it last flew, on May 17, but that didn't matter to the clearly peeved Piniella after the 7–5 defeat. "We didn't have three good at-bats with the bases loaded. We didn't swing at strikes," he grouched. "If we would have showed a little more patience at home plate, the outcome might have been different."

It was the 26th save of the season for Sherrill, an obscure reliever signed out of independent ball by Seattle in 2003. The next afternoon, he and teammate Dennis Sarfate visited Skybox on Sheffield. Sarfate was in uniform, filming a pregame spot for Baltimore's TV carrier. Skybox owner Dave Abrams told him how the biz got started and shared stories, like when he goaded former Cubs pitcher Jim Bullinger to toss a ball onto the rooftop, and Bullinger's short-armed throw broke the third-floor window. Then there was the one about Bret Saberhagen, who had sprayed bleach on reporters and spent his subsequent suspension by indulging himself on Skybox in 1994.

"I was sitting right there last night," Abrams said, pointing to a seat on the top deck. "I thought the Cubs were going to win."

Baltimore PR man Jeff Lantz cupped Sherrill's shoulder. "You can blame this guy right here."

Dave smiled. "That was you? That was a heckuva close. We kept saying, 'Why aren't they having anybody warm up?'"

Among players around the league, Sherrill and Sarfate agreed there's a curiosity about the rooftop experience. Sarfate spotted a teammate taking batting practice across the way. The stadium was void of fans. "Hey Ole!" he called out, and Garrett Olson turned. "You tanked!"

"You can heckle. Obviously, when there's 40,000 people, they can't hear you," Sarfate said. "But you always wonder if people feel like they are part of the game here. This is pretty cool."

As afternoon turned to evening, I found BleedCubbieBlue Al and his gang devouring a Lou Malnatti's Chicago-style pizza in their left-field bleachers section. Harry the Rookie used our address to have it delivered and waited on the curb. The driver steered around barricades at Seminary and got questioned by a policeman in front of the firehouse. "Delivery for Harry?" he asked. Harry paid the man and entered through the bleachers gate under the left-

Orioles George Sherrill (left) and Dennis Sarfate join Skybox on Sheffield owner Dave Abrams for a tour of the famed rooftop facility. *Photo by Jim McArdle*

field foul pole. The guard there didn't seem surprised, telling us one guy who lives across the street has his wife bring over dinner every night. Now that's Cubs baseball utopia!

Al's blog that morning alluded to a report on another website that the Cubs were stealing signs from the center-field scoreboard, not the first time that accusation has been made. So when the Cubs jumped on Baltimore with four runs in the first and two in the second, that topic came up again. "Could it be that the Cubs finally have built a team tailored to win in this ballpark?" Al asked rhetorically.

The O's closed the deficit to 6–4 with a pair of two-run homers. After Edmonds made it 7–4 with a solo shot in the fourth, Ronnie Woo came walking down our aisle. Jeff teased with his usual wry sense of humor: "Al, your girlfriend is here."

That sent Al on a rant. Ronnie is able to woo fans who make an occasional game at Wrigley. They take photos with him, high-five him, and "woo" right along. Those who are there every day, however, are wooed out and shoo the Woo away. "If Mark Cuban would get on the record that he would ban him forever, I'd get on the Mark Cuban bandwagon," Al quipped.

The Cubs finished with 12 hits and 10 walks. When the bases were loaded in the eighth, Al pointed out that they'd already stranded 11 men. The Cubs didn't score, making Woody necessary to close out the 7–4 victory by striking out the side.

The next day I dropped in on a neighbor I haven't introduced just yet. They're longtime neighbors but keep a low profile in their trailer. It's not their home, but with the amount of time the WGN-TV production crew spends in their mobile TV studio parked outside the western edge of the stadium, it must seem like it. Close quarters beget close relationships and good banter. When I walked into the Trio Video trailer for the finale of the Baltimore series, the first person I encountered was Marc Brady. "Are you doing a profile on me?" Brady asked. "I like long walks—"

Mark Stencel, sitting next to him, cut him off: "I prefer he takes them after the first pitch."

Brady, who grew up in the southeast neighborhood of Hyde Park, has been with WGN since 1998. Stencel, who is an, ahem,

White Sox fan from Highland Park, started in 1989. In front of them, Danielle Denning updated stats graphics displayed on viewers' TV tubes. In the front row, Pete Toma sat in the chair Arne Harris made famous. Toma, the Philadelphia-born producer of Cubs baseball on WGN, learned from the master before Harris' sudden death in 2001. Now he kicks around one-liners with Skip Ellison in front of a massive wall of monitors. A Georgia native, Ellison came to Channel 9 in 2002 via TBS. In his Southern drawl, Ellison commanded, "Let's go red, B slo-mo, A," dictating a replay of a Fontenot single that showed the view from the Harris-pioneered center-field camera, followed by a side angle in slow motion of Fontenot connecting on his swing, and a shot from behind the plate of Fontenot driving the ball into right field.

With 10 cameras going, these guys are more dialed into the game than the fans who are at the stadium. They're all wearing headsets while listening to cameramen, broadcasters Len Kasper and Bob Brenly, and the studio a few blocks west of the ballpark.

Both Toma and Brady had their laptops open, scanning the latest news. Albert Pujols had come off the disabled list...umpire Paul Runge was suspended. Brady even had an instant-messaging window open, talking to his counterpart on the Cardinals broadcast. A Gary Sheffield homer had tied their game in the ninth in Detroit. They constantly updated Len and Bob.

And why not? The Cubs were getting creamed, and the game was becoming stodgy. Kasper asked off air to know the last series the Cubs lost at home. "We haven't been mauled in a long time," said Brady as he went flipping through the game notes to find an answer.

Cubs media relations director Peter Chase could be heard announcing over the press box PA that Piniella had been named to coach in the All-Star Game. Ellison had a cameraman find Lou in the dugout, and seconds later Kasper passed along the news on-air. Then came time for the seventh-inning stretch, and Toma played a tape he'd put together on guest conductor Yosh Kawano, who was honored that day for 65 years of service in the Cubs organization. Bored late in the game, a cameraman found a squirrel scurrying along the base of the outfield vines. One camera stayed on it, and

Stencel started goofing around with a cartoon graphic of Bullwinkle the moose. Viewers never saw it, but it humored all of us and helped pass the time.

Piniella wasn't amused. He hates losing any games, but is usually more irritable after a close loss, not a 11–4 blowout such as this. Big Z had thrown that morning and looked to be on target for a return the following weekend in St. Louis. But Fukudome missed his second straight game with a calf strain, and Eyre pulled a groin muscle in the series finale. The suggestion was made that they weren't hustling. "We're so banged up right now. Let me tell you what—let's just get through the damn game," he said. "Emotion, to me, is good pitching and good hitting, and solid defense. I call that emotion. You want the other kind of emotion, you can go to a rock concert or to church."

The Trio Video truck was cleaned out and towed 70 blocks south to U.S. Cellular Field. It was time for Cubs-Sox, Weekend II.

•   •   •   •

IF A CUBS–WHITE SOX World Series were ever to occur, it would be known as the Red Line Series, because 13 stops on the CTA's Red Line train separate the two ballparks.

My 50-minute ride to the opener of the series ended with the train essentially emptying at the Sox–35th Street stop, and the conductor saying: "I figure this is the destination for many of you. Please make sure to remember your paraphernalia, that you have your mitts, caps, shirts, all your Cubs things. And give your favorite White Sox fan a hug for me."

The Sox didn't show any brotherly love the weekend before, but the Cubs were careful not to wage a war of words despite the media's attempts to goad them. Big Z was asked if he'd ever seen a rat at U.S. Cellular Field. Nope. Edmonds had once knocked himself out on the Cell's warning track but remembered fondly playing in the 1993 All-Star Game there. Marmol said it was "a nice park."

Huh? Didn't he remember the Sox calling Wrigley a dump a week earlier?

"I don't get into that," he said.

Neither would Piniella. "Are the Cubs the most popular team in town?" he was asked.

"Let the fans decide," he said.

"I don't put any restrictions on what people say. I don't have any reason to be critical of [the Sox]," Hendry said. "Lou runs the ballclub, and I think Lou thinks it probably would be a big waste of time....Who cares who says what?"

Nevertheless, "the Cell" seems an appropriate nickname for the White Sox's ballpark. It's been unfriendly territory for Cubs fans since the two teams started meeting annually in interleague play. The Cubs have played near-.500 ball there, but Sox fans are batting 1.000 with the heaps of abuse they dump on visiting North Side fans. My mission for the day was to look for "friendlies" from the confines.

I found BleedCubbieBlue Al and Miriam in Section 154, just foul of the left-field pole—almost home for them! Back in February, a pair of singles, one row in back of the other, was all Al could find in the 100 level.

I have to admit, the Sox taking the field with fans clapping to the beat of AC/DC's "Thunderstruck" was pretty cool. Then the fireworks went off, and the lights on the scoreboard's trademark pinwheels flickered and spun wildly.

"It's such overkill," Al said.

The banged-up Cubs started Patterson in left field, and he played a forgettable game, allowing a runner to tag up on a routine fly ball in the first (leading to the Sox's first run) and making a two-base error during a seven-run third. Al took out his phone and checked the weather radar. "It's coming but too late," he said. Soto and Fontenot made thunder with solo homers in the fifth, but three outs made the game official. The skies never opened, and the Cubs were blown out for the second straight day, this time 10–3.

An idea hatched by Crankshaft and an old Toons bartender years ago finally came to fruition the next afternoon. He and another Toons regular named Matt put together the inaugural "Cub Crawl." Why be locked in the Cell when we have a neighborhood concentrated with more taverns and watering holes than any other in the city?

There are 35 bars in an area along Clark Street from Grace Street south to Roscoe Street and from Sheffield Avenue north from Roscoe to Waveland Avenue. That's not counting the music clubs, like Metro and Wild Hare, and the restaurants, like Tuscany and Chens, that have liquor licenses. Nor does it include places off the beaten path, like Underground Lounge and Guthrie's. It's perfect terrain for pub crawls. Nine bars in nine innings sounded intimidating. What if notoriously fast-working Sox pitcher Mark Buehrle had been pitching? Against Greg Maddux? Talk about chugalug.

Both teams scored in the first, the Sox answering two Cubs runs with three of their own while we gathered at Redmond's. We soon discovered two other bar crawls doing our "original" idea. Crankshaft carped and ordered a second beer. I warned him not to run up his pitch count early.

There already was one out in the second by the time I ordered my next beer at Houndstooth. Then came the second out. This was going to be tough. "Take a pitch!" someone pleaded. By the time

The author and Crankshaft at the eighth bar of the Cub Crawl.
Photo courtesy Jim McArdle

we got to Irish Oak in the fourth inning, some seriously dark clouds hovered above, moving slowly south toward the Cell.

"By the time it gets there, it'll be the seventh inning," Crankshaft said.

A rain delay surely would be the death of us all and a great register ring for whatever bar we were at when play stopped. A three-run fourth, capped by D-Lee's two-run double, gave the Cubs a 5–4 lead. The deluge came and went before we headed to Mo's Cantina for the fifth inning. A second wave of rain came, and the Sox tied it 5–5. Gadzooks! If it hit the Cell now and the game was suspended, we'd have to return on Sunday to finish this bender.

The rain never reached the Cell. The sixth inning went quick, and the Cubs went 1-2-3 in the top of the seventh. In our haste, we forgot to sing "Take Me Out to the Ball Game" during the commercial break, the whole reason we slotted Harry Caray's for the seventh inning! So we broke into it as the Sox batted—and Carlos Quentin hit a go-ahead homer.

By the eighth, Matt, Crankshaft, and I were the only three to make it to Sports Corner. We reassembled at Murphy's, hoping to see that W flag in our mind's eye. D-Lee started the ninth with his fifth hit of the day, a double. But he never got past third base as the Cubs lost 6–5. For the tenth inning, we played Wii video games at Big D and Tree's across the street.

For the series finale, a softball buddy offered to take me on another mini pub crawl of the South Side's version of Wrigleyville. "It's not named after a gum. It's named after a bridge," White Sox Pete said of the neighborhood where the Cell and Comiskey Park before it were built. The bridge was too low to allow safe passage for boats on the Chicago River, so cargo had to be unloaded. Hence, the oxymoron of Bridge*port*, a historically Irish community in which five of Chicago's 45 mayors have lived, including Richard J. and Richard M. Daley. Just south of Bridgeport, the Union Stock Yards gave rise to Chicago's reputation as "hog butcher for the world."

"White Sox Pete" works in City Hall in the mayor's planning department. His mother worked for the previous Mayor Daley. The irony of ironies: Pete's wife, Terry, got her baseball allegiance from her grandfather, who no doubt took his lumps growing up as a Cubs fan in Bridgeport.

We met at Jimbo's on 33rd and Princeton, the equivalent to Cubby Bear for its close proximity to the stadium. It's worth noting that Jimbo, the bar's namesake, is a Cubs fan. Pete, with black hair and a goatee, walked in wearing a gray ringer T-shirt with the South Side Hit Men logo of the 1977-era Sox. I wasn't surprised to hear Journey, the band whose music the Sox had adopted during their '05 World Series run. But I was dismayed to see a Cubs fan picking out the songs on the juke box in the corner.

We headed out through Bridgeport's neighborhood homes toward First Base, a watering hole at 32nd and Normal. "It's like Melrose Park threw up on Bridgeport," Pete lamented as he looked around. "It's the worst architecture ever. They're big on these concrete front yards."

This is the land of sleeveless T-shirts and mullets. Fitting the part, we met a musclebound guy with a voice like Harvey Fierstein at the door of First Base. Above the bar, a bust of Richard J. Daley sat among bowling trophies. The bartender heard we were doing a quick pregame crawl and recommended Redwood on Wallace Street. "You can't swear there, but you can smoke!" she said excitedly.

With 1950s-esque décor, Redwood was on White Sox Pete's list and is a favorite hangout of Gene Honda, the Cell's public-address announcer. We walked in to Frank Sinatra crooning and left one beer later to a Jimmy Durante song. At the VFW across 32nd Street it was Dean Martin playing on the jukebox.

We finally caught up to modern civilization at Mitchell's on Halsted, where a sports talk radio station was doing a live broadcast. After a final beer at Schaller's Pub, we headed to the game.

Should've stayed at Schaller's. I hear the owner's son is a Cubs fan. Other than taking White Sox Pete's recommendation to eat a corn off the cob concoction mixed with lime, cayenne pepper, salt, butter, cheese, and mayonnaise, the game experience was bland. The Sox destroyed the Cubs 5–1. I left before the brooms swept me out. The City Series was even again, 33–33. It was the 82nd game of the season. Our story's heroes were on the back nine and still leading on the NL Central scorecard.

6

JULY

THE CUBS WERE GETTING HEALTHY. Aramis Ramirez left for the Dominican Republic after the White Sox series for the birth of his second son. He missed the first three games of the opening series of July in San Francisco, causing the team to play short-handed with 24 players. Ramirez returned for the finale, and Reed Johnson was activated off the disabled list. During the following series in St. Louis, Carlos Zambrano came off the DL, and Alfonso Soriano was cleared to start hitting.

The Cubs split four on the Bay. Mark DeRosa, subbing for Ramirez, blasted two homers in the series opener, and Mike Fontenot clubbed a tie-breaking solo shot in the eighth inning of the third game.

Big Z returned on Independence Day to beat St. Louis 2–1 in the series opener. Jim Edmonds received a rousing ovation at Busch Stadium for his eight years of service despite fireworks set off by Cards manager Tony LaRussa, who exhorted fans to ignore Edmonds because of comments he made earlier in the season about now wanting to be identified with the Cubs.

As the sun rose the following morning, six of us diehards already were headed south on I-55 for the final two games of the series. Big Joe borrowed his mom's minivan. At risk of being grounded for two weeks with no Cubs or cell phone if there were any crumbs, spills, or cigarette burns, Joe had Christie and Ginger pack drink boxes and fruit rollups, and it was Gateway City here we come.

We went to the beer garden at Mike Shannon's restaurant to meet friends. Between Shannon's and the stadium was a giant hole that is to become a retail/residential district they are calling "ballpark village." Part of the plan is to have areas where fans can view the game atop the village from beyond the bleachers. Sound familiar?

I sat with Melanie, a Wrigley season-ticket holder, in the center-field bleachers. DeRosa's third-inning homer landed in front of us and was thrown back onto the field. "Copycats!" Mel charged.

Peanut Tom and Big Joe were sitting over the Cubs' bullpen a couple sections over. One thing to know about these guys is they love their Budweiser. We even made a pregame stop at the brewery's gift shop. Well, when they alerted us to open seats in their section, we mobilized. "C'mon, let's go. They're right over th—" I said, spotting them standing at attention and saluting the video board as the Clydesdales clomped in a between-innings commercial set to Bud's "Here Comes the King" jingle. Even Cardinals fans appreciated that.

Ramirez snapped an 0-for-28 slump with a two-run homer in the eighth, but Edmonds was thrown out three plays later trying to score on a fly-out to right. It was a close play that stuck in manager Lou Piniella's craw long after the game ended.

We watched Kerry Wood warm up below and enter the game to protect a 4–2 lead. Three walks and a double later, Rick Ankiel drove a two-out, two-run single into center field to end it. We were seeing red.

Which reminds me of a pet peeve: fans who wear red Cubs caps and shirts, and accessorize with too much red. We are blue; the Cardinals are red. Keep it straight. Christie had been given considerable grief on Saturday for her cute—but red—Keds. The next day, Melanie wore red capris she tried in vain to pass off as orange.

Before Sunday's series finale, raffle tickets for free passes to a Cards game were issued at the Broadway Oyster. During the drawing, Peanut Tom harrumphed with a keen, clamorous observation: "Notice the tickets are blue!" In the first inning, Ginger scanned the Internet on her cell phone and informed us that seven Cubs had been named All-Stars: reserves Woody, Z, Ramirez, and Ryan Dempster, along with starters Soriano, Kosuke Fukudome, and Geovany Soto.

Our seats in the third-base loge box revealed a sprawling view of the Gateway Arch looming over the St. Louis skyline. Sean Marshall was also looking good, limiting St. Louis to a Ryan Ludwick homer in a 7–1 victory. As the final out was recorded, Peanut Tom unfurled a giant W flag that had once flown on Wrigley's centerfield scoreboard. We dangled the mother of all W flags off the balcony and sang "Go Cubs Go" a cappella.

The Cubs had gone 17–15 during a 35-day stretch that included two West Coast trips, two series against the White Sox, and a day trip from Canada to Upstate New York to South Florida, not to mention injuries to their ace, their leadoff man, and their center fielder.

The Cardinals were dropped into third place. On our way out of Busch Stadium, we asked a guy in a Milwaukee jersey if he had gotten lost. "We're coming for you!" he trumpeted. That night, the second-place Brewers were finalizing a trade with Cleveland for reigning AL Cy Young Award winner CC Sabathia, which made me wonder if maybe the bigger enemy also was in blue.

· · · ·

THE CUBS WERE HOME for the first time in 12 days. In the clubhouse, hours before game time, seven Cubs entertained queries from reporters working on All-Star stories. Edmonds wore his usual Gallagher T-shirt. Standing by the dugout while Matt Murton stretched with his teammates before batting practice, I was asked by a Cubs employee if a player transaction had been announced. It hadn't. "I keep hearing things," he said. I later found out he knew exactly what was happening.

When neither Piniella nor general manager Jim Hendry showed their faces for b.p., the scuttlebutt started. All the radio, TV, and newspaper reporters were on their cell phones to their bosses. At 5:25 PM, Cubs media relations director Peter Chase told us Hendry would be in the interview room momentarily. "I'm sure Hendry is talking to give us the status of the team," one reporter said as we filed through the catacombs to the dungeon. When Hendry arrived, he revealed the details of a six-player trade that sent Murton, Gallagher, Eric Patterson, and minor-league catcher

Josh Donaldson to Oakland for pitchers Rich Harden and Chad Gaudin. At 5–1 with a 2.34 ERA, the 26-year-old Harden was one of the more highly regarded young starters in the game. A day after the Brewers announced their acquisition of Sabathia, Hendry had countered. He commended Cubs chairman Crane Kenney and even Sam Zell for adding $2.5 million to the payroll in order to obtain Harden. Then he rejected the notion he was done dealing. "We don't look at it today like we're going to get in [the play-offs]," Hendry said. "A year ago, look at the standings, and look who ended up playing in it."

Good point. Exactly a year earlier, the Mets, Brewers, and Padres led their divisions. None played in October, and the Rockies, who were in fourth place in the West on July 8, 2007, went on to the World Series.

As our story's heroes built an early 2–0 lead over the Reds, I walked down to El Jardin for the monthly gathering of the Lovable Losers Literary Review. There was the usual toast to hope, and Ted Norstrom performed a song called "Just One Bad Century" off his CD *Believe It, Achieve It — Music For Cubs Fans*. As Robert Goldsborough read from his novel *Three Strikes You're Dead*, Fontenot extended the Cubs' lead with a two-run homer. "A big hand for Bob Goldsborough, and a big hand for Mike Fontenot," emcee Don Evans said as he introduced the next speaker.

Sitting at a front table with an earphone tuned to the game was Ballhawk Kenny, who was proud to report he'd recently gotten a new job. Then his face turned sullen as he admitted he wouldn't be standing on Waveland during weekday games anymore. Fellow 'hawks Moe Mullins and Rich Buhrke also were there. They are the subjects of a documentary called *Ballhawks* being completed by Chicago-born filmmakers Mike Diedrich and Kyle McCarthy. They gave a preview of their movie, which centers on the ballhawks' perseverance after the bleachers-expansion project threatened their sustenance. Diedrich played a few trailers and shared stories, like the one about the fan shouting down from the bleachers one day: "The only thing sadder than the ballhawks is a bunch of guys making a film about them!"

Mullins and Buhrke fielded questions, and Buhrke summed up the number-one requirement to be a ballhawk: patience. "Anybody can catch a baseball. It's a just a matter of waiting it out," he said. "A lot of people stay there for five minutes, and if they don't get anything, they walk away." While the three 'hawks held court, Dave Davison had Waveland Avenue all to himself. Soto homered in the Cubs' 7–3 victory, but luckily (for them) the ball stayed in the park.

Mixed emotions hung in the clubhouse after the game. Gallagher became weepy as he said good-bye to Scott Eyre, his ride to spring training and a teammate he referred to as "Dad." The next day, though, it was full steam ahead.

In 15 seasons in the majors, Edmonds had reached the playoffs six times and the World Series twice. He had one ring for all that. So the media went to him, noticeably not wearing his Gallagher jersey. "You have to realize how hard it is to win," he said. "This is the chance. You might not get it again."

When Harden and Gaudin arrived, the media was asked to vacate the clubhouse. "Okay, everybody out so Rick can come in," Edmonds said, turning his cap backward. "Everyone's gotta go!"

I commended BleedCubbieBlue Al in left field for ripping *Sun-Times* columnist Jay Mariotti, who on consecutive days had called upon Hendry to acquire Harden, then waffled about Harden's fragile health (six DL trips in four seasons). Sue Land, a semi-regular with Al's group and a corporate travel executive from Barrington, was setting up a game of home-run derby. The rules were simple. Pick a player by putting your initials next to his name on her scorecard. If he homers, you get a dollar from everyone; $2 if it's a pitcher; double your money for a grand slam. It's a game they only play when "Derby Sue" is there. "I'm the keeper of the card," she said. "If there's only four of us here, I'll keep passing it around. Do you think I have a gambling problem?" Heck, I think it's a problem if you're *not* gambling in the bleachers. By the time I got the card, D-Lee, Rammy, and Soto were taken. "Can you pick an opposing player?" I asked. "You can, but it's frowned upon," she said.

Considering Big Z was on the mound, one homer shy of tying the Cubs' all-time record for homers by a pitcher, I chose him. Returning from my No. 1 duties in the press box, I was in the left-field upper deck when Adam Dunn homered to right-center. Below, I could see the group standing up, digging into their pockets and extending a hand to Miriam.

Ramirez snapped a 1–1 tie in the sixth with a blast to left field, and we paid Al. Hawaii Jeff asked where the rich couple was going to dinner. Big Z, working on a one-hitter, appeared to beat out a sacrifice bunt in the seventh. We turned around to watch the replay in the third-floor lounge of the rooftop building across the street. *Hmm...*, I thought, *maybe we needed to turn our TV around in the Swank*. Z looked to be safe, and Piniella argued, but doubles by Fukudome and Rammy and a single by D-Lee gave the Cubs three more runs. It was a cushion they'd need because Woody had to put out Carlos Marmol's bases-loaded fire in the ninth.

Coming off two night games, the Cubs didn't take batting practice the next morning. In the clubhouse, Big Z did impressions of Piniella, and Gaudin showed off a wolverine pelt he acquired after being given that nickname by Jason Kendall when both were with Oakland. But it was the Reds who showed off during a drippy afternoon. I watched from the rooftop at 3639 Sheffield Avenue. Draped off the stairway to the roofdeck was a Japanese flag, added a few weeks earlier to make Fukudome feel at home as he trotted out to right field. Up top, I met Al and Michele Daspin, a husband and wife team hosting their annual outing for their Chicago-based law firm. They've been doing this event at 3639 for 12 years. Clients fly in from all over the country. "They look forward to it every year and ask, 'Hey, when is that rooftop day?' They book their flights and hotels early," Michele said. "This is a beautiful baseball tradition."

Fontenot, whose sudden power surge had earned him the nickname "Little Babe Ruth" from Cubs broadcaster Ron Santo, cut Cincinnati's fourth-inning lead to 8–5 by yanking a two-run homer inside the right-field foul pole. As it began raining lightly, Al explained his firm specializes in real estate law. So I offered food for thought: perhaps no two streets in Chicago have boomed quite like Waveland and Sheffield in the last 15 years. Al considered the recent renovation at 3639. "Before, there was just a rooftop with some metal bleachers. The infrastructure shock is incredible," he said. "There was a weather fear factor. Now you no longer have that. You just go downstairs."

Which was what many people started doing. Those who stayed were offered blue rain ponchos by the staff. The rain intensified, and I was standing on the corner of the rooftop when Dunn jacked a monstrous shot that hit two doors down off the third-floor façade of the Lakeview Baseball Club, just missing a window. The topspin shot the ball downward, it ricocheted hard off the concrete entryway, skidded up a wrought-iron fence, and shot 40 feet into the air. Finally, it landed in the fenced-off construction zone in front of the Ivy League Baseball Club, where a young ballhawk outraced his counterparts for the souvenir. Naturally, he chucked a decoy back over the bleachers.

It was the most majestic of seven homers the Reds hit for the day as they overpowered the Cubs 12–7, averting the sweep.

· · · ·

THE GIANTS WERE IN TOWN for the weekend, and that meant Scoop Steph and her crew in front of the center-field concessions stands had some guests. Oftentimes, diehards from opposing teams befriend each other. Such was the case with Connie Hohimer, a bleachers regular who reeled in Sharon Ann "S.A." Kushinka when she was consulting on business in Chicago in the early 1990s. S.A., 53, grew up rooting for the Phillies in Pennsylvania. She moved to San Francisco in 1976 and after the Phils won the World Series in 1980, made a clean break to the Giants. She organizes an annual outing of Giants fans who sit with Stephanie's group. It's reciprocal, as Steph visited the Bay a few years back and was lined up with tickets and a place to house-sit. (We won't get into the story of her losing the family cat!) "It's fabulous," S.A. said of her Wrigley hosts. "These guys are the real deal. They're not yuppies in search of a tan."

There were 12 of them in black-and-orange Giants apparel. Stephen Calvert and Leah Nanni sat in front of Howard and me.

Calvert greeted old friends and owned up: "I fully expect to get swept this weekend."

"I don't know. That [Tim] Lincecum is pretty good," Howard said of Sunday's scheduled starter and *Sports Illustrated* cover boy.

The game turned into a pitcher's duel between Matt Cain and Jason Marquis. At the end of the third, we walked to the top of the aisle, one section toward right field, to sing "Happy Birthday" to Bill Shannon and share some cupcakes. He was with his son, Tim, and their own pocket of bleachers regulars. Asked his age, Bill responded, "Forty-seven...in reverse!"

Fortunately, I had Holly Swyers to sort out this communal conundrum. A military brat, Swyers grew up rooting for her father's team, the Dodgers. The Cubs hooked her shortly after she returned to the United States in the mid-1990s. Swyers, 37, has been a regular on Scoop Steph's perch since 1997, when she was attending grad school at the University of Chicago. Today, she is a professor of anthropology at Lake Forest College and has written extensively on Wrigley Field bleachers culture. "What I find makes this possible is the general admission seating. You can sit by whom you want to....A lot of these people started coming to the ballpark by themselves," Holly said. "Everyone knows everyone. It's one big group. It's sort of like your immediate family versus your extended family. They have petty feuds, and all the joys they share, too. You're in it for the long haul together."

Cain and Marquis both were out of the game after the seventh, and The Riot led off the eighth with a single. Piniella had Fontenot bunt him over, forcing Bruce Bochy to pick his poison: D-Lee or Rammy. The Giants skipper intentionally walked D-Lee, and Ramirez creamed the first pitch onto Waveland Avenue. Bending around the foul pole, the ball bounced off the street, hit my apartment building, and came to rest in the small front courtyard, where a young ballhawk named Matt reached through the fence and scooped it up.

"I came 2,000 miles to see this?" Leah bellowed. "And it was going so well!"

I found Rammy in the locker room later and told him he damn near broke my window with his baseball tomfoolery. "Oh, no!

You're kidding!" he said, chuckling. He assured me if he ever did leave a baseball in my living room, he'd pick up the tab.

The next morning, with work being done on the Red Line, Dandy Don took the No. 22 bus up Clark Street "with about 500 Cubs fans." He phoned that he was running late, so I went ahead and asked for his usual front corner table on Tuscany's patio. When Don arrived, our waiter brought over a carafe of iced tea and asked, "The usual, Don?" That's a salad and a portobello mushroom sandwich. It's no longer on the menu, but they make an exception for their best customer. Dandy Don apologized for his tardiness, explaining that he and Pat were booking their spring-training accommodations. Flights had been booked in May—same American Airlines MD-80 jet, same row, same window seat for Don, same aisle seat for Pat.

We ate and chatted about spring training as the game-day crowd thickened. It came time to join them inside for Harden's first pitch as a Cub. He threw 95 of them that day, mostly strikes, as he fanned 10. An inward-blowing wind changed directions in the third inning, gusting out to right.

"Boy," Dandy Don said, "if someone could just get it up in the air to right, the wind will take it." Moments later, Edmonds did just that. His two-run homer made it 3–0. The Cubs added four in the fourth and still held a commanding 7–2 lead at the end of the eighth inning when Dandy Don clasped his hands together. "This is great," he summarized. "Harden pitched a great game, and we've won the series no matter what happens tomorrow with Lincecum."

With that he bid farewell, hoping to beat the crowds to the bus. The Spinners blared over the speakers, as Marmol warmed up. But the Rubberband Man snapped. Worrying about a runner charging home from third, he booted a soft liner near the first-base line. "He tried to prevent a run from scoring, and five scored," said an agitated Piniella later. "I thought that was the biggest out of the inning that got away from us." Single, single, walk, hit batsman later, Theriot made an ill-advised throw on an infield hit, and the error allowed the tying run to score. I called to update Dandy Don, who was on the bus near home on Division Street. Marshall, who pitched two spotless innings of relief, singled to open the eleventh.

Rich Harden delivers a pitch to home plate during his Cubs debut, in which he fanned 10. *Steve Green photo courtesy Chicago Cubs*

Two batters later, Johnson grounded a single to right, and DeRosa barely beat the throw home to give the Cubs an 8–7 victory.

After the game, it was revealed that a blister on Woody's hand would keep him out of the All-Star Game. Marmol would be taking his roster spot. For the final midsummer classic at Yankee Stadium, there would be nine Cubs (including Piniella) in uniform, more than any team in baseball, even the Bronx Bombers. "It's flattering," said Piniella, who's played his share of games in the House That Ruth Built. "We've played well in the first half, and these guys who are going are, in a way, largely responsible. We have a few others, but these guys have all done their jobs and done them well, and they're being rewarded."

On the final day of the first half, however, Lincecum, another NL All-Star, was on his game. I went next door to borrow a cup of beer and a Polish sausage from the neighbors at Brixen Ivy, a rooftop run largely by friends and family. Matt Marron checked me in at the door, and his wife, Jennifer, poured a soda at the 20-foot mahogany bar in the third-floor lounge. Somerlie DePasquale worked a portable beverage stand on the roof deck, as her husband, Jared, busily managed the building. All four are in their thirties and are musicians from all over the country. Jared is a studio guitarist, and Somerlie is an oboist who freelances in various orchestras and teaches. Jen is a singer, and Matt is front man in a Midwest-based pop-rock band. Other than music, their common thread is religious faith. They all met building owner Mark Schlenker through Park Community Church. "It's just so easygoing," Somerlie said. "He just surrounds us with all of his friends."

Friends populated the rooftop, as well, for the first-half finale, and Schlenker worked the crowd. From the top Sky Deck, the tops of the Sears Tower and John Hancock Center peeked above the rooftop over Wrigley's first-base side. In the seventh inning, the popping gloves of Cubs bullpen catchers Edgar Tovar and Corey Miller were audible as they warmed up relievers.

An inning later, Schlenker was talking about how he got into the business, leaving a sales job rather than transfer to California. Having commuted to games for years with his friends from west-suburban Wheaton, he moved into Wrigleyville in 1989 to be near the energy. Today, Brixen Ivy is his primary income. "This is a full-time job," he said. "Imagine throwing 81 weddings, with all the different people calling you, asking you particulars about this, that. There's a lot of coordination."

Ramirez came to the plate with two on and one out. Schlenker lost his train of thought and fixated on the stadium's fast-flapping flags. "Man, if we get a fly ball," he said, "a three-run homer would be really nice."

Lincecum got Rammy to bounce into an inning-ending double play and went on to hand Dempster his first loss at Wrigley Field, 4–2. Nevertheless, tied with the Angels at 57–38, the Cubs headed into the All-Star Game with the best record in baseball for the first time in their history. Fookie Dookie would be making the trip. My right index finger, despite All-Star first-half numbers (.438 batting average, 6 walks, 7 runs), did not get the invite.

•   •   •   •

AS A BOY, I ALMOST looked forward to pregame introductions of the All-Stars more than the game itself. So I was sure to get down to Bernie's to see all those Cubs lined up in a row along the third-base line. Even the commercial breaks seemed Cubs-themed, including the one filmed in front of my apartment back in April.

It had been awhile since I'd seen Rob the Vet and Ray, who were at the front corner of the bar. Crankshaft, Willy B, Peanut Tom, and Big Joe soon joined me. At a table behind us was a group of Wrigley stadium operations employees, fresh off their annual picnic in Lincoln Park, where they played a tournament for the Golden Softball Trophy (a spray-painted, Chicago-style, 16-inch ball).

Cubs hitters went 0-for-the-evening, but Big Z pitched shutout innings in the third and fourth. The NL put runners on the corners in the tenth with one out—perfect timing for Demp's first road win of the year after he'd struck out the side in the ninth. But Dan Uggla grounded into a double play, then made two errors at second base to start the bottom of the inning, giving birth to a new phrase: *He pulled an uggla!*

Somehow, Aaron Cook wiggled out of that jam and another pickle in the tenth. Marmol came on in the thirteenth and fanned two batters after Uggla made yet another *uggla*. Rob the Vet joked with the stadium ops peeps that they'd need special detail on Uggla for the Marlins' visit in two weeks.

I caught some grief for keeping a scorecard and was working my last column in the fifteenth. Both teams were down to their final pitcher when the AL ended the longest midsummer classic in history on a close play at the plate. J.D. Drew got MVP honors, but Tampa's Evan Longoria sent the game into extras with an RBI double in the eighth. Longoria had nabbed the final roster spot via online fan voting. "Maybe I should have voted for [the White Sox's Jermaine] Dye instead of Longoria 25 times," Rob said. "I would have been in bed already."

· · · ·

I HEADED TO NEW ORLEANS for the start of the second half. Naturally. Actually, it was en route to Houston with my Crescent City friends in a five-hour drive (think Chicago to St. Louis, only over bayous). It allowed me to contribute to a Cubs "altar" in a city where Marie Laveau practiced her legendary voodoo.

The Cubs altar in New Orleans included Mike Fontenot's spike (lower right), Ryan Theriot's batting gloves (top left), and Chad Gaudin's empty tin of Copenhagen (center). *Photo courtesy Ye Olde College Inn*

DUSTIN EGLSEDER

The NL's defeat in the All-Star Game meant that if the Cubs reached the Fall Classic for the first time since 1945, they would yield home-field advantage to their Junior Circuit opponent. Theriot ranked sixth in NL batting average (.320), eighth in hits (111), and was tied for first in multi-hit games (37). But he was left home. However, life and death matters at the break offered perspective. For one thing, Theriot's wife, Johnnah, gave birth to their third child, Georgie Grace. "There's a reason why I wasn't [in New York]," The Riot said. "I needed to be here with my wife, and I would've been here regardless."

Edmonds got married, and my friend Big D proposed to his girlfriend, using me as a ruse to get her to see his brick paver on Marquee Plaza. He asked what the heck Jim's brick with three lines of gibberish said. Then he covered it with a template, blocking out letters until it read, "Will you marry me, Valorie?"

And Dustin Eglseder, the fan who conducted "Take Me Out to the Ball Game" on the final day of the '07 season and at the Cubs Convention, passed away at the age of 23 from cancer. Theriot had befriended Eglseder, and they became phone buddies. He'll never forget one conversation they had late in 2007, when Eglseder was in the hospital. "We talked for a while. It ended up going okay, but he had to have his arm amputated," Theriot said. "Here's a guy who was preparing to go through a pretty serious surgery, and he's asking me about the Cubs. I wanted to say: 'Man, who cares about the Cubs? Let's talk about you.' But he was interested in my life."

At the convention, Theriot introduced Eglseder at the opening ceremonies and got to know Eglseder's family, who drove in with him from Iowa. Dustin was only five years his junior. The last time they spoke was early in the season. "This is a guy who was in the prime of his life, who had to live life for a long time in a lot of pain, but you never once heard him complain about it," Theriot said. "It's not about how much money you make or winning a World Series. It's about living life the right way, being able to get up out of your bed, open your eyes, and see the sun. He was somebody who was able to appreciate those things. ⋯⋯⟩

"His story should be told. One thing I've always tried to keep at the forefront is just how lucky I am, and it was just kind of fate that we were able to hook up."

Friends at a Mid-City restaurant called Ye Olde College Inn (they also own the Rock n' Bowl, my favorite music venue/bowling alley) performed a similar oblation to a Red Sox deity in 2004. And they won!

So when items were requested for the consecration, I faithfully collected an illustration of Tinker, Evers, and Chance, some fresh-cut Wrigley Field ivy, and a mason jar filled from Peanut Tom's 2003 bag of nuts. The Louisiana Cubs donated, as well. The Riot gave me some game-worn batting gloves, "Wolverine" Gaudin coughed up a freshly emptied tin of Copenhagen, and the Little Babe handed over his left spike. Dennis Waldron, a New Orleans criminal court judge, presided over the ceremony. I read "Baseball's Sad Lexicon," one of the game's most famous pieces of literature. Sportswriter Franklin Pierce Adams, a Chicagoan and Cubs fan who covered the Giants for the *New York Evening Mail*, wrote it in 1910:

> *These are the saddest of possible words:*
> *"Tinker to Evers to Chance."*
> *Trio of bear cubs, and fleeter than birds,*
> *Tinker and Evers and Chance.*
> *Ruthlessly pricking our gonfalon bubble,*
> *Making a Giant hit into a double—*
> *Words that are heavy with nothing but trouble:*
> *"Tinker to Evers to Chance."*

When everything was put before the altar, a candle was lit, we all sang "Go Cubs Go," and the second-half vigil began. Unfortunately, the next verse started in a hostile place. The Cubs went to Houston with a winning percentage of .402 (128–190) in that city since the expansion Astros joined the NL in 1962.

We stayed at the Inn at the Ballpark, a baseball-themed hotel kitty-corner from Minute Maid Park with a statue of the Ryan

Express in the lobby. During Friday's series opener, I met 43-year-old Ken Dwyer sitting next to me in a blue Cubs T-shirt. He's been in Houston for 20 years after growing up in Chicago-suburban Glen Ellyn. His friend was from Downers Grove. They're both aerospace engineers for NASA. Smart guys!

It's been tough living in Astros country, so when Edmonds hit a solo homer in the fifth, Dwyer beamed. "I've gotta text my friends," he said, pulling out his cell phone. "I've been catching a lot of crap for four years and then [the Astros] get to the World Series...playing the White Sox! It was my worst nightmare. What team do you root for in that?"

Carlos Lee hammered one onto the railroad tracks in left, and a choo-choo train tugging a cart full of what looked like pumpkins tooted away. The game stayed that way into the ninth, when Bob Howry yielded a double and single. Cubs lost 2–1. The NASA engineers shook their heads, and I knew exactly why. It wasn't rocket science. The Cubs had only four hits and were retired in order in six innings.

Late the next afternoon, a zydeco band dodged batting-practice blasts while jammin' on the deck in left-center. A place called Lefties, situated about where the Swank is in Wrigleyville, served up boiled crawfish. "Aaayyiiieeee!!" howled my Cajun friends. The Cubs continued to slump. Big Z's seventh-inning homer was all they could muster in a 4–1 defeat.

Piniella canceled Sunday's batting practice, and the Cubs responded with a nine-run outburst. Joining Big Joe and Co. for the finale in the upper deck, I reminded Ginger to put her new padlock on Peanut Tom's backpack. Joe had lamented how Tom had been breaking out his gigantic W flag prematurely and cost the Cubs two ninth-inning leads.

With two outs in the bottom of the ninth, Tom fumbled with the pack and stammered, "What the...? How'd that get...? Take that....D'oh!" *After* Marmol got the last out, we brandished the W banner from the upper deck façade, catching some 10th *Inning Show* TV time.

Back home, a makeshift hockey rink had been constructed across the street for a press conference to make the New Year's

With Peanut Tom and Ginger on the left and Big Joe on the right, the mother of all W flags flies again in the top row of Section 312. *Photo by Jim McArdle*

Day Blackhawks–Red Wings date official. Spying through binoculars, it was odd seeing all those red Indianhead sweaters at Wrigley in July.

The Cubs continued to be cold in even hotter places. They got blanked 2–0 in the desert by Randy Johnson and lost 9–2 the next night. I found Murph, Lee, and Jim shaking their heads at the television set inside the firehouse. They sauntered down the driveway for the soothing of a nice summer evening. "We gotta win tomorrow," one of them pleaded.

Was our gonfalon bubble being ruthlessly pricked? The Louisiana boys were hitting .438 since the break; the rest of the team was at .083. It was Theriot to Fontenot and leave the rest to chance. Piniella canceled batting practice again, railing: "We're going to come out here and stretch and play. That's it. I'm tired of seeing balls flying all over in batting practice and, when the damn game starts, see very little or nothing."

If it wasn't Skip's magic touch, it was Soriano's return to the top of the order. D-Lee homered for the first time in 26 games, Johnson hit a grand slam, and Lilly got his 10th victory to keep the Brewers, who had crept to within a half game, in second place.

Meanwhile, the Tribune Co. had culled the list of potential buyers of the Cubs down to five bids all exceeding $1 billion. NBA bad-boy owner Mark Cuban reportedly made the cut, but an offer from a group headed by John Canning, the supposed favorite of baseball commissioner Bud Selig, was rejected. Revised offers would be submitted in September, and the Cubs hoped to recommend a buyer to MLB by November.

·   ·   ·   ·

WOOD WAS PLACED on the disabled list. With any luck, he'd be back during the critical Milwaukee series at the end of the month. "We felt for the past few days it would end this way," Piniella said. "We rode it as long as we could."

Marmol took Woody's place at the end of the bullpen. I took mine with another group of bleachers regulars. They sit in left field, in the first three rows before the wall jets back toward the foul pole in what's historically been referred to as "the well." Ron Hayden sits here, with a kit Velcroed underneath his bench that has various hooks and clips to hold his binoculars, scorecard, pencils, and sharpener. An attorney, Hayden is a sort of unofficial liaison between the bleachers regulars and the Cubs. He mapped out where the season ticket holders sit, so they can get those seats for the playoffs, when the bleachers no longer are general admission.

I sat next to 49-year-old Mary Ellen Gourley, a nurse who's been a regular since the early 1970s. In front of us were "Radical Tim" Shockley and his wife, Ellen, who met in the bleachers and married in Arizona during spring training in 1992. Ellen, 46, works at the Board of Trade and grew up a mile south, off Sheffield. She's an expert at the dying Wrigley tradition of popping cups and does a pretty good Carol Burnett–like Tarzan yell. Tim, 49, an IT specialist, was a South Sider who moved to this section from right field in 1985. The blackened concrete at our feet was proof it's one area that was left relatively untouched during 2005–2006 reconstruction. "We always say we have the same seats as before the renovation," Ellen said. "This is our living room."

It's also been dubbed "Ground Zero" for batting practice. Why? "Big Mike" Reinserman showed off a welt on his inner thigh from a missed catch. That's why. Ken Keefer sits here with his sons, Joe, who's 12, and Jack, 13. Joe swaps out his Cubs cap for that of the visiting team when they start hitting. "Hey, it's my first game; throw me a ball!" he'll yell. Works every time.

To my left, Jeremy Morganegg had gloved 32 batting-practice balls after being adopted by Ground Zero early in the season. He quit his job as a mortgage broker and moved from Scottsdale, Arizona, for the season. "I had just gotten married in November. I ran it by my wife, thinking it wouldn't even be an option. But she went for it," said the 35-year-old native of Yorkville, Illinois. He and his wife rented a blue frame house two doors down from the Taco Bell on Addison, where Theriot had lived the previous year. "Arizona Jeremy" sips his morning coffee while gazing at Wrigley's red marquee. "What can be better than that?" he said.

After the first pitch in the bottom of the first, I got introduced to a tradition that dates back to the yellow hardhat–wearing Bleacher Bums of the 1960s. Hayden led the cheer, aimed at Marlins left fielder Josh Willingham in front of us:

HAYDEN: Gimme a Will!
CHORUS: Will!
HAYDEN: Gimme an Ing!
CHORUS: Ing!
HAYDEN: Gimme a Ham!
CHORUS: Ham!
HAYDEN: What's that spell?
CHORUS: Willingham! Willingham! Willingham! Fee fi fo fum, Willingham's a stinkin' bum!
KEEFER: You're a bum, Willingham!
HAYDEN: And don't you forget it! Get outta town, you bum!

They rag on the other team's left fielder the entire game. Sometimes the players joke back. One time, as they sang, "I'm a little teapot, short and stout..." Houston's Lance Berkman put a hand on his hip and extended the other arm "...here is my handle; here is my spout."

When the Cubs clinched in 2003, left fielder Moises Alou sprayed them with champagne and threw a second bottle up for drinking. Ellen later had Alou autograph it.

Ground Zero was busy on this night. Cedeno homered above to our left, Henry Blanco to our right, as the Cubs built a 6–2 lead. DeRosa prevented a big inning with a diving catch in the eighth inning. In the ninth, Marmol issued three walks but somehow pitched out of it for a save in the 6–3 victory. "It's never easy with the Cubs," Mary Ellen groused. "They're killing Santo."

Rookie Jeff Samardzija arrived the next afternoon to take Woody's roster spot, but Piniella still hadn't chatted with his new pitcher by the time the media entered his office for their daily briefing. "What do we got?" he asked to no one in particular.

"A new pitcher," Cubs.com reporter Carrie Muskat replied.

"Yeah," Piniella said. "How's his hair? A little long?"

The former Notre Dame star wide receiver reported to spring camp in 2007 with long jet-black locks that his manager ordered cut. Samardzija had some thick locks again, but also a 3.13 ERA in six starts at Triple A. What's more, the Cubs signed him to a five-year $10 million contract in 2007 to make baseball his profession over a possible NFL career. BleedCubbieBlue Al and the rest of Cubs Nation were anxious to see the 23-year-old "Shark" that day—and they would.

Al's girlfriend, Miriam, brought her father out. Until last year, Bob Romain hadn't been to the bleachers since the 1940s (see sidebar, p. 162–63). He sat with Miriam and Al twice last summer, both losses. "We better win today, or I'll be banished for good."

Al's son, Mark, also had a streak going. The club was 8–0 when he was attending. Something had to give. The intensity in the middle of a sweaty afternoon was cooled a bit when Robert, a vendor familiar to the group, stopped by, and Dave treated everyone to frosty malts.

Solo homers by Soto and Johnson—the former landing in Ground Zero—also relieved some stress and gave the Cubs a 2–1 lead. Samardzija came into the game in the seventh and turned the heat back up, eliciting "ooohs" and "aaahs" when his fastball hit 99 mph. But Jorge Cantu pulled an RBI double toward us down the left-field line. The Shark got his first big-league lesson: guys at this level can hit 99 mph—and turn on it—so movement, command, and changing speeds were critical.

Howry, he with the 6.97 ERA in July, gave up a homer to Jeremy Hermida to open the ninth. The Cubs lost 3–2. "Well, I think that's it. You can't come back," Al said as he winked at me, smiled, and threw an arm over Bob's shoulders.

The next day, Dominic D'Angi's eighth birthday, was an afternoon he'll never forget. Attending his first Cubs game July 10, D'Angi had been hit in the head by a liner off Lilly's bat. After the boy awoke from an induced coma, the concerned pitcher and D-Lee visited him in a nearby hospital. On his birthday, D'Angi's parents surprised him. He returned to Wrigley, met several Cubs before the game, and threw out the first pitch—covering all 60′6″ from mound to home plate and then some. Lilly leaped to catch it. "I came up in front of the plate, and he told me to scoot back. And I actually got a note from him telling me to make sure to wear two chest protectors, just in case," Lilly said. "I don't think he stopped smiling at any point he was here, especially when we had him in the clubhouse."

On a sun-baked, 78-degree afternoon, they were smiling on top of the Lakeview Baseball Club, too. I saw a guy wearing a purple LSU golf shirt in the first inning and barked, "Geaux, Tigers!" New Orleans native Mitch Aucoin and his friend Doug Saint were in town from Washington, D.C., on a work trip, sort of. Their rooftop day with a group of 40 was a precursor to a golf outing and dinner the following day. "It's a non-business weekend," said Sean Corrigan, their host and LBC member. "We talk to each other all the time on the telephone, so it's good to be seen and just hang out."

Plate umpire Gerry Davis got hit in the throat by a pitch and had to leave. The 14-minute delay gave us a chance to go downstairs for a burger and a beer. As we chatted, Ramirez broke a 1–1

THE LAST BLEACHERS SEAT

Bob Romain, Miriam's father, had a poignant story about ignoring his mother's orders that he wasn't to go to Game 6 of the 1945 World Series by himself. He got up at 4:00 in the morning and made himself a peanut-butter-and-jelly sandwich. He had attended his first Cubs game with his uncle and cousin only a year earlier, sitting in a section of the bleachers in center field that eventually was closed to create a solid background for hitters to better see the pitches coming. The youngster knew the 30-minute route along the Clark Street streetcar from his home in Rogers Park, a neighborhood north of the ballpark, and had just enough coins in his piggy bank to finance the forbidden adventure.

"When I was 12 years old, a bleachers seat was 25¢ if you were under 12 or 13. It was not $45, I'll tell you that!" Bob said. "Streetcar fare for a child was 4¢."

The trolley car conductor questioned what he was doing out alone so early, and Bob guilefully said he was going to help a cousin deliver newspapers. When he arrived, the line for bleachers tickets started at Waveland and Sheffield, where the old bleachers box office was located, went west to Clark, wrapped south toward Addison, and snaked across the other side of Clark back to Waveland, where it turned east. Bob got in line and waited. The box office opened around 10:00, and the line moved painfully slow. Finally, he was one person from the window...when it closed after issuing the guy in front of him the last day-of-game ticket. Bob cried all the way home, unsure whether the tears were for his own misfortune or what awaited him when he arrived.

His mother was compassionate, saying only, "When Dad gets home, he wants to talk to you." She took his sandwich bag, set it down on the kitchen table, poured a glass of milk, and tuned the radio to the game. Bob listened to the Cubs' thrilling 12-inning victory, the last fall classic game the franchise has won. His father got home and lectured on the importance of obeying his mother. "Then he said how sorry he was that I had been so disappointed by not being able to get into the game," Bob said.   ····⟩

Bob watched a few more games in the bleachers in the 1940s but otherwise hadn't been back behind the ivy until Miriam brought him out twice to sit with her new boyfriend in 2007. Make no mistake, Bob didn't stop coming to Wrigley. He's shared upper-deck season tickets in the first row of Section 416 with two friends since 1983 and attends about 30 games a year. "The biggest thrill in the world was when I could afford a ticket in the grandstands," he said. Next to having a guaranteed seat for the next World Series game at Wrigley, of course.

tie with a third-inning solo homer. Brett Conrad joined us, and the Indiana native and Notre Dame fan started trading barbs with Aucoin. "I got him tickets to the Sugar Bowl [when the Irish played LSU in 2007]," Conrad teased. "I got a call that he couldn't get tickets. I said: 'Let me get this straight. He grew up there, he's a fan, and he's going to stay home and watch it on TV?' I couldn't let that happen."

Conrad became a Cubs fan by tuning in their games in South Bend on WGN-TV, before it became a superstation. Similarly, Carl Elder started following the Cubs by picking up WGN Radio at his job in a furniture factory in Southern Indiana. Six days shy of his 70th birthday, he and his wife, Mary Kay, watched on TV from a shaded roofdeck table under the bleachers.

Up top, Elder's son, Brian, and son-in-law, Tim Moman, explained they had picked up four tickets to LBC at a charity event for Cathedral High School in Indianapolis and given them to Carl as a birthday present. "The only better birthday present was my dog, Buddy," Carl said.

Unfortunately, the day turned sour late. In the eighth, Hermida's second homer of the game tied it. An inning later, DeRosa was thrown out on a close play, and first-base coach Matt Sinatro and Piniella both were ejected for arguing the call. In the twelfth, doubles by Hermida and Cantu ended it. The pitching staff logged 20 strikeouts, and Harden had another dominant start. But the Cubs lost for the seventh time in 10 games, and Milwaukee won that night. The Brewers had been coming, just like that fan in St. Louis promised in the beginning of the month. And now they had pulled even for the division lead.

Seeking a little tension relief the next morning, I visited Ground Zero to see two friends reunited. After taking his swings in the cage, Marlins outfielder Luis Gonzalez went out to shag in left field. Gary Stromquist stepped down two benches to the wall and yelled, "Gonzo!" Gonzalez turned, smiled, and walked to the warning track. He removed his mitt and tossed it to "Loudmouth Gary," who threw his down. Gonzo practiced with the glove for several minutes before they traded back, and Gonzalez signed a Dodgers cap and jersey that the fan dropped down.

The two had struck up a relationship when Gonzalez was a Cub in 1995–1996. Loudmouth Gary asked during b.p. if anybody wanted to break in his new mitt. Gonzo obliged, giving birth to a tradition. Gary, 50, grew up in the shadows of Riverview Park, an amusement park that used to stand at Belmont and Western. He moved out to the suburbs a few years back, and with three college-age sons, he doesn't get to many games anymore. But he's there whenever Gonzalez is in town. "I expect to see him there," Gonzo said. "There's a certain core of people always out there, who I always say hi to. They've always treated me well as a visitor."

Having watched this scene, I joined my sister, Judy, in Section 108. Armen, my brother-in-law, brought me crashing back to fans' vexed mood. "People are down on Derrek Lee. Is he leading the league in double plays?" he asked. "If I was a pitcher, I'd walk the guy in front of him." Indeed, D-Lee's 21 GIDPs led the majors. Arm's approach, however, was impassioned if not a little severe. But things were getting worse. Mike Jacobs hit a pair of homers to give Florida a 5–0 lead, and the Astros were losing 4–1 in Milwaukee.

We were trying to teach my 10-year-old niece, Lucy, how to keep score, but she found a more important chore when she dripped ketchup and mustard from her hot dog onto her new 1978 Cubs road jersey. While Lucy scrubbed the stain, her white-striped powder-blue shirt was cause for Judy and me to reminisce about Cubs games with our parents. "Dad used to make us yell, 'Charge!' as loud as we could," she said after organist Gary Pressy's attempt to rally the crowd. "And I always hated it when the other kids would be eating Cracker Jack and popcorn, and I'm eating a plum."

The Cubs picked up two runs in the third and tied the game on Soriano's three-run homer an inning later. We got *uggla*'d when Uggla blasted a solo homer down Kenmore Avenue in the fifth, but moments later a 7 was put up on the scoreboard in Houston's half of the fifth. The crowd roared.

D-Lee tied it with a homer to start the seventh, and after they loaded the bases with two outs, we could tell the Little Babe's twisting liner to left was just out of the reach of Willingham, that stinkin' bum! Three-run double! Samardzija registered his first big-league save, with Edmonds making the final out of the 9–6 win on a spectacular sprawled-out catch in the gap.

The Brewers lost; the Cubs were back alone on top. Our story's heroes boarded a bus across the street for a 90-minute drive up I-94.

. . . .

THE STAGE WAS SET for what would be the most important series of the season—and perhaps the single most important game. The Cubs had been teetering on top, losing seven of their last 11. They headed to Miller Park with a road record of 23–30, and the Brewers had gone 16–7 to that point in July. Milwaukee sent Sabathia to the mound to open a four-game set, and he had gone 4–0 with three complete-games since coming over in the trade exactly three weeks earlier.

In front of a mixed crowd of 45,311 Brewers and Cubs fans creating a playoff atmosphere, D-Lee drove in a run in the first, and Soriano homered in the third for an early 2–0 lead. Milwaukee fought back against a tiring Lilly in the sixth, and the game went to the ninth tied 4–4. Lee drove in the go-ahead run, and a DeRosa run-scoring single put the Cubs over the top for a 6–4 victory. Nobody knew it then, but Milwaukee was swatted away for the last time. The tone of the NL Central race changed permanently, with the defending division champs composed and boring ahead to retain what was theirs, and the high-strung Brewers fighting off the vultures for the wild-card consolation prize.

Wrigley was an ancillary arena the next night. As long as I can remember, "CUBS," painted white on a green panel, always has been in the bottom left of the center-field scoreboard. On Tuesday afternoon it was three games up, on the visiting side, *above* "MILWAUKEE." In its place was "PEORIA" beneath "KANE COUNTY." Billed as the "Road to Wrigley," a minor league game would be played here for the first time, featuring Ryne Sandberg as manager of the Cubs' Class A Peoria affiliate.

Shortly after the Kane County players arrived, they were snapping photos in a visitors clubhouse where Babe Ruth, Jackie Robinson, and Stan Musial once lockered. On the home side, the Cubs' personal belongings in their lockers were covered with thick sheets of plastic. Think October!

A week earlier, Peoria had a huge brawl with Dayton, leading to some national publicity and the arrest of Chiefs pitcher Julio Castillo. The Lite billboard on Sheffield was changed that afternoon. "PLAY NICE," it read. "Boy," said Oneri Fleita, Cubs vice president of player personnel, "they don't miss a trick." When the gates opened, the bleachers regulars took their customary posts. Outside, Moe Mullins waited in his usual spot on the Waveland parkway next to the Bud building. "A big bore...one ball!" he said. "I'm missing a nap for this. I was gonna go home and take a nap so I could watch the Cubs game. I get up at 4:00." Spotting in the back row of the bleachers, an exasperated young ballhawk started gesturing at hitters. "Hey, Mikey!" Moe yelled up. "Don't beg. Ballhawks don't beg."

Before the start, Willy B got a gig shooting sponsor photos of Sandberg in the on-deck circle, and Ryno's uniformed minions signed autographs in the concourse. The game featured T-shirts and Frisbees being tossed into the stands, a mascot playfully chucking a third baseman's glove into the bleachers, an umpire doing the worm, and a creature called "Clammy Sosa" eating a man and spitting up his trousers. Back-to-back homers by Rebel Ridling and Brandon Guyer got Peoria the lead, and gained those two players memories they'll cherish. Fans followed the Cubs-Brewers game on the inning-by-inning scoreboard, cheering when a 1 went up for the Cubs in the fourth. Watching Big Z working eight shutout

Cubs Hall of Famer and Peoria Chiefs manager Ryne Sandberg was back in the dugout at Wrigley for the first time in almost 11 years.
Photo by Will Byington / www.willbyington.com

innings, they huddled around TVs in the concourse and behind the bleachers, reacting often before the entire stadium roared when a 5 was posted in the sixth inning.

At Ground Zero, Ballhawk Kenny, who took the 'hawking inside, listened to the Pat & Ron Show with his earpiece. Brad Martin wore a 1984 Cubs cap and held a small Casio TV tuned to WGN-TV. The Cougars and Chiefs went into the ninth tied 6–6. The Cubs' 7–1 victory gleamed across the message board, opening up a three-game lead…and then the rain came. After a long delay, the game was suspended (and resolved the next night in Peoria in a 12-inning Chiefs win). More than 10,000 kids who lined up to run Wrigley's bases after the game, however, went home wet and disappointed.

Only two rooftops had been open. The Lakeview Baseball Club offered two free passes to each member, and Brixen Ivy hosted Sandberg's charity, Ryno's Kids Care. But with 32,103 attending, it shattered the Midwest League attendance record. And Sandberg wore No. 23 in blue pinstripes at Wrigley for the first time since September 21, 1997. "Cubs fans are incredible, the fact that we're talking 30,000-plus tonight," Sandberg said. "Anything that the Cubs do, anything at Wrigley Field, anything with the Cubs logo on it, I've been around long enough to not be surprised."

The next night, about a dozen Wrigley crowd management staffers headed to Miller Park for a busman's holiday. A flat tire didn't stop them from arriving in time to tailgate. I joined them in the parking lot, where charcoal-burning grills and accordion-playing polkas pervade. In Milwaukee's time-honored tradition, our pregame feast included burgers, hot dogs, and brats. We sat in the top deck in right field, about 30 feet from the top of the foul pole—the Bob Uecker seats! When DeRosa's RBI single made it 2–0 in the first, Katelyn, a dark-haired twenty-something Wrigley worker sitting next to me, stood, applauded, and danced a dance of joy as she pointed to the 7 and *DeRosa* on the back of her blue T-shirt. A three-run Cubs sixth started sending Brewers fans to the exits. Just before the Cubs added two more in the ninth to complete the 7–2 blowout, one staffer called his boss back in Chicago to ask if he'd be fired for going down Bernie the Brewer's left-field slide. Needless to say, he remained in his seat.

The following day I was tethered to Chicago via spending a few innings in the WGN Radio booth sitting in on the Pat & Ron Show. Pregame host Cory Provus and producer Matt Boltz support the stars, trolling the Internet for news and keeping in touch with the studio back in Chicago. The tight-knit foursome works together home and away. Boltz, 32, even rooms next to Santo on road trips. Provus, 30, spells Hughes every game, doing an inning of play-by-play. Provus, who grew up in Highland Park, Illinois, and Boltz, from Missouri, both listened to their mentors during their formative college years. "I consider them to be friends and fathers," Boltz said. "Ronny has a little grandfather in him, too. We call him the Godfather."

Distracted by one of their frequent guests, Boltz missed a cue during the pregame show. Santo's mike wasn't on initially, and he stumbled but laughed it off and talked excitedly about the potential of a sweep with Harden on the mound. At the commercial break, he spewed a harsh but fun-spirited lashing at Boltz, who smiled sheepishly.

As the game got going, Hughes painted his listeners' imagination, describing the uniforms, the outfield dimensions, the sellout crowd, and the fact that second baseman Ricky Weeks was playing Ramirez to pull by positioning himself behind the bag. Hughes' hands were animated as he described a play in which Lee fell down while smothering a throw from Soriano, corralled the ball, and beat Weeks to the bag to complete a double play.

Pat's scorebook included an empty column for him to write interesting stats and facts to mention. His Brewers media guide was open to the bio of starting pitcher Dave Bush. Hughes noted Bush's double major at Wake Forest in psychology and sociology. "So he could really straighten his own self out then," Santo joked.

Bush couldn't solve Edmonds, who missed the series' first three games after getting a cortisone shot in his knee. After pulling a solo homer to right field in his first at-bat, Edmonds stepped to the plate an inning later with the bases full, and, well, I'll let Pat and Ron tell it:

> HUGHES: Here's the 1–1. Edmonds drives one in the air, deep left field. Back goes Braun. Braun back near the walllll...grand slam!
>
> SANTO: All right! Yes!
>
> HUGHES: Jim Edmonds, the grand slam to left, and the Cubs lead five–nothing!
>
> SANTO: Oh, ho, my God! How 'bout that? Oh, my God! He really hit that ball, Patrick!

Strange sight seen: the next time he strode to the plate, Edmonds, a former Cardinal, received a standing ovation by a pro-Cubs crowd of 45,346, second-highest in Miller Park history. Harden gave up just a run in seven solid innings, while Sori and Fookie added homers to complete an 11–4 pasting. The four games ranked among Miller Park's Top 10 attendance dates, but local fans saw Brew Town turned into Broom Town. The Cubs outhit their hosts 49–30, outscored them 31–11, and outpitched them (2.75 to 7.25 in ERA). The four-game sweep knocked Milwaukee five games out, momentarily into third place behind St. Louis.

"Oh, I don't know about statements," Piniella told the media at the completion of the series. "We've got baseball to be played in August, in September, but certainly, coming in here and beating a good opponent in their own ballpark four times is something to feel good about."

Peanut Tom, Ginger, and Mel held up the giant W flag in the lower deck. We celebrated the sweep in Friday's beer garden outside the stadium. We were somewhat surprised to hear the live band cover "Go Cubs Go." Just like being at Bernie's!

7

AUGUST

WHILE THE CUBS RETURNED HOME as conquerors and would be playing 22 of their next 31 at home, a familiar antagonist awaited them in Chicago. I knew because as I left Miller Park, I bumped into Pirate Matt, looking very much like Blackbeard. *Yo ho ho, and a bottle of rum!* The last-place Pirates were in town, having just unloaded top run producers Jason Bay and Xavier Nady. I watched the opener from Wrigley Done Right atop Willy B's apartment building. It was the same view I'd had two days earlier at Miller Park, only about 30 feet lower and with Sheffield Avenue wedged between the foul pole and me.

WLUP-FM was having a promotion for 130 listeners. A film crew followed party host Jonathon Brandmeier as the morning shock jock arrived at game time, climbed the rooftop's aluminum bleachers, and hammed it up for pictures. "Let me check this out a minute," he said, pausing, bobbing his head up and down and surveying the panorama. "What would this feel like in October?"

A Wisconsin native who watched Milwaukee Braves Hall of Famers Eddie Mathews and Hank Aaron at his first live major league game, Brandmeier was making his rooftop debut on a day sweatier than cheese in an oven. He was shocked to learn from his family that his cousin had been conceived in that very building!

Since first arriving in 1983, Johnny B's goofy antics, song parodies, and prank phone calls have made him hugely popular among Chicagoans.

"They're real people. They give a hard day's work. They believe in something, and they've always believed in it. That's the weird part," he said. "I get this vibe. I get this party. I get this. It's not just baseball here, believe me. I think they want to be there [when the Cubs win] to say, 'I was there.'"

They need not be there on this day. Matt Karstens, making his Pirates debut, pitched six innings of a 3–0 shutout. On Saturday, Willy B and I played wedding crashers, as Josh Austin and Brianne Sharp tied the knot atop Murphy's Bleachers Rooftop with Wrigley Field as a backdrop. Their 75 guests were bussed up early that morning from Streator, Illinois, about 100 miles southwest of Chicago. The ceremony started at 11:30 AM as the grounds crew was making final preparations across the street for a noon game.

"Welcome," said the Reverend Phil Landers after Brianne, in her off-the-shoulders wedding gown, was escorted to the rooftop's front railing by her father. "We gather here on this great baseball day to celebrate one of life's greatest moments."

The attendees donned blue T-shirts with the Cubs' walking bear logo on front and the words "Hey, Chicago, what do you say, Josh and Brianne got married today" silk-screened in red on back. A wedding banner was draped from the balcony with white lace wrapped around the iron railings, and they designed their own baseball-themed wedding program.

The Cubs were stretching and throwing while the late-twenties couple took their vows. Fans in the bleachers and on the rooftop next door watched and snapped photos. "Josh," the priest said when it was official, "you may kiss your wife." The applause spread across the street as the newlyweds smooched. A tape of Harry Caray singing "Take Me Out to the Ball Game" played as guests passed through a makeshift receiving line on their way to the bar under a gable displaying Harry's caricature on a giant pinwheel.

Longtime Cubs fan Brad Angelico was feeling like his stout friend "Hoss" stole his thunder. Pointing at home plate, Brad declared he would be married there someday. "I'll do it," said his girlfriend, "as long as I can wear a dress!"

By the time the Cubs opened a 4–1 lead in the fourth, Brianne let her brown hair down and changed into casual baseball clothes, and Josh loosened his tie and shed his tan suit jacket. The Cubs ran

Brianne Sharp and Josh Austin exchange vows on Murphy's Bleachers Rooftop.
Photo by Will Byington / www.willbyington.com

their lead to 5–1 on Derrek Lee's sacrifice fly an inning later. "Ring that bell!" someone shouted from the back row of the bleachers, and the bartender obliged by whacking a hanging ship's bell.

By the seventh, the heat had driven many under the shaded bar-room, where they tried to catch unsuspecting victims beneath an old-fashioned pull-chain showerhead. A shirtless friend named Ben jumped under and basked in the cascading cool water. He peeled off his cargo shorts, kicked away his sandals, and stripped off his tighty whities...revealing swimming briefs. Ben took in the rest of the game dressed that way atop the bleachers. For their big day, the happy couple had something blue to remember (the Cubs' 5–1 victory) and something blue to forget (Ben's Speedo).

Before Sunday's series finale, I connected my friend Rob Glaubke with Peanut Tom and Big Joe's group in the right-field bleachers. Glaubke, 43, grew up in Evanston but has lived in New York City for 22 years. He went to school there and now runs his own graphic design company. "It kills me because I love Chicago so much. I look for any kind of reason to come back," he said.

Glaubke saw an article about the West Side Rooters Social Club and volunteered to design their website as a labor of love. He came to town in part for business with the Rooters and for his mother's art show. The son of professional artists, "Rooters Rob" followed his parents' career path. His father turned him and his mother into Cubs fans. He was doing the same for his girlfriend, Stephanie Abell, whom he met through a Cubs meet-up group in Manhattan.

The Ohio native may have been a bleachers virgin, but she was a quick study. Stephanie removed her No. 38 Carlos Zambrano T-shirt and watched the game in her bikini top on the 75-degree afternoon. Big Z came out after five with a 5–1 lead, but the Pirates tied it in the eighth, and after Geovany Soto walked with two outs in the bottom of the inning, the Cubs sent up a pinch-hitter. "Reed Johnson is my mom's favorite player," Rooters Rob said.

Johnson pulled the next pitch into the bleachers for a go-ahead homer. Sori followed with a solo blast, and Peanut Tom and Big Joe unfurled the giant W minutes later. "My mom must be jumping up and down," Rob said. "This is a team where everybody's stepping up and picking each other up, all 25 guys."

Johnson called his first career curtain call "the best moment for me on a baseball field." Nobody in attendance the next night will forget that game, either. Except Peyton Knorr, that is. Just over two months old, Peyton and her mother, my friend Kathleen, joined me in field box seats behind the home-plate screen. The guy taking our tickets at Gate K told KT and I not to forget to "baptize" Peyton after the game using the water spewing from the red hydrant in front of the firehouse across Waveland. Nice idea!

Peyton's mother fashioned a "My 1st Cubs Game" sign that morning, and we held it in front of Peyton as she posed in a pink Cubs onesie for her first Wrigley pictures. During the first three innings, she finished a bottle of her favorite beverage. As Houston added a fourth-inning run to its 1–0 lead, Peyton napped, only to be startled awake in the bottom of the inning by the crowd reacting to Jim Edmonds' double.

A guy in his seventies sitting next to KT touched his finger to Peyton's itty-bitty nose, smiled, and told vivid stories about his first Cubs game. He sat in the first row of the center-field bleachers when fans were allowed to sit in what's now called "the batter's eye." He went through their entire lineup that day: Bill Nicholson in right, Don Dallesandro in center, Augie Galan in left…

Two-month-old daughter Peyton enjoys her first Cubs game with her mother, KT, before the rain arrived. *Photo by Jim McArdle*

Peyton's first game was memorable for other reasons. Noticing ominous clouds, Kathleen turned to me. "Uncle Jimmy," she said, "we were going to ask you during the seventh-inning stretch, but in case we get rain and have to hustle out...will you be her godfather?"

It was an "aw, shucks!" moment as I lightly kicked the ball of my foot across the concrete beneath me. Moments later, as the sixth inning was about to start, big, fat raindrops fell from the sky, and we ducked into the first-aid room to feed and change Peyton...and waited it out. No longtime employee could remember the tornado/air-raid siren in front of the Bud Building clamoring while Wrigley was full. It roared during a storm that included 90-mph winds, a breathtaking lightning show, driving rain, and fans in the upper deck being evacuated to the lower concourse. Peyton cried, and I leaned over and said softly, "I hate rain delays, too."

When it let up, we walked Peyton home in her stroller, stopping at the firehouse so KT could swipe a thumb full of water from the fireplug across her forehead. Next time would be my turn. Peyton was cooing in her crib when I headed back to the game. Bone-crackling thunder and radiant flashes of lightning chased me to shelter and about made Astros first baseman Lance Berkman jump out of his cleats. Marooned at Hye Bar on Southport, where television reception was down, I was told by the barfly next to me that the game had resumed—only to end on this latest wave. The final score made it official: our story's heroes lost 2–0, and Peyton was a Cubs fan.

The blister felt 'round Wrigleyville was healed; Kerry Wood came off the disabled list the next morning. To make room, Scott Eyre was designated for assignment. Having pitched once since coming off the DL on July 23, Eyre was traded to Philadelphia days later. "The hardest thing is to say good-bye to your teammates," said the wistful veteran, apologizing after pausing to compose himself. "I'm sorry, but I like this place...I'm gonna hop in my RV and drive home."

The Cubs cruised to an early 6–1 lead. Mike Meade, 26, manages George Loukas' Wrigleyville Rooftops business two doors east of my building. It's a summer job for the blond-haired and bespectacled physical education teacher at nearby Walt Disney Magnet School. He had herded his guests from the lounge into a wide inner stairway for 20 minutes while the siren wailed the previous night.

Sunshine baked all that rain into a sweat-rolling-down-your-back kind of afternoon. Many fans watched on one of the televisions in the air-conditioned third-floor lounge downstairs. Before I joined them, I sized up the view from the wide aluminum bleachers up top and wondered how Cubs outfielder Glenallen Hill had ever hit a home run all the way up here back in 2000. Ballhawk Kenny was standing in the apartment entryway that day. *Cool, it's coming right to me,* he thought, and went out into the street. *That's over my head,* he realized, running back. *Wait a minute, it's going to hit the building,* he deduced, running back into the street for a rebound that never came. "It never occurred to me that he could hit it on the roof," Kenny said.

The Astros didn't hit any roof shots, but they scored two runs in each of the fifth, sixth, and seventh innings to take a 7–6 lead. A.J. Gandhi, an accountant on a company outing with KPMG, loved it. He's that rare native North Sider who hates the Cubs and cheers for the White Sox. He described Cubs fans as the lambs of baseball.

"Cubs games are like a Grateful Dead concert. It ain't about the music. It doesn't matter if the Cubs win or lose. It's about having a good time," he railed. "Believing in the Cubs is like the child equivalent to believing in Santa Claus."

Having gotten my fill of loathing, I headed back upstairs and sat behind a guy wearing an Alfonso Soriano jersey. He was 19 years old, impressionable, hopeful. The Cubs tied the game, and Sori blasted a three-run homer into Ground Zero to punctuate his 10-game hot streak (.419 average, 11 RBIs) and the Cubs' 11–7 pasting.

Piniella was trying not to get ahead of himself the next morning, but he was thinking about boating on Lake Michigan with his grandkids during Thursday's day off. "I've never been swimming in the lake," he said. "It doesn't sound like a lot, but in the middle of a hot summer, we haven't had a day off since the All-Star break. Yeah, we're looking forward to the day off."

Having just finished hitting, Mark DeRosa dripped sweat as he caught up with Paul Assenmacher in the Cubs dugout. They'd met in Atlanta's spring camp in 2000 before Assenmacher, the one-time Cub, retired. "I just got off the schneid yesterday," DeRo said as he smiled and gave his batting practice bat to Assenmacher's wide-eyed son. "I just want to build off that."

DeRosa, who hit .195 in July and was benched in two of the first four games of August, had an RBI double in the second inning and a grand slam in an eight-run third that put the Cubs on top 9–4. Loukas' 3609 Sheffield rooftop, the southernmost rooftop on Sheffield, has bleachers angled toward the field. From the bleachers and patio furniture on the fifth-story deck, the diamond is perfectly visible between Wrigley's lower grandstands and right-field upper deck. Up there, I met 33-year-old Jon Hershenhorn while the Cubs built on their eventual 11–4 victory. Five years earlier, he would've been my neighbor.

From 1998 to 2003, Hershenhorn lived in a first-floor apartment facing Waveland Avenue in the building I'd visited the previous day. Jon and another tenant holding a fishing net once climbed a ledge above the entryway and were photographed in *Sports Illustrated* during Sammy Sosa's epic 1998 home-run battle with Mark McGwire. He used to go up top for as many as 60 ballgames a season.

"You knew everyone in the building. On Saturday afternoon we'd put a keg on the back porch," Jon said. "I would equate it to almost a fraternity-type atmosphere, where you could walk into anybody's room anytime. I miss it. I just look at it as a great time in my life. But it was time to move on."

•   •   •   •

TWO SCHEDULING ODDITIES intersected: 12 days short of a full calendar year since the Cardinals had been to Wrigley Field, St. Louis was in town for a matinee contest—on the 20th anniversary of Opening Night at Wrigley Field. An agreement with the city barred night games at Wrigley on Friday and Saturday, and the Cubs had used the timing to lobby in the news to lift that restriction.

August 8 also was 100 years to the day that the West Side Rooters Social Club, which touted itself as the first official fan club of the Cubs, had a "tallyho" fan rally and paraded to the West Side Grounds, the Cubs' ballpark in those days. Grant DePorter revived the Rooters and organized a tallyho from Harry Caray's Steakhouse on Kinzie Street to Harry Caray's Tavern in Wrigleyville. Two double-decker buses waited out front for the first 100 club members who signed up. Inside, fans gathered around Rooters chairman Ernie Banks and treasurer Dutchie Caray, Harry's widow, who was sitting next to a glass case displaying remnants of the infamous Bartman ball. A little girl named Addison climbed up on Dutchie's lap.

Ward Tannhauser was in his "Ivy Man" outfit. Originally "Tree Man" for Halloween in 1998, the 47-year-old father of three modified the costume. Standing on stilts and using crutches to balance himself, the 6' Crystal Lake man stands 8'6" tall in a getup adorned with ivy leaves, berries, and a gold 368 sign set against a brick background. The giant, walking Wrigley Field power alley is a regular outside the ballpark on Opening Day.

"I don't normally wear it in the summer," said Tannhauser, who said he's won more than $18,000 in various costume contests outfitted in ivy. "It's too hot. I wore it for about 45 minutes for the first Red Sox game [at Wrigley, in 2005] and lost eight pounds."

The ride to Wrigley was raucous. Buses decorated with signs and balloons went north down Dearborn and cut over to Clark, going past the Division Street bars Harry frequented. Speakers blared "Go Cubs Go," "Hey, Hey, Holy Mackeral," and Harry singing "Take Me Out to the Ball Game." Ronnie Woo hung off one side of the first bus, and a mascot in a cow costume named Holy Cow hung off the other—both madly ringing cowbells. I learned to beware of low tree branches after standing up to take a photo and nearly getting decapitated.

Everyone, Rooters Rob and I included, shouted, "Oof wah!" as we drove past honking cars and pedestrians holding up and waving their Cubs gear. We arrived in Wrigleyville to hoots and hollers just as three Navy Leap Frogs parachuted into the stadium, one holding a W flag.

"A Journey with Ernie": Mr. Cub led the West Side Rooters' first "tallyho" in 100 years. *Photo by Will Byington / www.willbyington.com*

I popped up on Skybox on Sheffield for a corporate party Big Joe's company was hosting. Someone blocked my view of Edmonds' long fly ball in the second inning, but I saw him dismissively flip his bat toward the Cardinals dugout and knew where it was going.

Peanut Tom had spare upper-deck seats and dropped them to me from the bleachers, weighted with a peanut, of course. St. Louis led 2–1 in the sixth by the time my friend and I got up there, a perfect vantage point to see Sori gun out a runner at home plate. After Edmonds' second homer an inning later came something I never could've imagined…a former Cardinal getting a curtain call as a Cub after killing his old team at Wrigley.

The game went 11 innings, when Henry Blanco became the latest hero by driving a bases-loaded single through a pulled-in infield. "Every day it's going to be nine guys that go out there, but at some point in the season all 25 count," Blanco said. "That's what this team is all about."

But for one of those 25, hits were becoming elusive. Fukudome's .224 average in his last 38 games was concerning, especially with Mike Fontenot, DeRosa, and Johnson swinging hot bats. The Japanese rookie seemed to be spinning himself in to the ground on strikeouts. "We need him to start hitting, or we'll have to look for more options," Piniella told the media. After a 12–3 Cubs loss in the second contest, The Riot was given a day off, and Fukudome was inserted into the number-two hole for the homestand finale.

I wondered if I was to blame. Babies, rooftops, and rooters clubs had caused me to miss my No. 1 duties several days in a row, and Fookie Dookie was 0-for-5 in those first at-bats. "Where've you been?" Scoreboard Rick scolded when I arrived in the first inning. "Do you remember how to do it?"

Maybe I didn't. Fukudome rolled into a double play. Fortunately, Ryan Dempster scattered six hits in six-plus innings. When Sori did his hop on a couple fly-outs in the third, the gals in Scoop Steph's group sang, "Here comes Peter Cotton Tail, hoppin' down the bunny trail..." In the sixth, D-Lee's RBI single made it 2–0, and Howard rang his cowbell feverishly, the first of many bell-ringing sessions in the five-run rally.

As we sang during the seventh-inning stretch, I caught Steph changing to words to "...if they don't win it's the same..." A right-field regular named Ken Kunce taught them to her, warning against interpreting as gloom and doom. Rather, it meant the spirit of Cubs fans would persevere. Kunce died suddenly in the early 1990s at age 38, two days after the annual North Halsted Market Days street fair, which coincidentally was happening just two blocks east. "That was the last time I saw him. I haven't gone back to Market Days since," Steph said in a forlorn tone.

She recalled an informal memorial service in which a plane flew over Wrigley, towing a sign that read, "Ken Kunce says left field

EMIL VERBAN, WE HARDLY KNEW YE

I sat with members of the Emil Verban Memorial Society on the afternoon of August 9 for the second of a three-game series against the Cards at Wrigley. Bruce Ladd started the club, named after an obscure former Cubs second baseman, 33 years ago. Ladd, 72, has been a Cubs fan since coming to Wrigley from his Avalon Park neighborhood on Chicago's South Side as a boy.

Having retired to Chapel Hill, North Carolina, from his job as a lobbyist for Chicago-based Motorola Inc. 13 years ago, Ladd is closing the Verban Society down at the end of 2008. The Society, which grew to 700 members, virtually ran itself. There were no dues and only a biennial meeting. But Ladd, who wrote up and mailed a quarterly newsletter, wanted to finish writing his book on Abraham Lincoln.

"I did this as one of the most clever lobbying techniques ever invented. I needed to get a leg up on Microsoft and my other competition," Ladd said. "I got the idea to start a Washington, D.C., fan club. Now you've got them."

"Them" included political high rollers like charter member Dick Cheney, former President Ronald Reagan, former Speaker of the House Dennis Hastert, and presidential candidates Barack Obama and John McCain, not to mention John Paul Stevens and Antonin Scalia from both the liberal and conservative sides of the United States Supreme Court.

Ladd named the Society after Verban, a native of downstate Lincoln, Illinois, even though he only spent parts of three seasons with the Cubs. "He seemed to represent the kind of plodding, Chicago, Midwest work ethic," Ladd said. "Do spring training right, come out early to practice, hit to right field, be a solid defenseman...that was Emil Verban."

For what likely would be the Society's last tallyho, about a dozen members came in for the game and dinner at nearby Tuscany. Cubs versus Cardinals seemed fitting for this final Verbanite game since they were two of the three teams on which Verban played. "He can't lose," said Verban's oldest son.

Emil Verban Jr., sitting next to me for the game, proudly noted how his dad had driven in the Series-clinching run for St. Louis in the ⟶

1944 World Series. Meanwhile, Zambrano hit his third homer of the season in the third inning but gave up four homers and trailed 9–2 by the fifth.

The senior Emil Verban died in 1989. His namesake played one season of minor league baseball before going into dentistry in Bloomington, Illinois, where loyalties are divided among the Cubs and Cardinals. As St. Louis built on its 12–3 thrashing with three runs in the ninth, Emil talked about the storied rivarly. "I kind of go back and forth," he said. "For sentimental reasons, I always favor the Cubs because they haven't won. The more elusive something becomes, the more people want it."

sucks!" The left-field patrons, of course, retorted, and during the vocal bickering, Andre Dawson belted a home run into the batter's eye between infighting sects of fans, several of whom were releasing Kunce's ashes onto the field at that moment.

Meanwhile, after Demp posted his 13th win, by a 7–2 count, he admitted afterward what 41,000-plus had been feeling all summer. "I've been here five years, and it's never felt like this," he gushed. "I've played in other cities, and it's never felt like this. It's a tribute to our fans and how great they are and how excited they are about our team."

. . . .

AN OFF DAY AND RARE RAINOUT in Atlanta gave the Cubs consecutive days off. In their first day/night doubleheader sweep on the road since 1992, they pounded the Braves 10–2 and 8–0. Former Cub Randy Hundley held a fantasy camp at Wrigley for Tribune Co. bigwigs that afternoon across the street. Which begged a question I'd been asking myself all summer: exactly how far *was* home?

So between innings of Rich Harden's victory in the nightcap, there Crankshaft and I were, two eejits stretching a metal tape measure across Waveland Avenue on a quiet night. Until the guy speeding up on a bike shrieked. *Think fast!* We both dropped the tape measure to the ground, and the cyclist rode harmlessly over it. For the record, it was 460 feet from home plate to our sun porch.

"You're not the first tenants to do that," Landlady Lara laughed after we fessed up our story. "They've all been guys who have to know that."

The Cubs' offensive onslaught continued in the series finale, as Aramis Ramirez's three-run homer and Soriano's two-run blast paced an 11–7 win that gave the franchise its first season sweep of the Braves in the NL's 132-year history.

The Blue Angels were buzzing our apartment the next afternoon during the Air & Water Show, and Willy B stole my thunder that evening by beating me to the publishing punch. He had a release party at Harry Caray's for *We Are Cubs Fans*, his coffee table photo book, signing copies as we watched the Cubs game on TV from South Florida.

Trailing 5–3 with one out in the ninth, Daryle Ward pinch hit with two runners on base. I abruptly interrupted a friend's story, saying: "Hold on. The Cubs are about to win this game." Ward crushed the next pitch into the right-field seats. It was the Cubs' ninth straight road win and first win in Miami since July 2005. Ward was given a beer shower by his teammates after snapping an 0-for-13 slump. "He got doused," Piniella said. "Just a huge at-bat. We needed it, and he delivered."

The clutch hits dried up on Saturday. After scoring at least six runs in nine straight road games for the first time since 1880 and averaging 8.4 runs per game during the stretch, the Cubs stranded 13 runners and were limited to Blanco's solo homer in a 2–1 loss.

While the Cubs were pounding the Marlins 9–2 the next afternoon, high schoolers played at Wrigley in an all-star game. I passed Dave Davison on his way inside the stadium to return the nine balls he'd ballhawked on Waveland during batting practice. "They'll mean more to them," he said.

•   •   •   •   •

FOLLOWING THEIR FOURTH DAY OFF in 12 days, the Cubs figured to be well-rested, happy to be home, and, well, just plain happy. And they were, joking around as they stretched before batting practice. Piniella was asked about his club's 36 come-from-behind wins. "It's two-fold," he said. "Number one, there's no quit on your team. But number two, your pitching staff is giving you the chance to win."

Although the Cubs were embarking on a 16-game stretch that included 13 home contests and only four games against contenders, YMCA Dorothy was reserving judgment. Back in 1969, when she and her oldest son would walk to Wrigley from a two-flat she's owned for 51 years in Lincoln Square, there was a team that was nine games up on August 16. "They look good, but we've got a tough road in September," she said. "I've been disappointed too many times."

Nevertheless, the team was growing on her, even though she knows fewer of the players personally than in the days when she frequented Wrigleyville bars after games. "Mark DeRosa can put his shoes under my bed anytime!" Dorothy said. She's slowed down as an octogenarian and was hospitalized twice over the winter. But she only missed four games all season and still spends pregames in the Stadium Club, a routine she started when she first got season tickets in 1986.

Everybody seems to know her from her seventh-inning-stretch cameos. Four girls once came to a game wearing YMCA Dorothy's face on their T-shirts, and ushers helped them find her so they could snap a photo together. Wearing a pastel-striped shirt and a wide-brimmed visor before Cincinnati opened a mid-August homestand, Dorothy held court with the staff from her usual Stadium Club barstool. A woman introducing herself as Kim approached. "Today, on my 50th birthday, I said if she's here, I'm coming up to say hello," she told Dorothy. "You're kind of a celebrity!"

Dorothy used to travel with the famed "Wild Bunch," a group of crazed fans who organized Cubs road trips. One time, Dorothy got her buddy Mark Grace to sign autographs in the team hotel for her roommate's son. In his twenties now, the son had invited Dorothy to his wedding in July. "They made me do the 'YMCA'!" she said.

Reds starter Johnny Cueto didn't let her do the song and dance until the eighth inning, when he was lifted with the Cubs holding a slim 1-0 lead provided when Soto tripled and made a well-calculated dash from third base on Harden's sacrifice bunt. "[Third base coach Mike Quade] said if it's a bunt, read the play," Soto said. "I just followed the third baseman. I was far down the line, pretty much right next to him when he threw."

"Good heads-up baseball," Piniella added. "The second baseman's moving to first, the shortstop's moving to second, so there's nobody at third [to hold the runner]."

The Cubs blew it open with a four-run eighth, and after Woody finished the 5–0 shutout, a new wrinkle was added to the "Go Cubs Go," W-flag tradition. The words to Steve Goodman's fight song scrolled across the center-field messageboard, karaoke style, for fans to sing along. In the catacombs behind the dugout, Soto barked like a pit bull on his way to the clubhouse.

The Piniella Quiz Show was going on in the dungeon the next afternoon. Did he prefer the wind blowing in or out at Wrigley? Was he satisfied with his bench? How much impact do managers have on winning? What did he think of the Cubs being in position to take their biggest division lead in 24 years? "I wasn't aware of that, and I really don't care," he said. "You can't look too much ahead in this business."

Just then, Reds broadcaster Marty Brennaman and a Cincinnati beat writer barged in, both wearing pink shirts. "Whoa! It's hot pink in Cincinnati," Piniella cackled. "What is it, Sadie Hawkins Day?"

The homestand against the last-place Reds and Nationals was threatening to turn the usual dog days of August into comic relief. BleedCubbieBlue Al challenged anyone to find a Washington fan during the upcoming weekend series. "First place is two tickets to a Nationals game," he said. "Second place is four tickets to a Nationals game."

I went to the press box for my No. 1 duties, and by the time I returned, the Cubs had taken a 1–0 lead as DeRosa tied his career high for RBIs. The red trim surrounding a white C on Hawaii Jeff's Cubs cap flickered like a neon sign. "I only use it for night games," he said with that wry grin. "It's lit when they're winning."

Leading 1–0, Lilly's no-hitter was broken up to open the sixth. DeRosa, who snared a one-hop liner to limit that damage to a run and leaped to snag a would-be RBI hit three innings later, came to bat with two outs and the Cubs down 2–1 in the bottom of the ninth. "He's made the plays on defense; it's time to make one on offense!" Harry the Rookie beseeched.

Our caps were turned inside out, and Hawaii Jeff's blinked like mad. DeRo lofted the first pitch high our way...it drifted into the grandstands a few feet shy of the foul pole. Plate ump Tim McClellan rang him up four pitches later to end the game.

For the series finale, I reported to Ground Zero early with my outfielder's glove, ready to pull my first souvenir of the season. Radical Tim was living up to his nickname, the former Dead Head sporting long salt-and-pepper hair that he'd let grow for months. "I'm not cutting it until they fall out of first place!" he pledged.

The Cubs skipped batting practice, but the Reds, with seven hits for the series, were working on it. Arizona Jeremy had caught his 49th ball of the season the night before and dropped it down for Carlos Marmol, No. 49, to sign. He also said Theriot had stopped by his old place, where Jeremy now lived, to enjoy a beer in the backyard.

Seated in the third row, I had just finished writing these cute little tales into my notepad when I turned and saw it. On a fast decline coming right at me was a projectile on a path of a whole lot of hurtin'. *Incoming!* I tried to switch from pen to glove in a tizzy, but it was fruitless. I scooted right, and Jeremy reached around my back, but the ball bounced off the heel of his glove to a cherry-picker in the first row.

"I felt it graze the hair on my left forearm," I told Arizona Jeremy.

"That's probably why I didn't get a clear shot," he responded. Rookie mistake.

Later, a fan a few rows behind us hollered for the attention of Cincinnati coach Billy Hatcher, standing in left field. The former Cub turned and hit a baseball with a fungo bat. It was coming right to me. Could it be? A second chance? A guy one row down stuck his bare hand in front of the palm of my mitt and snagged it! *Curses!* And that was that. I was shut out. My only chances would be "a throw" from an outfielder after between-innings warm-ups or that mother of all Ground Zero trophies—a "gamer." Unlike the previous two nights, a gentle outward-blowing wind might make that possible.

With the Cubs up 1–0 in the second inning, DeRo blasted one. But Fookie Dookie was on deck, and so was I—in the press box. The ball landed a section to the right of Ground Zero and several rows up. The sky started spitting as Big Z homered to right for a 3–0 lead in the third. Like the Boy Scouts, Ground Zero's motto is "be prepared." They all dug into their backpacks for ponchos and plastic to cover their benches.

Zambrano cracked a molar on his chewing gum in the fifth, spit the tooth out, waived Piniella and the trainer off when they came to the mound, and soldiered on, giving up a solo homer in the sixth before being pulled. We joked how Joey Votto's name sounded like it was straight out of *The Godfather* trilogy, but when the rookie homered for the seventh time against Cubs pitching, this one onto Sheffield Avenue, the laugh was on us. "Mary Ellen," Arizona Jeremy said, "call Don Corleone and make sure Joey Votto sleeps with the fishes."

We settled for the Cubs' sixth series win in a row after Woody rung up Javier Valentin for the final out. Cue the lyrics: "Baseball season's underway. Well you better get ready for a brand new day…"

•   •   •   •

LIVING ACROSS WRIGLEY for five seasons, the sound of engine-idling tour buses waiting on Waveland and Sheffield avenues has been constant. But there are other ways they come here. Jenna Mammina, a pop/jazz vocalist and songwriter I met in New Orleans, took a South Shore Line train full of Cubs fans from as far away as South Bend, Indiana.

When she was a little girl in southwestern Michigan, her dad, who worked in the Sears Tower, would whimsically pull her out of school to catch a Cubs games. Once, her principal spotted her and friends on television and called them down to his office the following day. "Next time," he chided, "bring me." Just a handful of feet from my apartment building, Jenna pointed out where she stood in the street during the 2003 NLCS, the last time she was in the neighborhood.

Inside the park for the first time in "maybe a decade," Jenna smiled through an hour rain delay and my bad joke about good timing for SpongeBob giveaway day—to soak up all that rainwater. We sat with Peanut Tom, Big Joe, and their lot in high right field. Leading 4–0, Marquis got knocked out of the game in the sixth, and Washington took the lead on Willie Harris' first career grand slam.

The Nationals piled on in each of the next three innings. Subbing on Tom's scorecard while he sharpened his skates, Ginger held up a Rockies pencil Tom had been using since our trip to see the Rockies hammer the Cubs 15–2 at Coors Field in 2007. "I hate this thing. Look at this scorecard. There's more black diamonds than Aspen! Just like when he got it." she said, vengefully snapping it in half.

Washington's 13–5 rout proved that on any given day the team with the worst record in baseball can beat the team with the best. But were any of their fans there to see it? Al's joke became my examination of team loyalty. I set out Saturday in search of a fan who actually would splurge on a road trip to see the worst team in baseball. Standing under the red marquee before the game, maybe I'd find one trying to slink past incognito.

It was Elmer Fudd on a stakeout: *Shhh! Be vewy, vewy quiet...ovah dare, in bwack and wed...* I found them, a whole family of Nationals fans from the District of Columbia. The teenage son was in a wheelchair, having been injured on the Delaware Shore last year. "We're actually a minor league team," he joked. "Stop that! Don't say those kinds of things," his mom scolded. The father explained the trip was more of a pilgrimage to see Wrigley Field; it just happened the Nationals were in town. So they really didn't fit the profile.

I checked the concessions stands, the ramps, standing-room only. Nothing. Maybe the upper deck patio, hiding in a corner? There were two guys in the right colors—one was in a Phillies cap; the other bore the University of Utah logo. In the souvenir shops, I found Cubs mini bats, wristbands, socks, snow globes, even a martini-glass-and-shaker set. Nary a Nats' knickknack could be found.

In the concourse, I saw a guy in a Washington cap walking hand in hand with a little boy. They hurried into the first-aid room. No wonder. Ramirez had just slugged a three-run homer to give the Cubs a 4–0 lead. In the bleachers, Al pointed me in the direction of the far left-field grandstands, against the fence. They'd spotted a guy wearing Washington's red alternate jersey with the *DC* logo.

I never found their guy, but in that vicinity I met John Myers wearing a navy blue Washington Senators cap. "It's the 1924 design, when they were world champions. Which is still more recent than the Cubs," he said. Touché, John! He and his wife, Megan, flew in to watch the weekend series with friends Jason and Sarah Rice, who live three blocks from Wrigley. Sarah and Megan went to Drake University together. Megan is actually from Kansas City, but John hails from the District of Columbia. They have a 20-game package to games at new Nationals Park.

John admitted it's been a tough season as DeRosa belted a solo homer to make it 6–0. "There's still growing loyalty," he said. "But there are a lot of the old-timers there still, who remember we lost the Senators twice."

I headed outside, where Ballhawk Kenny laughed at me after I explained my task. I kept going, turning south onto Sheffield by the bleachers gate. Like the beacon on the Washington Monument, a vinyl Nationals banner hung from the façade of Murphy's Bleachers Rooftop. I talked my way up and met 16-year-old Clarke Lindsay. The Nats have been in existence a quarter of his life.

"You want to say you're rooting for a team in the pennant race," Clarke said, about the time Rammy blasted his second three-run homer. "But, hey, I saw a win yesterday. They pounded them. It's fun when you get to see that."

"Say," I asked, "what's a youngster like you doing all the way out here in Chicago, up here?" Clarke told me his father does advertising work with the Nats, and this was a team-run sponsorship outing. Tod Rosensweig, vice president of corporate partnerships for the Nationals, took them to Friday's game, too.

"I'm not sure if this is what you're looking for. These people's loyalties are largely business," Rosensweig conceded. "You've got to really be loyal to be loyal to us now. It's easy to be a Red Sox fan. You have to work harder to be a fan of the Washington Nationals. You have to have patience. You're a Cubs guy, so you know patience. Our people are struck by what great fans these are here."

And there it was. As the Cubs put the finishing touches on a 9–2 victory, I realized my analysis of faith could've been answered by looking inside my own soul. Cubs fans' fortitude has been tried and tested many a season, but this wasn't one of them. Our story's heroes set out the next afternoon to win their eighth consecutive series for the first time since 1937. Dandy Don was at his customary front patio table at Tuscany, sipping iced tea and eating a portabella mushroom sandwich late that morning.

His wife, Pat, was there, too. They met at Butch McGuire's Division Street pub in the late 1960s when it was one of the hippest singles bars in the country. "In those days, I wasn't real big on the Cubs," Pat admitted. "I went to a lot of White Sox games, because my dad was a season-ticket holder. But I had a lot of other things on my mind. I was 24 years old."

Dandy Don and his wife, Pat, enjoy a pregame meal on the patio at Tuscany with Wrigley as a backdrop. *Photo by Will Byington / www.willbyington.com*

"Of course," Don chimed in, "she hadn't been to Wrigley Field and seen where my seats were."

It didn't take long for Don and the Cubs to hook Pat. More than the games, she treasures the friendships and memories. She skips most of the night games but is there on most weekends. Sometimes when the Cubs are playing late games on the West Coast, she gets up in the middle of the night to use the bathroom and will switch on her AM radio. "She knows I'm not a really sound sleeper," Dandy Don said. "So she'll come back, and there will be a slight whisper in my ear, 'They won!'"

Finished with lunch, Don fixated down Waveland at the scoreboard. "That's another thing about sitting here," he said. "You've got that clock, so you can keep track of the time. And you've got those flags. Boy, this wind is blowing right in off the lake. Any pitcher would love to see that."

Harden certainly did in a 6–1 win. He two-hit Washington over seven innings, registering double-digit strikeouts for the fifth time in eight starts as a Cub. DeRosa continued to rake, homering in his fourth straight game and raising his average to .390 with 22 RBIs since "getting off the schneid" in that early August Houston series. "You've really got to thank Jim Hendry for this team," Dandy Don said. "He checks out everybody, besides just their stats."

Harden was getting more and more comfortable with the relaxed clubhouse feel and his confident teammates—not to mention the playoff atmosphere in the stands. "There are a lot of places where the fans just go to the game to be seen and aren't really into the game," Harden said. "Here, if you get behind 2–0 to a hitter, you can hear a kind of grumbling in the stands. They like first-pitch strikes; they get excited on an 0–2 count. That's one real good thing I've noticed."

. . . .

I WAS IN THE MIDDLE of a three-week period in which I was attending all but one of the Cubs' 19 games—daunting, if not fun. The first of two road trips in that stretch took me to Pittsburgh. The opener would be the only game I'd miss, so the day before leaving, I had a burger at the Newport Bar & Grill so I could tease Pirate Matt, who wouldn't be making the trip.

"I'm keeping it," he said of his beard, combing his fingers through the thick, black whiskers. "My luck changed since I grew it. Nothing bad has happened."

"Except," I mocked, "that the Pirates suck ass."

"They'll always be bad until they get new ownership and spend some money," he said. "It's a shame, because it's such a beautiful ballpark."

Once I stopped teasing, Matt gave a few travel tips—the sandwiches at Primanti Brothers, the view atop the Mount Washington tram, and the ferry to the ballpark from Station Square. The Cubs pounded the Pirates 12–3 on 17 hits that night in the series opener. Fukudome had three hits and four RBIs a day after ripping a pinch-hit two-run homer at Wrigley. "He sure does have a keen eye for a lot of little things," Fukudome said of Piniella, who had him shorten his hitting stride during a recent coaching session.

Toons owner Danny Beck and I flew out the next morning. "DB" hadn't been to a game in Pittsburgh since road-tripping there as a teenager from Kansas with his dad, who grew up in the area. The bar business is a tight network, and DB's buddy who owns Hye Bar, where I ducked for cover the night of the tornado sirens earlier in the month, knew some very important folks in Pittsburgh.

He hooked us up with an afternoon tour of PNC from Jim Trdinich, the Pirates' media relations director, where we learned the Allegheny River is a 10-foot shorter home run than my apartment window. The company that constructed the park provided our free pregame meal and seats in the Lexus Club right behind home plate. The only caveat was we couldn't wear any Cubs gear, which of course was all we brought. I even had my "gamer," a weathered Cubs cap I bought during the 1989 playoff run that's been soaked in playoff-clinching champagne celebrations in 1998 and 2003. It stayed in my bag. DB went out and got us a couple $10 shirts. "At least yours is blue," said Peanut Tom, who met us at the ballpark.

In the first inning, DB was "that guy," talking on his cell phone on television. One of the regulars called from Toons, and DB could hear Cassandra the bartender exclaim in the background, "Danny's talking on the phone!" "Yeah," said the caller. "He's talking to me!"

The Cubs' 82nd victory of the season guaranteed a winning record but wasn't pretty. They made three errors, trailed 3–0 early, and blew a 5–3 lead before finally breaking loose with a seven-run eighth. Soto had a pair of three-run doubles and his 20th homer, breaking Randy Hundley's team record by a rookie catcher. The highlight for us was running into Jalapeno Hanna and the Running Pierogis mid-game and snapping a picture in the Lexus Club. After the four-hour marathon, we met up with Peanut Tom and Ginger to fly the mother of all W flags.

It was out again the next day after a 2–0 shutout by Marquis, Marmol, and Woody. The Cubs scored their runs on a swinging bunt and a suicide squeeze. DB and I were first-row home plate this time, right on the rolling message board—on TV for every center-field camera shot. "Christ, i c more of u in pittsburgh than at home," read Crankshaft's text message. I was busy texting Pirate Matt: "Ahoy matie! We made ya walk da plank! Cubs sweep!"

The Cubs had gone 14–4 against his Bucs and were 33 games above .500 for the first time in 63 years. As our flight full of Cubs fans taxied from the gate, the pilot indulged us by playing "Go Cubs Go" over the intercom.

·   ·   ·   ·

FOLLOWING A STRETCH AGAINST NL mediocrity, the East-contending Phillies were in town on Piniella's 65th birthday. Eyre was back three weeks after being dealt to Philadelphia. He said hello to old friends before batting practice and seemed touched by fans saying they missed his friendly face around the Confines. He offered his take on the 2008 Cubs, as an outside observer formerly on the inside.

"I think it started with Dempster in spring training, in all honesty, with his attitude coming in," he said. "A lot of guys took notice of the effort he put in over the off-season.

"I know Lou talks about Cubbie swagger," Eyre continued. "Lou wants you to walk around with the attitude that 'I'm going to win. Don't come into our house and think you're going to beat us.' A lot of guys over there have that now. They really, truly believe that the game's not over until the last out."

Case in point that evening. Trailing 4–1 with Dempster lacking his best command, the Cubs went to work after the hypnotic spell of Philadelphia lefty Cole Hamels was lifted with his exit to start the eighth. The Little Babe rousted the crowd with a leadoff homer. Soriano one-hopped the wall for a double; Theriot singled to right; D-Lee walked.

Not a butt in a seat as Rammy stepped in. On cue, he crushed a 1–0 Chad Durbin fastball deep into the bleachers. Center fielder Shane Victorino didn't budge or even turn around. Bedlam, pandemonium, jubilation—pick a noun. With Wrigley in rhapsody, Ramirez had an out-of-body experience as he rounded the bases, realizing, "I just hit a grand slam to put us ahead!" He had driven in 15 runs in a six-game stretch and suddenly sat at 99 RBIs with 28 games to play.

Dempster heard the deafening cheers in the concrete cave of the clubhouse. "Aramis Ramirez," he said, "with the guys I've ever played with in my career, is as clutch a hitter as I've seen. He smells it."

Piniella praised: "He's an RBI guy. He likes to be up there in big situations. He knows how to hit, and he rises to the occasion. He takes it to a different level. The good ones do that. What a great come-from-behind win. That was exciting. This place really got loud."

So loud that attendants at the Cubs' remote parking lot west down Addison heard it—almost two miles away! "It was like the heavens were screaming out or the clouds," a longtime stadium ops staffer told me. "I called the ballpark to find out what in the hell just happened."

That lot, where patrons are bussed to and from the ballpark, is an example of another neighborhood plankton I haven't yet touched upon. They're key in a place where ballparks have more acreage than car parks. The parking culture has evolved with Wrigleyville. Instead of 10,000 people coming to games in a blue-collar neighborhood, it's 40,000 fans coming to a hip, crowded urban bar district.

Four of the best spots are behind my building, where Landlady Lara sells garage parking for $30 a car. She was working on Friday and offered to let me park cars and pocket the gate. So there I was, standing on Seminary just west of the firehouse, looking like a tool with a handmade sign that read "PARKING" in thick, black permanent marker on creased cardboard.

There was a furrowed, gray-haired older man out there, too. Tom parks cars behind Rooftop by the Firehouse before doing cleanup and odd jobs up top. He grew up near Wrightwood and Halsted, and went to Cubs games as far back as the 1950s. "I went to Lake View High School," he said. "We used to leave after school and come over here. They'd let all us kids in for free in the seventh inning."

We got to talking about fishing when I got my first nibble. Ray, a middle-aged man from south-suburban Orland Park, pulled in his red Nissan Quest. Next, Tom sent a black Impala my way. I asked if the guy requested an indoor spot, which Tom couldn't accommodate. Nope. Apparently, the Confines were friendly out here, too, in this give-and-take competition.

Mostly, there was a lot of standing around. I got to recognize that cars with neighborhood stickers weren't going to stop and those with Chicago Fire Department decals would be pulling into the lot behind the firehouse. As it got closer to game time, I started to worry. But traffic increased, and soon I was filling my final spot to a girl who couldn't have been happier since she had dropped off her sister and daughter in front of Brixen Ivy next door. "I have a little girl with a disability, and I don't know how long she'll make it," she said. "Can I leave early?" No problem.

I sat with BleedCubbieBlue Al's group, so I missed only a half inning when I met them back across the street in the top of the sixth inning. The Cubs had just cut a 2–0 deficit in half with a run in the fifth. Right after I got back, they tied it by coaxing four walks. An inning later, Soriano blasted a go-ahead homer into the left-center bleachers, as the Cubs matched their victory total from 2007—with a month left to play.

"I don't believe in destiny," Cubs manager Lou Piniella said, laughing. "I believe in good pitching and good defense and timely hitting. That's destiny. You do enough of that; you create your own destiny."

The last of my four garage guests reveled for an hour after the game at Cubby Bear. I didn't mind waiting. Patience was being rewarded these days in Wrigleyville.

Marty Lennartz and Lin Brehmer, the two WXRT radio personalities who ushered in Opening Day at Yak-Zies, learned patience in very different ways. Together, they share a thirst for that special Cubs season. The son of a Chicago policeman, Lennartz, aka "the Regular Guy," grew up three blocks from Wrigley in a building that was razed for a parking lot behind the Irving Park Road post office. He got an Alex Grammas foul ball at his first Cubs game, went to Ladies Day games with his mom in the 1960s, and took in games with friends from George Loukas' Waveland/Kenmore rooftop in the late-1980s.

Brehmer was born in 1954 in Queens. The Yankees were in the World Series nine of the first 10 years of his life. "I thought the World Series was a series where somebody else played the Yankees. I had a kind of skewed perspective," he said.

He still has the scorecard from Mickey Mantle's 500th home run. By that time, however, the powerhouse Yankees had become a second-division club. "I saw Mantle in his declining years. I saw him strike out with the bases loaded. It prepared me for being a Cubs fan," Brehmer deadpanned.

So did a family of Cubs fans who moved into his neighborhood. Their games of stickball were always the Yankees against the Cubs. They formed a fan club honoring Cleo James, an obscure Cubs outfielder of the early 1970s. Brehmer was spinning records in Albany, New York, in 1984 when he interviewed for the WXRT job. They bribed him with tickets to the World Series, and the moving truck arrived in Chicago during Game 5 of the NLCS, which he watched on his landlord's television three blocks from Wrigley.

Brehmer has been to 23 of 24 Opening Days since and attends 40–50 games a year. He considers himself a Cubs fan now and could care less if the Yankees ever win another championship. "I've been brainwashed, like in *The Manchurian Candidate*. People ask where I'm from, and I say the North Side of Chicago," he said. "Then I realize I'm living Marty's life."

Lennartz playfully reminds Brehmer that he'll never have the pedigree of a true Cubs fan. "He doesn't have the experience of only rooting for the Cubs. He doesn't have the 1969 experience—that kind of pain. He was here in 1984, but not really," a smirking Lennartz said loud enough for Brehmer to hear on the other side of me at Uncommon Ground's diner counter on Clark and Grace streets. "But he's learning his Cubs pain."

I joined the deejays in terraced reserved seats Lin's shared with two buddies for 20 years. Brehmer pegged Lennartz as a baseball savant, accurately spewing all sorts of obscure numbers. Ramirez came up with two men on and no outs in the third, and Lennartz noted how Rammy had 45 RBIs after the seventh inning.

He flew out, the Cubs came up empty, and after Brehmer left to get a round of beers in the fifth inning, Jayson Werth's solo homer tied the game 1–1. "I'm never getting up for beer again," Lin decreed as he returned.

Werth had a two-run single in the sixth and another homer in the eighth, as the Phillies built a 5–1 lead. His cap turned inside out, Lin started passing out "magic peanuts" in the eighth. It worked! Three straight singles opened the inning. "Here it comes," read a text Brehmer received from Magic Marc, his producer with the supernatural gum in Scoop Steph's group. What is it with these radio guys and sorcery? On our feet for Johnson's at-bat, we sat down with the crowd of 41,511 after he fanned. "That strikeout took the wind out of this place," Lennartz said. Two more Ks ended the threat, and the Cubs' seven-game winning streak was history an inning later.

With that loss, anxiety once again replaced assuredness. Complaining of a "dead arm," Big Z was bumped back a couple days in the rotation. Southpaw Sean Marshall started against ageless former Cubs lefty Jamie Moyer, meaning the lineups on two of the top-slugging NL clubs would be stacked with right-handed bats. Perfect day for ballhawking on Waveland Avenue! The Cubs weren't taking batting practice, so I showed up just after Philadelphia started hitting. "You're late!" my sensei, Ballhawk Kenny, chastised. "Now, if you tell me you were sitting in the air conditioning inside because you could see from your window that the Cubs weren't hitting...I'll let it go."

Eight balls had come out during b.p. the previous day, so I was encouraged I'd see some action. But there were lots of 'hawks circling, including Moe Mullins, Dave Davison, and Rich Reisman, a 50-year-old physical education teacher in Lincolnwood, with teenagers Matt, Mikey, and Mitch representing the "next generation."

Kenny and I stood in the middle of Kenmore, staring up. A ball peeked over the top of the bleachers, but I could see it wasn't coming out. Kenny sidled forward into Waveland Avenue; the ball landed on a stairway leading to Ground Zero and bounced down. "That was in the aisle, so it had prime bounce-out potential," he tutored to me in my cement sneakers.

Just before it left the ballpark, another ball was snared by a young guy wearing a Zambrano jersey in the walkway behind the bleachers. I realized it was Arizona Jeremy, adding number 56 to his season's tally.

I remarked to Ballhawk Kenny how all the pretty women in foot traffic on a 78-degree, sunny day can be distracting during the abundant downtime. He warned against it...and then, moments later, after he started yapping with a girl he knew, a ball came rocketing well over the bleachers, headed for the building to my right. It slammed into the yellow bricks about 12 feet high and took two bounces back across Waveland. Davison and I were hot on its trail, but the alpha dog was a step ahead. Under the bleachers overhang, a guy walking with a baby girl on his shoulders used his foot to pin the baseball to the sidewalk. Davison reached down and latched onto it with two fingers and a thumb before releasing it so the man could kick the souvenir over to his wife.

"Dave," I said, "I've heard of stealing candy from a baby, but that was ridiculous." He laughed. "I told him I was going to give it to him," Dave said, "but he said he didn't believe me."

I returned to my spot alongside my 'hawking guru. "You played that well young Pad-Wan," Kenny said in his best Darth Vader voice.

The author (left) and Ballhawk Kenny, patiently waiting for that special prize from the sky. *Photo by Will Byington / www.willbyington.com*

Only one other ball came out, joggling through a tree in the parkway of the Bud Building and into Moe's waiting glove. The Cubs were having their best season in memory, but the 'hawks were famished. As Moe relaxed in a lawn chair under an umbrella Dave had duct-taped to the fireplug on Kenmore, an acquaintance stopped to say hello. "This is the worst summer we've ever had out here," Moe reported. "Everybody's numbers are way down."

As the game started, I got the ballhawks' version of a hot foot when Ryan Howard, the majors' home-run leader and a left-handed hitter, came to the plate in the first inning. "You young guys better get over there," Moe barked, gesturing toward Sheffield Avenue. I started running, but Howard's at-bat was over before I reached the center-field bleachers gate.

The Phillies scored three runs in that inning—without a home run. "If you're gonna lose," Ballhawk Kenny griped, "at least lose with some homers."

The Cubs cut the deficit to 3–2 with four singles in the second inning, but Werth homered in the fifth. That blast landed a few rows above Ground Zero and skipped on some hands up to the top row, where fans were digging for it under their seats. In the sixth, the heat had taken its toll on Moe, who pulled away with Dave hanging out the window. "Where ya going?" I yelled. "I'll be right back," Dave said. "If any balls come out, just leave them here on the curb."

He returned with a two-liter bottle of soda. After draining it, he and Mikey made a game out of trying to place-kick it into a garbage can on the corner. Football season was upon us! The Cubs picked up a run in the eighth, but Sori fanned with two men on to end the inning. They went 1-2-3 in the ninth, and that was that. I was still 0-for-the-season. Worse yet, with the 5–3 win, the Phillies had won the season series 4–3 between two teams that might be meeting again in October.

8

SEPTEMBER

WILLY B AND I WERE wedding crashers again, albeit late. In fact, we almost were part of the procession down an aisle of stairs separating 150 stadium-style seats atop Tom Gramatis' year-old rooftop at 3619 Sheffield. Kara Ferguson and Rob Gillman were tying the knot on Labor Day as the Cubs opened a series against Houston on the back end of a seven-game homestand.

Her brunette hair pinned up, the bride promenaded past in her wedding gown to the tune of Israel Kamakawiwo'ole's "Somewhere Over the Rainbow." My BlackBerry vibrated with a press release from the Cubs, who had added six players as rosters expanded in September. The couple was heading into a life together; baseball was merely in its final month.

Rob bought a condo on Sheffield between Addison and Clark in 2000 and has shared season tickets with nine other guys in section 518 for nearly 10 years. During a session of pillow talk in March, he half suggested a rooftop wedding. A bee in her bonnet, Kara got up and started surfing the Internet as Rob rolled over and went to sleep. They signed a contract in April—two months before he officially popped the question—sent out invitations that looked like game tickets and spent substantial time explaining exactly what type of ceremony their guests would be attending.

"Out-of-town people were like: 'What? On a rooftop? How do we get the owners to let us go up there?'" Kara said. "I still think to this day there were people who thought we'd be sitting in folding chairs on a hot tar roof."

They took their vows over the sound of Cubs bats smashing balls during batting practice across the way. Michelle Miller, pastor at Holy Trinity Lutheran Church just west of the ballpark on Addison, delivered a sermon drawing parallels between the institutions of baseball and marriage. She held up items common to baseball and related them to the union of husband and wife. The scorecard was a reminder to stay involved, yet not keep track of all the runs and errors. The hot dog and a beer were symbols to provide nourishment in the form of love and compliments and to share, as in, "I'll get this round." We all sang "Take Me Out to the Ball Game," a mental note to take an occasional break, stretch, relax, and enjoy the game. And the Cubs shirt and cap represented faith in your team and perseverance through the hard times. "There's something about Cubs fans' spirit that is unmistakable," Miller said. "There's almost an insane optimism about what next year can bring."

Even more insane is that Rob is a converted Cardinals fan whose parents are Missouri dairy farmers, and Kara grew up rooting for the Tigers in Oxford, Michigan, just north of Detroit. They met in a Wrigley mezzanine suite during the Cubs–White Sox series in 2002.

While the newlyweds mingled with guests, Houston's Roy Oswalt was stymieing the Cubs. WGN Radio was playing on the rooftop deck in the fifth inning, and Pat Hughes announced a final from Milwaukee: Mets 4, Brewers 2. Cubs fans, Cardinals fans, and even a few Astros fans found common ground and cheered. Sitting up top in a comfortable white camp shirt on an 80-degree, cloudless afternoon, Rob showed that unmistakable Cubs optimism as they headed into the ninth inning down 3–0: "What's this gonna be, our 58th comeback win?"

One-out singles by Daryle Ward and Alfonso Soriano raised eyebrows—not to mention Wrigley faithful from their seats. But Houston closer Jose Valverde came out of the bullpen to hand the Cubs their first three-game losing streak since being swept by the White Sox in June. Not exactly the way Rob and Kara wanted to begin their marriage, but they were postponing a honeymoon in

Italy with hopes of more important games in October. I reminded them of Miller's homily and asked if they could make sense of the Cubs' blemish on their day. "It's not how much you score," Rob said, his arm wrapped around his wife's waist as he looked into her eyes. "It's how you play the game."

The Cubs weren't playing well. The next evening I met Willy B and our friend, Andy Skretta, at Messner's Wrigley Grille, which is off the beaten path on Southport. Andy, who has a share of season tickets in the upper deck, was chattering while nervously shoveling French fries into his mouth. "The Cubs haven't had an extra-base hit since Friday," he said. "The season is peaks and valleys, so maybe it's better we have a valley now and peak at the end."

Wearing a Carlos Zambrano 2004 All-Star Game jersey, Andy was trying to maintain his always-positive disposition, and enjoying his staple pregame meal at Messner's was part of that. It's healthy on the pocketbook, if not the body. The Cubs Game Express Menu included a choice of two hot dogs, a pulled pork sandwich, a sloppy joe, or 10 mini corndogs with fries and a pint of beer for $6. Andy picked up the tab. "Where else can you buy dinner and beers for two of your friends for 18 bucks?" he said. "I tell you what. There are deals in Wrigleyville. Only the locals know."

At the firehouse back on Waveland, I was regaled with Engineer Lee's stories of corking his bat while playing college baseball and in Chicago's 16-inch softball beer leagues. A Chicago policeman pulled up on his motorcycle and asked if he could park behind the bench we were sitting on. He bragged about the policemen beating the firemen 14–3 at the Cell recently in their annual charity baseball challenge. "Lee," I said, "you should have been there with your corked bat!"

Lee's chuckle stopped as he sniffed the air. "Uh-oh, somethin's burnin'. Mike, we've got some rubbish in that garbage can," he said. Mike dumped a bucket of water from the fireplug into the smoldering can. Chicago's finest, indeed!

Just then, the crowd roared on the first pitch of the Cubs' fourth. "Hey! Hey!" Lieutenant Steve said, jumping out of his seat inside the garage to get a look down Waveland. He ducked back in, and the delayed TV broadcast showed Mark DeRosa homering to snap a 1–1 tie. A batter later, Geovany Soto clubbed another. Steve predicted a phone call from his wife, a huge Soto backer, and *brrriiing!*

But it was a stale night with little wind. Even though Wrigley pushed past the 3 million mark in attendance at the earliest point ever, it was a tired and listless assembly. I'd attended 29 games in 40 days, but what I got for my rain dance earlier in the day was a 4 hour, 17 minute, 9–7 loss in 11 innings.

Zambrano bugged out after five with a sore shoulder, Bob Howry gave up four runs without getting an out, and Jim Edmonds leaped into the wall for a long fly ball, and two balls came out of the ivy. Still, the Cubs battled back from a 7–3 deficit and tied it on Edmonds' solo homer in the seventh. But Derrek Lee grounded into an inning-ending double play with the bases full in the eighth.

In the clubhouse, Carlos Marmol walked past Howry, who'd been booed riotously. Marmol gently slapped his behind, and Howry turned to face reporters. "You can't expect them to cheer when you're going out there and putting your team down four runs," Howry admitted. "Walking a guy who's trying to bunt, that was unacceptable."

D-Lee was equally dismayed yet accountable. "My team put me in a situation to get a come-from-behind win. I kind of let the air out of the balloon," he said. "We're in a skid, obviously. Four in a row. We've got to get it fixed."

Three hours before the finale of the Cubs' second-to-last home-stand of the season, no announcement had been made on the status of Big Z. There were mixed reports on whether his SUV with the "TORO 38" plates was in the parking lot or if he was at the ball-park at all. The media surrounded DeRosa, their old standby. "We've put ourselves in good position to enable our guys to skip their spots in the rotation and get healthy," he said, "but the bottom line is the guys you're asking to step up are not as good as the guys you lose."

In a lengthy session with lots of lines to read between, the media peppered Piniella in the dungeon. Zambrano had been examined by team orthopedist Stephen Gryzlo but left short of taking an MRI. "Did he just leave?" Piniella was asked. He sighed. "He was supposed to take an MRI today. It was available to him, and he didn't take it today. That's it," he answered. "Until he takes the MRI, we're not going to know anything. That's the final part of the examination, as I've been told, and probably the most important part."

Questions turned to Harden, whose turn in the rotation was being skipped that night for what initially was characterized as a precautionary breather. "Harden?" Piniella said. "If he were available to pitch today, or tomorrow, or the next day, why would we wait for St. Louis? Doesn't that make sense? He's not available right now is all I'm trying to tell you."

Writers pressed. "Look," Piniella said, using a word I've come to identify with him being agitated with a line of questioning. "He's had some discomfort also," Piniella affirmed, patting his right shoulder with his left hand.

To cut the tension I had to look no further than inside my own trousers. I was bold enough—or maybe it was just flirtatious—to make a wager with a lady friend in Houston before the Astros series started. Each game's loser had to go commando the next day, so while I was saving on laundry expenses, cool breezes and the threat of rain took on a whole new meaning. At least the gals in Scoop Steph's group got a kick out of hearing about the particulars of my particulars.

Colleen Manzella, 49, was sitting next to her best friend, as she does for most games. At the age of 15, she'd met Judy Caldow on Opening Day 1975 in the right-field bleachers. Colleen's dad wrote a letter to her high school teachers, excusing her for "Cubitis," and she's made every home opener since. That includes 2000, when she climbed the ramp and said a brief hello. "I had my son, Christopher, on April 8. I told my husband I had to come to Opening Day—on our way home from the hospital," she said. "I came in, got my magnet schedule, got my scorecard, and went home."

This was to be another long night, and the women of Aisle 311 identified it early after five of the first seven Cubs struck out. "Wow! The Cubs are really coming out hitting," Colleen scoffed. "Kerry Wood's record is in jeopardy," Judy added.

Randy Wolf fanned eight, not 20, but went the loop in a 4–0 shutout. "Do you know the Cubs and the Marlins are the only two teams in the National League that haven't lost five games in a row?" Colleen said as the Cubs were going down in order in the ninth. "Until tonight!" Milwaukee also got swept, so at least the 4½-game lead remained intact.

• • • •

PINIELLA WANTED TO SPEND Thursday's off day in Chicago rather than take the charter for the team's longest road trip of the season. So he and first-base coach Matt Sinatro, a sort of traffic cop if you will, decided to drive and got lost on their way to a city in which Piniella managed for three years!

Somehow, their directions had them headed toward someplace called East Liverpool, Ohio, near the Pennsylvania state line. Piniella took a nap along the ride, and when he awoke, Sinatro was closing in on Cleveland. The skipper changed signs, went into a filling station to buy a map, and they headed south through Columbus. "I wanted to get my mind off baseball for a little bit. I sure as heck did," Piniella joked after arriving at Great American Ball Park two hours before first pitch.

The five-hour trip took eight hours. At least it only took us six. Big Joe borrowed Mom's minivan again, but our problem was detours upon detours while trying to get southbound on I-65. Despite cell phones, laptops with wireless cards, and all our technology, we found ourselves on a two-lane rural road splitting two expansive cornfields.

Finally, we reached civilization. "There's a Best Buy. Maybe we should get a radar detector," Peanut Tom said. Christie amended, "How about a GPS instead?"

The Cubs hadn't lost to Houston in two days, but they hadn't won a game, either. So I felt it necessary to continue my own version of a cilice, which is no doubt a bad metaphor coming from a guy wearing no underpants. The corporal mortification would continue into Saturday, as Ted Lilly had his worst outing of the season, Jon Lieber had his last, and the Cubs got pounded 10–2 in the opener of the road trip. On ballpark scoreboards, Reds graphics people lampooned a Wrigley tradition by flying a red W on a white flag. Curses!

It marked the Cubs' first six-game losing streak since one culminated in Mt. Piniella's eruption and first ejection as Cubs manager June 2, 2007. The skipper may have gotten lost on his way to Cincinnati, but he was finding his famous boiling point.

The next afternoon back in Chicago, my friend Mike Reischl helped honor the former site of West Side Grounds, where the Cubs franchise won four pennants and two World Series from 1893 to 1915. Mike the Cop started the "Way Out in Left Field Society," whose goal was to dedicate a plaque at the ballpark's old site, on the campus of his alma mater, the University of Illinois–Chicago. He took the society's name from the idiom "that came out of left field," which was derived from odd cries that used to come from a psychiatric hospital located beyond left field from the old park. "The marker is on the building that replaced the institution where the saying comes from," Mike said. "This is my one contribution to my city, my university, and my favorite baseball team in the world."

Back in Cincinnati, Arizona Jeremy and Ken Keefer added to their baseball collection that evening. I ran into them before the game, comparing notes about ballhawking just like it was Ground Zero—sort of. "It's a little different here. The ball has to come right to you," Jeremy said. "You can't go running over rows of seats like you can on bleachers." He scored his 60th of the season; Ken got two.

On his 33rd birthday, D-Lee got four hits and three RBIs, as the Cubs had 18 hits and matched their run total during the six-game slide. Even pitcher Jason Marquis homered in the 14–9 victory. Most of the sellout crowd of 41,204 was Cubs fans. They had to be, because I've never seen a visiting player so close to taking a curtain call after Soriano lined a three-run shot, his third homer of the night, to make it 6–1.

"He just loosened everybody up to go out and have fun. We were playing so tight," said DeRosa, who also had a three-run blast. "We really weren't panicking, but we were flat."

It was good to wear skivvies again on Sunday and have my boys back in a neighborhood. Sean Marshall kept his 'hood clean in a nice spot start for Big Z, and Ronny Cedeno's two-run double in the seventh gave the Cubs a 3–1 lead. However, an error, two walks, a bad-hop double, and a game-winning Jolbert Cabrera single in the bottom of the ninth off Woody kept Peanut Tom's giant W flag in his backpack and gave reason for another dreaded red W sighting.

Wood hollered at a celebrating Cabrera on his way off the field. Frustration was manifesting, and Piniella gave his troops a tongue lashing in the clubhouse. There were good signs, though. Zambrano threw off flat ground and felt good enough to goof around before Sunday's game, taking a lap around the clubhouse on a bicycle. Big Joe got us home without incident, and I was back in drawers again.

．　．　．　．

A RAINY MONDAY BACK IN Chicago wasn't a good day for baseball, but it was perfect for dark, esoteric wordsmiths. While the Cubs spent the day off in St. Louis, Don Evans emceed the final gathering of the Lovable Losers Literary Review at El Jardin. The theme was curses, befitting of the 39th anniversary of the black cat incident, in which a stray feline ran around the visitor's on-deck circle at Shea Stadium and engaged in a stare down with manager Leo Durocher during the Cubs' infamous '69 collapse. With all that had happened to the Cubs of late, Evans assessed, "We've got to examine if curses really apply only to us."

Renowned Chicago media personality Rick Kogan did the toast: "Here's to the children who fall in love early and for keeps....The ball is in the air, the catch is about to be made. Baseball is about to enter the bloodstream. We were all kids once. Here's to the children." They channeled for answers through a Ouija board, and a comedian/crooner named Dave Impey sang a customized version of "Witchcraft": "When Zambrano can't find the plate, the wind's blowin' off the lake, Soriano's wrist, it breaks, that's witchcraft."

Author Randy Richardson read from "Scapegoats," an essay written in the voice of a goat: "Not only do you continue to slander us as a species, you are blaming us for the failures and fortunes of a baseball team and, in turn, the pain and suffering its fans have endured. You have made us into, well, scapegoats." Introduced as one of the founders of the Cleo James Fan Club, Lin Brehmer, the WXRT personality who treated me to a game in late August, read from his Q&A style "Lin's Bin" radio feature in which a fan referenced the 2004 Red Sox and 2005 White Sox and asked, "Could we be next?"

> Only if the universe is ordered like sullen five-year-olds waiting to go down the slide in a Chicago playground. It's not your turn; it's my turn. Let me tell you something about cosmology and about Chicago playgrounds. Whenever you think it's your turn to go down the slide, some grubby kid with an overactive pituitary gland starts walking up the wrong way. Which is another way of saying, "Hey, pal, 2003 was your turn, and you just couldn't get down the slide."

Author James Finn Garner offered a closing psalm: "Sweet Lou is my shepherd, I shall not want to root for the Sox, or tune in to the Bears, just yet....Yea, though I walk through the valley of the shadow of 100 years of suckitude, I will fear no team, for Lou is with me...as long as he doesn't try to drive me all the way to Cincinnati."

Down on the Mississip after next evening's loss to the Cardinals, Sweet Lou raged red-faced in his postgame press conference: "We're playing like we're waiting to get beat," he hollered from his office loud enough for his team to hear. "You've got to get your damn shirts rolled up and go out and kick somebody's ass! That's what you have to do! Period!"

From home the next day, I saw lots of suits parading around Wrigley Field, as Cubs executives hosted various potential ownership groups in meetings and tours around the facilities. Lilly pitched eight solid innings in a 4–3 victory and bulled over catcher

ROSEY THE WRITER

Jack Rosenberg knows a thing or two about writing—and Cubs heart-break. I visited "Rosey" at his Lincolnwood home to watch the opener of the Cardinals series. Born in downstate Pekin, Illinois, Rosey came to Chicago in 1954, spending 40 years as a writer and executive with WGN Radio, WGN-TV, and Tribune Radio Network. Together with Chicago broadcast legends like Jack Brickhouse, Arne Harris, Vince Lloyd, Lou Boudreau, and Bob Elson, Rosey helped make WGN and the Cubs synonymous. "The camaraderie that was there was unbeliev-able. We came down the road, literally, together," he said of that group. "We went through weddings, births, funerals, bar mitzvahs, the whole of life. I'm very proud of that."

Perhaps most of all, he was proud of the succinct speech he wrote for Brickhouse when Brickhouse won the Ford Frick Award for broad-cast excellence in 1983. In part, it said: "It's a contradiction, baseball is. It can be the simplest of games, yet it can be the most involved."

Brickhouse received a wristwatch from the Tribune Co. after 40 years of service. Given to Rosey by Brickhouse's wife after his death, he wears it every day. Rosey, 82, has lived in the same home for 46 years and introduced Cubs pitcher Ken Holtzman to his neighbor's daughter across the street. They later married. A family man whose wife, Mayora, passed away in 2007, photos adorn Rosey's walls—of his two children and six grandkids, in addition to those of him with President Reagan, Willie Mays, and Ernie Banks, among other celebri-ties. Downstairs, he has a collection of signed baseball bats, ranging from Banks and Ron Santo to Dick Groat and Jim Hickman, my favorite player as a boy. Rosey had a special twinkle in his eye as he showed me a bat given to him in September 1972, the last time he saw Roberto Clemente alive. "I had two requirements to make my collection," he said. "He had to not only be a helluva player, but he had to be a hel-luva guy."

He brought out two cups of ice cream, and we settled into his fam-ily room to watch the ballgame. While the Cubs built a 3–0 lead, Rosey entertained with stories about Durocher and creating a three-man radio broadcast booth in 1990 by hiring both Santo and Bob Brenly ⋯⋯▸

to do color. And then with one swing of his bat, Albert Pujols tied the game with a three-run homer in the sixth. "Oh, man...Oh, man," Rosey groused. "The Cubs have been in some tough ballgames lately."

They hit into rally-ending double plays in the eighth and ninth, and St. Louis put runners on second and third with one out in the ninth. The Cubs pulled their infield in. On a 96-mph fastball, Marmol induced a weak check-swing grounder to DeRosa. Soto blocked the plate and took the throw, but Brendan Ryan slid backdoor, around the tag, to score the winning run. "Just like your speech, Jack," I said as the Cardinals celebrated. "We did everything right at the end of the game, pulled the infield in, tough pitch down in the zone, and still lost. It's the simplest of games, yet the most involved." Rosey nodded, his smile morphing into a grimace.

Yadier Molina in a fine response to Piniella's challenge. They won 3–2 the next night, too, as Harden returned to the rotation, Soriano and Kosuke Fukudome made late run-saving catches, and Woody nailed down his 30th save.

The fun was back in baseball that afternoon, as well. With Willy B as my photographer and Peanut Tom as my best grip, I had my first official entourage. We carried my desk across the street to shoot the cover photo for this book. It was September 11, seven years after that horrible day I had watched on television sets in Wrigley Field's front office. I'll never forget the pit in my stomach that day, created by the thought that I was inside an American icon that could be looked upon as a target. It was the only time I've ever wanted out of Wrigley, and I hate them for making me feel that way. From now on, I'll prefer the memories of 2008 when I think of September 11.

·   ·   ·   ·

HURRICANE IKE WAS BEARING DOWN on Texas' Gulf Coast, and before the finale of the St. Louis series, it was announced that the Cubs' road trip would not continue to Houston, and the team would be returning to Chicago.

A press release was issued just short of 9:00 on Saturday night: the Cubs and Astros would be playing Sunday night and Monday afternoon at Miller Park. The final game of the three-game series would be made up at the conclusion of the season if it had any bearing on the postseason. I got a text from Ballhawk Kenny minutes later: "I hear they're going to get Daryle Ward, Henry Blanco, Lance Berkman, and Carlos Lee to do the sausage race since it's a day off for the regular runners."

It had been raining in Chicago for two days, and even though the Astros would be the home team and had won 14 of 15 to enter the wild-card picture...c'mon, Milwaukee is 90 miles north of Chicago. We knew the fans would be wearing blue. So did the folks running ballpark concessions, selling cheese fries and ice cream in tiny Cubs helmets. The "home" Astros were booed. So was anyone wearing any Brewers attire.

Twenty-four hours earlier, nobody imagined they'd be making a whimsical trip to Brew Town the next evening to witness history. BleedCubbieBlue Al and Miriam were part of the crowd of 23,441; so were Judy and Colleen from Scoop Steph's crew, and Big Joe, Christie, and Melanie. Ken Keefer of Ground Zero left behind floodwaters that were inches from the electrical boxes in his back yard. I convoyed with Crankshaft, Willy B, Harry the Rookie, and others.

Bob Vorwald, WGN-TV's director of production, scrambled to assemble a staff and truck to broadcast the game, and didn't get permission from MLB to televise locally—on a night in which ESPN had national exclusivity—until that morning.

I've always coveted that one completed and treasured scorecard: a no-hitter. Knowing there wouldn't possibly be any scorecards printed, I brought a blank one from a 2007 Cubs-Reds series. The souvenir stands were passing out free scorecards from a Brewers-Reds series, but if I was going to be scoring on a card including the Reds, at least they were going to be playing the Cubs.

Zambrano, in his first start in 12 days, started hanging zeros on the Houston side, but following baseball protocol, nobody said anything. David Newhan smashed a line drive in the fifth; D-Lee snared it. As Big Z was striking out Berkman to end the seventh, fans chanted: "Let's go Z! Let's go Z!"

Three up, three down in the eighth, with kudos to DeRo for tracking a drive down the right-field line. Z had tallied 99 pitches on a night in which the Cubs wanted to limit his pitch count to 90–95. Piniella looked at bench coach Alan Trammell. "If he's got to come out of the game," Piniella said, "you go get him."

Fans were on their feet when Zambrano walked to the mound in the ninth. Two ground-outs to Theriot started the inning, and then Darin Erstad chased a full-count change-up to complete the Cubs' first no-hitter in 36 years and baseball's first on a neutral site. After briefly kneeling and pointing presumably to the heavens

Carlos Zambrano points to the sky after completing his storybook no-hitter.
Photo by John "Nunu" Zomot

beyond the closed roof, Zambrano was swarmed by teammates. "I was thinking [about it] the whole game," Big Z said. "In the ninth inning when I came out, the crowd was all crazy, and that helped me out."

We had a celebratory drink afterward at the lounge in the Pfister Hotel, where the team stayed. Pitching coach Larry Rothschild walked in. "Our pitcher looked pretty good tonight, eh?" I said. Larry chuckled, "Yeah...he was all right." Harry's girlfriend stopped Zambrano to snap a photo, and Z dropped his cell phone—the only error he'd made all night.

Remember, folks, this is nonfiction. I'm not making it up! Nor could I. Just consider this turn of events from the Brewers' perspective: a Cubs pitcher threw a no-hitter at their stadium, after which his teammates doused him with more than three cases of beer and several cans of shaving cream in the Brewers clubhouse (their gear was cleared out to make room for the Cubs). What's more, the Astros were no-hit and still gained a half game in the standings because Milwaukee got swept by Philly in a doubleheader.

Brewers manager Ned Yost was fired the next day, and Lilly took a no-hitter six-plus innings into an eventual 6–1 one-hit victory, the first time in major league history a team followed a no-hitter with a one-hitter. The Cubs' magic number was six, and they could clinch in front of their home fans by sweeping Milwaukee over the next three days.

• • • •

MY DOOR BUZZER WENT OFF AT 9:30 AM, as my scorecard delivery guy gave a reminder that Wrigley was heading into its final homestand. Milwaukee soldiered on with Dale Sveum as interim manager, and the switch was so sudden that Yost still was listed as manager on my scorecard. "You see the finish line, that's for sure," Piniella told a huge delegation of media before the game. "We're at the point now where we can sprint right to the wire. It's there for us."

I arrived at Ground Zero early for one more shot at that elusive batting practice smash. I tracked one to the wall, but hastily running down rows of bleachers while looking up at the sky is ill-advised. I pulled a rib muscle and nearly crashed. Worse, I was shut out again. So was Arizona Jeremy, but he did share stories of meeting Dempster and Lilly during recent walks in the neighborhood with his two dachshunds.

Mark Loiacano, a 28-year-old road construction worker, got six to increase his count to 59 on the season—in only about 20 games. "I usually average 4.2 per game," he said. "You have to watch what's happening down there. I try to watch their body, their front foot. They're trying to do different things." A Ground Zero veteran and regular bleachers ballhawk, he was given the nickname "Rambo" by Dempster several years ago. With shoulder-length, stringy black hair, a soul patch, and camouflage cargo pants, he looked the part. Rambo caught one on the run several rows behind me. When a group of lefties came up to hit, he ran over to right field and snared a couple more. That group finished, and he sprinted back, behind the high center-field bleachers, in time to catch a ball by snaking his glove at waist level through some oblivious fans descending the stairway down toward Ground Zero. The crowd around us turned at the commotion, and another ball bounced hard off two peoples' backsides. "The second one'll kill ya," Radical Tim said, sipping his beer.

The Cubs jumped on Milwaukee early with a run in the first and two in the third. I chatted with an earthy, blonde-haired girl sitting next to me. She had an old mitt, and the others were teasing her about her impending nuptials at the Stadium Club the following weekend. "Hey, I know who you are," I said. "Your Ballhawk Kenny's girl!"

Laura Cannata, an OB nurse at Illinois Masonic Hospital, grew up in my north-suburban hometown of Des Plaines. Her aunt once lived a few blocks west on Waveland, and her uncle lived in a rooftop building on Sheffield. In 1975 on her first outing to Wrigley in elementary school, she became hysterical when they mobilized to leave in the seventh inning. "The first time the Cubs disappointed me was when I realized I was a girl," she said. "I would say to friends, 'I want to play for the Cubs when I grow up.' And they'd say, 'You can't play for the Cubs. You're a girl!'"

As the Brewers closed to within a run in the sixth on Prince Fielder's mammoth homer off my old apartment building on

The Cubs celebrate another late-inning victory at Wrigley Field.
Steve Green photo courtesy Chicago Cubs

Sheffield, Laura told me how she'd been proposed to the previous year. She was looking for some hangover food after a night of concert-going and had just returned to Ground Zero with a hot dog. Radical Tim had a camcorder rolling, and Kenny took a knee and gave her a Cubbie-blue sapphire ring with diamond baguettes. "All I wanted to do was eat that damn hot dog," she laughed. "I had mustard all over the ring within seconds."

Just then, Soriano hit a seventh-inning homer into the basket to our right. Fortunately, the Cubs added another insurance run in the eighth, which became necessary when Woody yielded a run in the ninth before nailing down the 5–4 win.

In the morning, a work crew riveted a blank tarp over the Budweiser advertisement on Kenmore and Waveland, and the sound of glass being busted out of the Ivy League Baseball Club's façade filled the neighborhood. Tom Gramatis, the owner of both buildings, continued to wield his power in the Wrigleyville skyline.

Ronnie "Woo-Woo" Wickers is a pretty well-known character here, too. I'd been putting it off all season, but it was time to spend a day in Ronnie's kitschy shadow. We met at the Salt & Pepper Diner on Clark, where he often hangs out before games, hoping someone tosses a spare ticket his way. When that didn't happen, he drifted down Addison and exchanged whispers with a ticket scalper.

In the 7-Eleven parking lot at Sheffield, his friend Janet caught up to him with a box full of 8-by-11 photographs of Ronnie. "Have you got a Sharpie?" she asked him. "Sign one for Jim."

The game started, Milwaukee took a fast lead, and Ronnie Woo still didn't have a ticket. He started wiggling his body and waving his arms like noodles, saying: "It's time for me to slip and slide! Meet me in the grandstands in 10 minutes." And then he ditched me. Like the Batcave, I only was allowed to see the inside, not the journey. I arrived in time to witness Aramis Ramirez lining a second-inning homer into Ground Zero to close the deficit to 3–1. Keefer, who's caught 24 Cubs homers in 30 seasons, had it bounce off the heal of his glove.

Ronnie's 10 minutes turned into 20, then 30. I walked a lap around the stadium. It was like "Where's Waldo?" only "Where's Woo-Woo?" I asked a security supervisor if he'd seen him. "Thankfully, no," he said. "Just keep your ears open. You'll find him." I texted an all-points bulletin: BE ON THE LOOKOUT FOR WOO-WOO. Finally, in the sixth inning, Radical Tim pointed toward Beyond the Ivy's Waveland/Sheffield rooftop. "You heard him?" I asked. "God, did I ever," he said.

There wasn't anybody at the locked front door, so I rang my friend Big D's buzzer and went up through his apartment. Sure enough, there was Ronnie, jitterbugging to no music with a shapely, short-haired, pretty-faced blonde.

Ronnie also had procured a ticket—two, in fact. So off he went, down the stairs and up Sheffield, wooing, taking pictures, and shaking hands like he was the mayor. We arrived back in the stands in time to see the Brewers extend their lead to 6–1 in the seventh. We settled into Section 222 with two sisters who knew Ronnie from spring training.

The Cubs scored a run and had two runners on in the ninth. Ronnie wooed throughout The Riot's 10-pitch at-bat, and the crowd around us joined him before Ward grounded out to end the game. As we filed out, Ronnie gently kissed the back of a girl's hand. "We're still number one," he told her.

Wouldn't you know it? The next day when I joined Bleed-CubbieBlue Al's group, Ronnie was on the other side of the foul pole, wearing our ears out with his wooing from the far left-field grandstands.

After Harden worked out of a pickle in the first inning, Al asked if I was still punching in Fukudome, who was batting eighth. "You better get up there now," Al said. "They're gonna bat around." Liking his confidence, I threw my Cubs batting-practice cap on Harry the Rookie's head (there's no cheering in the press box), and off I went. I languished up there into the third inning before Fookie Dookie finally came up. He was batting .178 since the end of July and had not started the last five games. He popped out, and the slump continued.

I wondered if it was my right index finger. He was hitting .100 in the second half when I punched in his number. Should I switch to the left? Maybe watch tape of how I button-pressed in the first half? Do some finger exercises, like rapid pop-topping cases of beer cans?

Derby Sue's pool was going again, and Al remembered Edmonds homering twice off Dave Bush in late July. His scouting paid handsomely when Edmonds hit a solo shot in the second. Rammy hit one on the other side of our aisle in the fourth—pay up to Hawaii Jeff.

Harden worked a no-hitter into the fifth, but six walks ended his afternoon early. He left with a 2–1 lead, but an error in the sixth helped Milwaukee to four unearned runs. With two outs and nobody on base in the ninth, it didn't look good for our story's heroes. Ramirez doubled on a sinking liner that Ryan Braun nearly caught. Edmonds singled him home, and an extremely jittery Derby Sue said, "I could go for extra innings!" I cautioned, "We still need three runs you know." DeRosa singled, and the tying run stepped in with Fukudome on deck. Harry asked, "Do you walk Soto and pitch to the spinning Japanese dreidel?"

Milwaukee chose to pitch to Soto, and he hammered the first offering high into the left-field bleachers. We jumped up and down in an ecstatic group hug, leaving Harry's sunglasses trampled and busted. Sue got her extras and remained on the edge of her seat as Woody worked into and out of a second-and-third, no-out jam in the twelfth.

After two walks in the bottom of the inning, D-Lee snapped an 0-for-5 afternoon by lining a walk-off single to center. Al was beside himself as we filed out, proclaiming this as bigger than even the comeback against Colorado in May. "Biggest win of the year," he said assuredly. "Four runs down in the ninth inning with nobody on base? I don't know how to write up this one. I'll probably just say, 'The Cubs beat the Brewers today 7–6. Done.'"

. . . .

IF THE CLINCHING WOULD COME in the opener of the Fan Appreciation Weekend series against the Cardinals, it would be in the evening with a Brewers loss—provided the Cubs won their matinee. Piniella was asked about his evening schedule. "I don't have any plans," he said. "I don't like to count chickens. You people are getting ahead of yourselves."

The *Chicago Sun-Times'* front-page headline screamed, "THIS ROOF'S FOR YOU." Anheuser-Busch filed a lawsuit against Gramatis, their smarmy new leaser who terminated their contract because they were late on a quarterly payment. Hence the tarp covering the ad. "It's available," Gramatis told the paper. "It's known as the Budweiser Building, but it's the Whoever-Wants-to-Go-up-There Building."

Richard Harris' wife could be seen in an accompanying photograph of the iconic gabled rooftop. She actually was standing on the building next door to the north, where silent-film star Gloria Swanson lived as a little girl. About eight years ago, Harris, who grew up in Rogers Park and went to high school at nearby Lane Tech, bought the three-flat's top-floor condominium. Harris, 64, considered buying the Lakeview Baseball Club when it was for sale in 1987, but as an advertising copywriter working for DDB at the time, he reconsidered. "I looked out the third-floor window at the field, and I knew I would have never gone to work," he said, only half kidding. "I would have been doomed. I'm addicted to this team."

He enjoys several games a year in what he calls the "naked rooftop" experience. No, it's not a nudist colony. Yes, I was still wearing skivvies. It's a flat, parapet-edged, tarred roof with a four-foot tall door at the top of a winding, wooden staircase around back. A half dozen lawn chairs faced the ballpark in front of a row of bar stools. Two huge Styrofoam coolers sat in the middle. This is what the bare bones Wrigley rooftop experience used to be like.

"Most of the rooftops now, they're corporate. There's formality to it. You're talking to somebody who works in your office, maybe your supervisor. It puts a different spin on it," Harris said. "This is more democratic!"

Wearing a Budweiser bowling shirt, Harris mockingly positioned an empty case of Bud on top of a brick chimney. His friends, Donny Davis and Mike Duffy, did the milk run in the morning and carried the beer, sodas, water, booze, mixers, snacks—even sub sandwiches from an unnamed Italian deli—up top. "We were beat. Those are some serious stairs. We looked at each other and said, 'Why do we do this?' But look around," Duffy said, spreading his arms. "This is why."

They mixed Bloody Marys, and one woman served a tray of homemade deviled eggs she'd toted on the El. Across the way, Big Z's bid for a second straight no-no ended with the first batter. It was 5–0 at the end of the first, and as the Cards added three more in the second, a baseball came skipping across the rooftop and over

Friends of Richard Harris (far left in Budweiser shirt) enjoy the "naked rooftop" experience, the way it used to be in Wrigleyville. *Photo by Jim McArdle*

the side. Anne-Marie Sesti and Carrie Mondschean had been locked out, and ballhawk Dave Davison threw a ball up from the street corner below to get our attention.

After the girls climbed the stairway, the crowd was a comfortable 20. It was 11–0 before the Cubs finally got on the board in the fifth. Harris lives in Lincoln Park and rents the condo, so I wondered out loud, "Where does one find the loo?" Davis answered: "Murphy's. The girls make friends over at the fire station. They can get in there. Guys can't go over there." Unless you know Lee and Murph. Then again, my washroom was closer.

The Cubs scored two in the eighth and two in the ninth, but lost 12–6. But there's no last call here, so I mixed another vodka lemonade as Wrigley emptied. All that was left to do was fold up the lawn chairs and carry the garbage downstairs. And take down the empty case of Bud, because the tarp would be removed next door that evening in compliance with a restraining order approved that afternoon. Like Gramatis, the Brewers lost, too, reducing the magic number to one.

More than five hours before Saturday's game, fans lined up for the bleachers and filled the queue for day-of-game tickets. The barricades were going up, and Wrigley was buttoning up for a party. Piniella had gone to dinner the night before with his wife and two of his kids, where many fans stopped to say hello. "They're excited and rightfully so," he said. "I understand it's been a long, long time here, and I can empathize."

The Cubs invited Leo Hildebrand as part of Fan Appreciation Weekend. At 104 years old, he is believed to be one of the oldest living Cubs fans. "I was in Chicago during the Worlds Series [in 1908], but I didn't get to see it," he told a group of writers. "My dad said, 'You'll get to see them win another one.'"

Hildebrand was given tickets to the game, and several players greeted him and signed a baseball as he sat in a wheelchair behind the batting cage. Woody bent over at the waist and whispered a surprise the organization had been holding. "You're throwing out the first pitch!" Wood said, grinning like the Cheshire cat. "You've got 40 minutes to get loose."

Just enough time for lunch at Tuscany with Dandy Don, who'd arrived early, amped like everyone else. "We should start a pool. My guess is 6:15 PM for the final out," he said as he poured iced tea from a carafe. "Wrigleyville is going to start trembling. Over at Toons, that bar you go to, they'll hear the glasses start clinking together. Everyone over here is going to be banging their feet and stomping the ground. The emergency siren over there on Waveland, those doughnuts, they're going to be going off with one more out to go. This place is going to be unbelievable!"

He piqued my suspense by recounting clinching moments from 1998 and 2003, when players emerged from the clubhouse after the game and sprayed champagne all over Aisle 15, where we'd be sitting. "I should have called you and said to wear your old clothes," he said. "It's good you've got sunglasses. Keep them on. It'll keep the champagne out of your eyes."

Dandy Don picked up the last starting lineup sheet they had available at the Customer Relations Window, a good omen. A fielding error on Soriano's two-run single in the second inning allowed a third run to score. Pleading for insurance runs in the fourth, we got them on an RBI double by DeRosa and a perfectly executed suicide squeeze bunt laid down by Lilly. We were scoreboard watching, and Milwaukee had taken a 2–1 lead on the Reds about the same time St. Louis' Troy Glaus ripped a three-run homer to close the lead to 5–4.

In the bottom of the eighth, we noticed the electronic scoreboards in the upper deck had the Reds leading 4–2. The number 3 was about to go into the window of the manual center-field scoreboard for Cincinnati's half of the sixth inning when Edmonds grounded out to end the Cubs' half of the eighth. The crowd never got a chance to react. Cue "Welcome to the Jungle." It just didn't matter what Milwaukee did, because Woody was going to take care of this himself.

He walked the first batter, but got a fielder's choice and a strikeout. Aaron Miles' soft fly-out to Edmonds ended the game, almost an hour earlier than Dandy Don's prediction. But Wrigleyville was shaking, just like he said it would. Willy B joined us after the final out with his camera.

Edmonds trotted in and joined the celebration on the mound, giving the ball to Woody, the longest-tenured Cub who had framed the afternoon by catching Hildebrand's first pitch and hurling the day's last. "He has been here a long time, and he deserved that ball," said Edmonds, who assembled his teammates in the clubhouse for a team toast.

After 15 minutes inside, they came charging back out, wearing NL Central championship caps and T-shirts, and in some cases, swimming goggles. We were about to get a drenching. Dempster jumped on the wall in front of us and shook two bottles of champagne all over.

"Thanks for the shower," I told him later.

"Did you like that?" Demp laughed. "I loved it. I just thought I'd watch somebody else get sprayed for a change."

The team took a victory lap, Sori hosed down his friends in Ground Zero, and the celebration moved inside. Theriot was asked his favorite moment of the season, and September call-up Koyie Hill—a success story in his own right who had three fingers and a thumb sewn back on after severing them in an off-season accident with a table saw—emptied a bottle of bubbly over Theriot's head. "Probably this right here!" The Riot hooted with his eyes clenched.

Observers noted the celebration was more subdued than the previous season, and I was asking DeRosa about that. "We talked about it before the game," he said. "We want to enjoy it. You work so hard to get to this point. You should enjoy it but also realize that there's a lot more at stake. This team's been put together to…"

The author enjoys a champagne spraying courtesy of Alfonso Soriano on clinch day. *Photo by John "Nunu" Zomot*

With that, Marmol turned a bottle of champagne upside down over him. Ward, shaking another bottle and shouting, "De-ROOOW!!!" unleashed a hosing onto DeRosa, my notepad, and me. "I'll get you later, Mark," I said with a smile. "Go get 'em back."

They returned to Wrigleyville the next morning for Sunday's home finale with the best kind of hangover. Scoop Steph had gone from The Piano Man to Yak-Zies to Guthrie's Tavern on her roundabout journey of revelry toward home the previous night. "I stood outside Guthrie's and thought, 'Should I?' That lasted about 30 seconds," she laughed. "They gave me a blue shot!"

Thinking of Holly Swyers' portrayal of the bleacher community as immediate family and extended family, I decided to finish my journey with my "homies," Peanut Tom, Ginger, Big Joe, and Christie, in the right-field bleachers. Game number 100 for me started much the same way as the first one. I punched in Fookie Dookie's No. 1 a final time, and he led off the bottom of the first with a double to finish with a .364 batting average at the tip of my right index finger. Scoreboard Rick even let me run the balls and strikes for the entire inning. The Chicago Bears game was on his small TV next to me, and I peeked over to check the score. "Pay attention!" he barked.

Piniella gave his starters the day off, and the Cubs' second-teamers were cruising to a 5–1 victory. Between innings, Faith, Christie's adorable four-year-old daughter with curly blonde hair, was tickling Big Joe with a red feather. I called Scoreboard Rick and asked Faith what her favorite number was. She crossed her thumb over the palm of her right hand and held up four teeny fingers. I asked Rick to put No. 4 up at-bat and pointed up at the scoreboard. She whirled back with a melt-your-heart smile.

We split into teams of two and spent the last inning of the final home game figuring out the Cubs' playoff roster. Ginger and Tom picked the same 25 players that Big Joe and I did. Would Piniella choose the same way? I found it fitting that in my 100th game in the Cubs' 100th pursuit of that next championship, they won. Demp went five innings to pick up his career-high 17th victory.

With a sellout crowd of 40,551 on the same afternoon the Bears were playing their home opener, the season attendance of 3,300,200 set a city record. Wrigley had been packed to 99 percent capacity for this championship season, and fans saw the Cubs win 55 times at home, one shy of the club record set by the 1933 club and 1935 NL champs.

After the game, the group at Ground Zero gave a baseball to Arizona Jeremy that they all signed. It was his 71st and perhaps most-treasured souvenir. He had attended every inning of every game, and would continue to do so in the postseason. But his wife had started packing, and they'd be headed back to reality and Scottsdale. How soon would be entirely up to the Cubs.

Crankshaft and I hosted our new bleacher friends for a barbecue. After they had let me into their "living rooms" all summer, I figured I'd invite them to mine—36 steps away. I was out back, working the grill, while Al was writing his blog from my desk on our sun porch. The Rookie walked in, slightly misty-eyed, hugged Al, and thanked him for the ticket connections and friendship. Al held Harry squarely by the shoulders, and said, "You're part of the family now."

· · · ·

A FINAL ROAD TRIP that once looked intimidating turned into a victory lap in front of the snooty New York media and the fans whose team lost the race to the NL Central wire. If anything, the Mets and Brewers were battling it out for the wild-card berth, so the Cubs could help determine their first-round playoff opponent. Santo told me before the home finale that he would be skipping New York. Yeah, good riddance to Shea Stadium and recollections of the infamous black cat running past him in the on-deck circle during the 1969 Cubs' collapse. He giggled at the suggestion of Shea's impending date with the wrecking ball.

In the opener of that series, D-Lee hit his 20th homer, giving the Cubs five players with 20 homers for only the third time in their history. Marquis added a grand slam and beat the Mets 9–5 as Chicago clinched home-field advantage throughout the NL

Wrigley Field's famous red marquee delivers the biggest news of the season.
Photo by Will Byington/www.willbyington.com

playoffs and the Senior Circuit's best record for the first time in 24 years.

The Mets rebounded to win the second game 6–2 on the 100th anniversary of what's come to be known as Merkle's Boner. The story goes like this: New York Giants infielder Fred Merkle failed to touch second base on what would've been a walk-off, game-winning single. Instead, Merkle headed to the clubhouse amid celebrating fans flooding the field. Cubs second baseman Johnny Evers noticed this, retrieved the baseball, and touched second base. Umpire Hank O'Day ruled Merkle out on a force play. With chaotic fans on the field, the game was ruled a tie, and when the two teams finished the regular season stalemated atop the NL standings, they replayed the Merkle game. The Cubs won and went on to capture the 1908 World Series.

While walking past the 7-Eleven on Addison the next night, I ran into Rob Gillman, the guy whose rooftop wedding I crashed on Labor Day. He was obsessing about his upcoming playoff ticket draft. "I just want to make sure I get a World Series game," he said nervously.

Meanwhile, the Cubs were trying for their 44th comeback win of the season. D-Lee's go-ahead bloop double in the tenth inning preceded Rammy's two-run homer as Piniella became the 17th manager in big-league history to record his 1,700[th] win. Nevertheless, Lou still had to defend a story by a New York tabloid, which quoted him as calling 2008 a "tough year" and saying: "Sometimes it can really take a toll on you. I don't know how much longer I want to do this."

Micah Hoffpauir went 5-for-5 with two homers and five RBIs in the series finale to make a case for inclusion on the postseason roster, but the Mets came from behind to win 7–6.

I'd already hit my goal of 100 games, and the Cubs had clinched. So I bypassed Milwaukee over the weekend in favor of other activities in Cheeseland, like boating, tubing, and swimming on Lake Geneva with my best pal, John, and his wife, Linda, and boys, Joey and A.J. Chicagoans started "summering" there shortly after the Chicago Fire of 1871. William Wrigley bought a mansion, Green Gables Farm, around 1911. P.K. Wrigley, who grew up there and preferred spending time at the rural lake rather than the urban ballpark, bought property to add to the estate until it was said to include 1.25 miles of lakefront property.

Sixty miles west, the Cubs lost 5–1 to the Brewers on Friday but won 7–3 the next afternoon behind Lilly's six innings of no-hit pitching. His 17th win gave him the most by a Cubs lefty since Holtzman won 17 in 1970. That night, Ballhawk Kenny and his new bride, Laura, had their wedding reception at Wrigley's Stadium Club. They took photos on the field and in Ground Zero, had customized bobbleheads of themselves on their wedding cake, and Kenny gave his groomsmen Louisville Slugger bats on which he had their own autographs engraved. "The whole day was pretty much a blur," he said later. "But everyone keeps telling me what a great time they had, so I guess we did it right."

On Sunday, CC Sabathia pitched a 3–1 complete-game victory to give the Brewers their first playoff berth since 1982. Stopping at a Wisconsin corner farmstand on my way home, I found a pumpkin with a Cubs logo painted on it and brought it home, placing it in my sun porch window. The calendar was about to change; "Cubtober" was coming.

9

OCTOBER

THE CHICAGO CUBS' 100-YEAR drought has been well-documented. This fact has not: since division play started in 1969 and an extra playoff round was added in 1995, the Cubs have won one post-season series—in a winner-take-all fifth game against Atlanta in the 2003 Division Series. In 16 postseason series in their history, they only swept an opponent once, rolling over the Tigers four games to none in the 1907 World Series (and even that Series had a game that ended in a 3–3 tie due to darkness). Cubs fans have been conditioned that nothing comes easy to this franchise, so even though their team had the best record in the National League, a nervousness started building.

Fortunately, I didn't sense it in the team as I made the rounds to check in with some key Cubs during the last homestand. Perhaps it stemmed from the top. Lou Piniella has seen his share of Octobers—five as a player with the Yankees and six in his first 20 seasons as a big-league skipper. Finally, "the Peerless Leader," Frank Chance, was with peer. By guiding the Cubs into postseason play in consecutive seasons, Piniella had done something no Cubs manager had accomplished since Chance took his team to three straight fall classics from 1906 to 1908.

The Cubs weren't far removed from their season-high six-game losing streak and a stretch where they lost eight of nine. "We didn't lose confidence," outfielder Alfonso Soriano insisted. "Good teams get out of slumps quick."

Closer Kerry Wood admitted there was a worried sense in the clubhouse during the streak, but he intimated an underlying theme of picking each other up that had been there all season. It just had a sublevel players needed to realize. "You kind of get into that routine of, 'Okay, if I don't get my job done, [Carlos] Marmol will get it done. If I don't get the hit, the guy behind me will get the hit,'" Woody said. "Sometimes, you've got to be the guy to go up there and do it, like, 'I'm going to get us out of this.'"

Woody walked the walk, too, locking down a pair of one-run victories as the Cubs came out of that slump. Then Carlos Zambrano threw his no-hitter, followed by a one-hitter by Ted Lilly and the bullpen a day later. The Cubs had cured their most bothersome hiccup of the season, coasting to an 11–6 finish that gave them their highest victory total since the 1945 team won 98 games.

The team was now almost eight months removed from Ryan Dempster saying on the first day of spring camp that they would win the World Series. As the Cubs celebrated their division-clinching victory in their clubhouse, I brought Demp back to that bold prediction. He explained that it wasn't based solely on his own preparation to go from the end of the bullpen to the top of the rotation. He saw a look of determination in his teammates' eyes, as well. "There's not one guy in here whose goal isn't to win the World Series," he said with a bottle of champagne in his hand. "There's not a clear-cut MVP; there's not a clear-cut Cy Young Award winner. It's just a bunch of guys doing the same thing and setting about on the same goal."

Everyone had a role: Ryan Theriot, "The Riot," led the club in batting average; Alfonso Soriano, "Sori," was the home-run leader; Geovany Soto, "Geo," was the Rookie of the Year; Aramis Ramirez, "Rammy," was Mr. Clutch; Mark DeRosa, "DeRo" was Mr. Versatile; Marmol was Mr. Setup; and Woody was the 21st-century Mr. Cub. They had retreads Jim Edmonds and Reed Johnson anchoring the outfield in center, solid bench players in Mike Fontenot, Henry Blanco, and Daryle Ward, and anyone in the rotation proved capable of pitching like an ace on any given day.

And then there was Derrek Lee, "D-Lee," their captain. "He's one of the good guys," Ramirez said. "He plays every day, and he plays hard. You never hear about D-Lee getting in trouble off the field. He's a great role model."

Indeed, at 6′6″, the former basketball recruit of Dean Smith's at North Carolina is the biggest Cub in both stature and experience. He isn't the type to carry a loud conversation from one end of the clubhouse to the other, but when the Cubs bottomed out in 2007, it was D-Lee who called a team meeting to order, minus Piniella and the coaching staff. "I'm definitely more of a leader by example, no question, but if something needs to be said, I'll say it," Lee said. "This is my 11th season, so I think that's a responsibility I can take. I know guys took me under their wing when I was coming up as a young kid. It's just kind of a role you assume with more time in this league and more understanding of this game."

In contrast, Edmonds was one of the newest Cubs. He certainly was glad to be on the home side, even though it took some time to win over a fan base skeptical of a player they were used to despising. Edmonds had been in 61 postseason games and was one of only three Cubs who had a World Series ring. So I gauged the veteran's thoughts on the pitfalls that lay ahead. "Everybody just seems to get it here. Nobody is out just playing for themselves. Everybody wants to win," he said. "But when it comes to crunch time, you have to have a little bit of confidence to you. The energy level doesn't need to go up; the focus needs to go up. If you get too excited, you can't concentrate like you're supposed to."

The Cubs' team batting average of .278 was their best since 1937. They led the NL in runs, eclipsing 850 for only the third time since 1900, and their run differential of +184 runs led the majors by a wide margin. They spent the last 140 consecutive days of the season in first place, their longest stretch in that position since 1969. And they came one victory short of tying the club record for wins at home, where they would open postseason play. This was a very good Cubs team we were sending into war.

· · · ·

WRIGLEY WAS GETTING DRESSED UP for the first day of October. The grounds crew painted the Division Series stencils on the grass in front of both dugouts, bunting went up on the brick walls and upper-deck façades, and postseason graphics were tested on messageboards.

HARVESTING THE CUBS FARM

More than any postseason team in recent history, footprints of the organization's farm system were all over this club. Ten of the 25 men on the Division Series roster were either drafted by the Cubs or spent part of their development in the system, including two starting position players, one starting pitcher, their setup man, and their closer.

Oneri Fleita has been in charge of the farm system since 2000 and Latin American operations for 11 years. A few years back, I traveled with "Fleet" and *Vine Line* photographer Steve Green to check out the Cubs' new training facility in the Dominican Republic. During a rural drive one day, we came across a herd of goats walking single file along the side of a dirt road. (I won't go into what the locals were doing to one goat hanging upside down by its legs from a tree.) One of the goats caught Fleet's eye, and he stared intently as it walked. "See that one there, with a wobble in its walk?" he said. "He's got a bad hind leg." I chuckled inside, thinking about the curse of being a scout, but realized our development system was in good hands if the guy on top always is evaluating.

As he does every year, Fleet traveled to Arizona for the opening of Instructional League in late September. He described to the Cubs' newest recruits about being in the clubhouse days earlier for the division-clinching party. One by one, Zambrano, Soto, Marmol, Theriot, and others pulled aside the man who believed in them from the beginning. They hugged Fleita and doused him with champagne.

"It sounds a bit pom-pomish, but it's real. We are men, but there's no better job than being able to celebrate what you've accomplished at the end of the season," Fleita said. "When I told them about it, I could see a look in their eyes. I want everybody to be a part of this. I want guys to be saying, 'When is it going to be my turn?'"

Nagging injuries sustained in the final week by DeRosa (calf), Soto (wrist), and utility infielder Ronny Cedeno (shoulder) muddled decisions on the Cubs' postseason roster, but the spirit of Cubdom was proud and plenty for a fan rally held at Daley Plaza on the eve of the playoff opener. W placards filled the crowd of several hundred and were in windows of the skyscrapers surrounding the square. The Picasso sculpture was adorned with a giant Cubs cap, and so was Mayor Daley, a Sox fan like his dad, the longtime Chicago mayor before him.

Actor/Cubs fan Jim Belushi was the emcee, singing and dancing to "Sweet Home Chicago," and dismounting the stage with a backward somersault. Ron Santo, joined on stage by Hall of Fame teammates Billy Williams and Ernie Banks, declared, "I have just four words for you: *This...is...the...year!*" D-Lee, one of just a few players to attend, grabbed the mike. "I just want to say to the best fans in the world, thank you for having our backs and showing your support for the last six months," he said. "We need you guys for one more month."

Blowers rained Daley Plaza with blue and red confetti from the sky as the crowd dispersed to "Go Cubs Go," Belushi liberally changing the lyrics to: "Hey Chicago, waddaya say? The Cubs are gonna go all the way."

Back at Wrigley, the Cubs and Dodgers were preparing for their final workout before postseason play. Piniella and D-Lee spoke during a team meeting, and the media congregated under the first-base box seats in a much bigger interview room modified out of a storage area.

Derek Lowe, Los Angeles' Game 1 starter, helped Boston break its 86-year drought in 2004 and was asked about the Cubs staring down the franchise's 100-year infamy. "I think that's city-driven. What I mean by that is, the players don't necessarily feel it as much," he said. "It does kind of annoy you, I think, after a while, because no matter what [you] do, you're always going to get that question of, 'When are you going to stop the streak?'"

While the Cubs hit, general manager Jim Hendry revealed something even his media relations staff didn't yet know. The organization had picked up Piniella's $4 million option for the 2010 season. "It's a wonderful place to manage, and a wonderful organization," Piniella said. "If I'm going to continue doing this, I might as well do it right here."

I got back home and was in my sun porch when the Dodgers started their turn to work out. The guy with the dreadlocks was hitting, so I grabbed my mitt, popped a frozen pizza in the oven, and charged outside for a few bonus minutes of ballhawking. During breaks between cars driving past in rush hour, Moe Mullins was hitting a rubber ball from under the bleachers overhang to Dave Davison and two of the next-generation ballhawks across Waveland Avenue down Kenmore in a game of 500.

One gloveless guy walking past was thrown a ball by a groundskeeper. Dave asked, "Do you have your ballhawking license?" The guy shook his head. "Uh-oh, no 'hawking license," Dave said, turning to young Matt, who playfully demanded, "Street tax!"

One of the Dodgers—I think it was Chan Ho Park—came out to the bleachers and collected some baseballs, ignoring my pleas for a throw. I was talking with Dave about the oversized mitt on his hand when we heard the crack of a bat. "Oh, that sounded good," he said, looking east down Waveland. The ball soared over the bleachers into the Bud building's backyard, where Moe reached through the fence a moment too late. When batting practice ended, Moe counted five that had come out, none of which found their way into my glove. Shut out one last time.

That night, Crankshaft and I watched the White Sox beat Minnesota in a one-game playoff to give Chicago two postseason teams for the first time in 102 years. The field was set for the playoffs, and the calendar flipped to October.

"We know what everybody in this city wants," Piniella had said in the interview room earlier, "and we're going to try to give it to them."

·　·　·　·

CUBS CHAIRMAN CRANE KENNEY had been emailed in late September by a friend of the Reverend James L. Greanias, the pastor at Greek Orthodox St. Iakovos Church in Valparaiso, Indiana. The friend pleaded for playoff tickets for the diehard Cubs fan. Trying to do a good thing for a holy man, Kenney called Greanias himself, who was overjoyed at the invitation to see postseason baseball. The reverend showed up early on the first day of October to reciprocate with a brief blessing. Kenney told the pastor he didn't much believe in curses or superstitions, but it was seven hours before game time. What could be the harm?

The Cubs celebrate on the mound at Wrigley after clinching their second straight NL Central Division title. *Steve Green photo courtesy Chicago Cubs*

Well, a TBS cameraman setting up his equipment noticed the priest spreading holy water around the Cubs dugout and shot some footage. Like his players, Piniella didn't know anything about the ceremony until seeing it on television in the clubhouse during the pregame show. Hundred-year-old questions came up again. "There's no curses here. I don't know how many times I have to answer about curses," Piniella responded. "I'm a Christian guy, and I believe, and you can pray, but the other guy's praying, too. God doesn't care about a baseball game."

On my way to the ballpark, I ran into an off-duty cop outside my building—hired by Landlady Lara to keep the postseason peace. Barricades walled both sides of the parkways down Waveland, certain to add an obstacle to ballhawking. Even more challenging was a stiff wind blowing in off the lake. Piniella told the media prophetically before the game, "Walks can hurt you in this type of environment a heck of a lot." Near Gate K, I ran into Arizona Jeremy, who abandoned his plan of 'hawking on Waveland because of the wind and loaned his mitt to Ken Keefer's kid for batting practice. The bleachers no longer were general admission for the playoffs, so among the regulars in Ground Zero, and with BleedCubbieBlue Al, Scoop Steph, and Big Joe, only the season-ticket holders had seats reserved in their usual sections. Jeremy had a Terrace Box seat, but was always looking to "upgrade." Just then, Radical Tim arrived.

"If you hear anyone in your group selling for the next round, I'm buying," Jeremy told Tim.

"I like your thinking. What about the round after that?" Radical Tim replied.

Jeremy smiled, "That, too!"

The gates opened at 3:30 PM, two hours before game time. Kelly Houlihan, who hadn't been to a playoff game since she was eight years old in 1989, was the first one through the turnstiles and made a beeline for the seats adjacent to the home bullpen. She was a teacher from the South Side neighborhood of Beverly, but wanted to be clear: "I left work early; I did not ditch. I just wanted to be close, take some pictures. I know they're on a mission, too, so I don't expect autographs. I just wanted to take it in. I wanted to be there and see them lift up the gates and then come charging in."

Big Joe was shaking his head atop Section 312 in right-center field, realizing something that never had occurred to him before: the guy sitting one row down was in Section 313, Row 13, Seat 13. "If we lose, I'm looking at you," he said to him. I told the guy to find a Dodgers fan and switch seats.

During the first few innings, a guy chalked "GO CUBS GO" in giant letters on Waveland Avenue in front of my apartment. The enthusiasm inside, however, was oddly muted, even after DeRosa followed Edmonds' second-inning single by slicing a two-run homer inside the right-field foul post. My security staff friends told stories of lost fans unsure of which gate to enter or their seat location. We deduced many of the regulars sold their early round seats to bankroll into later-round tickets.

The bleachers regulars were there. Sitting across the aisle from Scoop Steph, Judy turned to me in the third inning with a skittish look. "Why are we so nervous?" she asked, half rhetorically.

"Because we lost our eight-game lead, and the standings reset to zero," I said. "But we're okay. Dempster looks good, and we're up 2–0."

Unconvinced, Judy fired back, "But he's got 61 pitches already!"

Her apocalyptic observation intersected with Piniella's pregame comment an inning later when Demp issued his fifth, sixth, and seventh walks, most by a Cub in a postseason game since 1935 and as many as he'd issued the entire month of September. Next up was James Loney, who barely tipped an 0–2 pitch before slugging a grand slam to center field. Flummoxed, Judy, Colleen, and Holly shook their heads.

"Hey," I said, trying to reassure them. "What's the one thing we've been able to do all year?"

Judy shot me another apprehensive look, and said, "Come back?"

Magic Marc, sitting in the same section but several rows below, showed up in the sixth inning and emptied his pack of gum. Rammy had a leadoff double but was stranded at third. Before the bottom of the eighth, "All the Way," a new song Pearl Jam frontman and Chicago native Eddie Vedder wrote at the behest of Ernie Banks, was piped over the PA system:

> *Heroes with pinstripes and heroes in blue,*
> *Give us the chance to feel like heroes do.*
> *Whether we'll win and if we should lose,*
> *We know someday we'll go all the way.*

Its weepy melody, however, was not the rally song for the situation in which we found ourselves. The stadium became increasingly quiet as the Cubs went down in the eighth, and Russell Martin sent some to the exits when he hit the Dodgers' third homer of the night to make it 7–2. The irony of ironies: former Cub Greg Maddux came out to mop up in the ninth inning. "I have mixed emotions," Scoop Steph said as 42-year-old "Mad Dog" warmed up. "This might be his last appearance here. Did you hear the applause he got?"

Dempster shouldered the blame but showed the resolve that's been the backbone of the team all season. "We'll be ready to go tomorrow. We'll come out and win a game. You don't have to win all five, just three," he said.

The next afternoon, I saw Moe Mullins in front of my building carrying a jacket and his faithful baseball mitt. "Look at this wind blowing out," he said, anxiously gesturing at the flags atop the scoreboard. "The players aren't here yet, so I'm going to go sit in my car." With a late 8:30 PM start to accommodate the TV schedule, Wrigleyville was on edge for a long afternoon.

Dandy Don had been to every playoff game Wrigley Field hosted for the past quarter century until giving away his seats for Games 1 and 2. Still, he came up to Wrigleyville to get a taste of the pregame energy, not to mention Tuscany's famous roasted garlic mashed in olive oil and Parmesan cheese. He was holding onto tickets for Game 5 but hoped his 2008 postseason debut would be in the NLCS. "We've seen our champagne celebration here this year. Let's let them do it out there," he said.

After keeping score of Game 1 at home, Dandy Don was awoken at 2:30 in the morning and couldn't get back to sleep, even after listening to some calming jazz on his headphones. "I don't know if I woke up as a result of that game or not. I think it was," he conceded. "We'll all be sleeping well tonight."

Don had made reservations for the rest of the postseason at the same window-front table at Tuscany, so he could watch the buzz grow toward game time. His confidence was shared. Arizona Jeremy was certain he'd be in a car after the game, driving his wife back to Scottsdale so he could fly back in time for Game 5 in Chicago and the rest of the Cubs' postseason run before moving back to the desert.

As the Cubs finished batting practice, Ballhawk Kenny tracked a line drive on its way out of the ballpark and made a nice running catch. Little did he know it would be the last Cubs souvenir deposited onto Waveland Avenue of the 2008 season.

Like most Cubs fans, I did my part to change their luck. I'd come across my father's World War II dog tags, and put them on a chain around my neck. I switched to my lucky "gamer" 1989 Cubs cap, kept score with a different pencil, and reverted to a streak-breaking practice that worked once before. That's right, I was going commando again, a considerably chillier practice than it was a month earlier.

The mood in the ballpark was a world of difference from the previous night. With a building energy fed by "Fanfare for Rocky" from the soundtrack of the Sylvester Stallone classic as Big Z warmed up, the crowd was on its feet well before the teams took the field.

When I arrived at Ground Zero, they were still giving Ellen and Mary Ellen grief about a recent Yahoo.com story in which Soriano affectionately described the forty-somethings as his "his grandmas." Two real grandmas, Marilyn and Roberta, joined them in Ground Zero. Mary Ellen wore her Reed Johnson jersey with her long, frizzy brown hair flowing out her Cubs bandana. Ellen accessorized in blue—fingernails, toenails, and ponytail. She had a sleeve of paper cups to pop, and her Carol Burnett–Tarzan yell was in full force. A guy on the end of my row rang a cowbell that hung from his neck. "Are we making enough noise tonight?" asked Radical Tim, clearly peeved by media charges of the fans being quiet in the series opener.

I wanted to get a taste of how Ground Zero treated Manny Ramirez, the Dodgers' enigmatic left fielder acquired from Boston at the trade deadline. In the top half of the first, he took an 0–1 pitch for a strike, and the crowd leaped to its feet and cheered. He swung through the next pitch, a 95-mph fastball, for the third out and sauntered out to his position in the teeth of Ground Zero's taunts.

"It's 1...2...3 strikes you're OUT at the old...ball...game!" they sang. The choruses morphed from "MANN-EEEE! MANN-EEEE!" into "Manny sucks! Manny sucks!" Ground Zero started into it's "Fe, fi, fo, fum, Manny is a stinkin' bum" chant after the first pitch, but they were drowned out by reaction to Soriano's single lined down the left-field line. "It's all your fault! It's all your

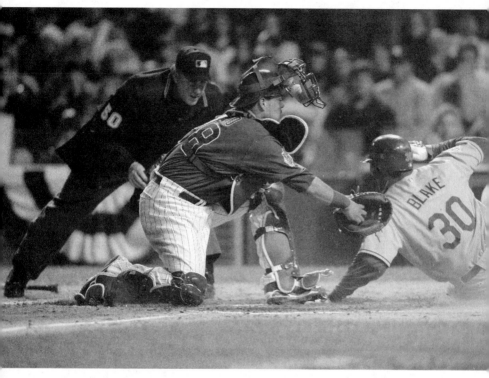

The Dodgers' Casey Blake slides around the tag of Geovany Soto during the Cubs' Game 2 loss. *Steve Green photo courtesy Chicago Cubs*

fault!" they hollered at Ramirez as he returned to his position. Then they broke out an old chant from the 1960s: "Manny's got a big ol' butt—oh yeah!"

The electricity, however, short-circuited in a second inning in which the Dodgers hit just two balls out of the infield and scored five runs. Andre Ethier and Loney both singled, the second ball bouncing off Theriot's bare hand as he tried to change direction on his way to cover second base on a hit-and-run. One out later, DeRosa and Lee mishandled consecutive ground balls that could've been inning-ending double plays. After Rafael Furcal's bunt single scored the second run, Martin's three-run double gave L.A. a 5–0 advantage. Ramirez homered onto the roof of the batter's-eye suite in center field in the fifth, and two walks led to another run in the seventh.

Aside from pleading all night unsuccessfully with Soriano for a throw to the sit-in grandmas—Tim and Ellen eventually handed over baseballs to their septuagenarian friends—Ground Zero grew quiet. Other fans were livid, and many booed throughout the final half of the contest. After Rammy made an error in the fourth, my sister, Mary Jo, texted, "What are the Bad News Bears doing out there?" Another fan, who refused to succumb to despair, held an "IT'S GONNA HAPPEN" placard.

"I'm going home to get drunk," a fan three rows back said. "That's what's gonna happen!"

The seventh-inning stretch came and went, with a listless version of Wrigley's daily sing-along. "That's the first time I've ever not sung 'Take Me Out to the Ball Game.' They don't deserve it," one fan ranted.

The crowd almost seemed disappointed in the bottom of the inning when Edmonds' RBI double broke up Chad Billingsley's shutout bid. In the final inning, Woody got into the game in relief, the first Cub to appear in four postseasons since Stan Hack in the 1930s and 1940s. Not that it mattered. Crankshaft walked up wearing his Cubs construction helmet sideways—rally cap. "I was trying to get this whole section going over there," he said. "I told them, 'C'mon, it's only a touchdown and a safety.'"

Make that a touchdown and a field goal. Theriot made an error in the ninth, leading to the Dodgers' final run in the 10–3 thrashing and giving every member of the Cubs infield an error, the first team to do that in the postseason since the Tigers in a 1934 World Series game.

Piniella was seething afterward, cutting off interrogators before they could finish. He knew what the questions were. "I don't think you can win 97 ballgames playing that way," he said. "The last two games, they've probably been the two worst games we've played all year from a walking and errors standpoint. It wasn't fun to watch, I can tell you that."

Kosuke Fukudome was hitless in eight at-bats over the two games, including a strikeout and weak grounder to first when brought to the plate by my right index finger. "I don't want to hear about Fukudome anymore as far as whether he's going to play or not," Piniella said. "I'm going to play Fontenot or Reed Johnson or somebody else, and that's the end of that story. The kid is struggling, and there's no sense sending him out there anymore."

In the afternoon, DeRosa had called it a do-or-die game. Piniella bristled when asked about that comment, too. "This is why I don't like talking about do-or-die things, and I hear that from a few of our players. I'll talk to them about it. This is not do or die," he said. "We're sending a pretty good pitcher out there on the mound in Los Angeles on Saturday in [Rich] Harden, and we're sending a darned good pitcher out to the mound Sunday in [Ted] Lilly."

I reported to Bernie's, hoping, pleading it wasn't our final postgame beer-swilling session of the year. Actually, the mood wasn't bad. One by one, as Peanut Tom and Ginger, Big Joe, Willy B, and Scoreboard Rick left for the night, they hugged and said, "We'll see you Tuesday."

. . . .

JUST THE FACTS: of the first 29 teams to go down 2–0 in a five-game series in major league playoff history, 21 went on to be swept, and only seven came back to win the series. The odds were definitely stacked against our story's heroes. I got an email from the West Side Rooters Social Club. It was a message of encouragement from the most positive thinker in the annals of Cubdom:

> Fellow Rooters, it's easy to "believe" when the Cubs have the best record in baseball and appear unstoppable. But at moments like this, it's real fans like the Rooters who truly believe in the team. As a former player, I can assure you that your belief when times are tough gives the team strength.
>
> As they did in 1908, the Rooters must join together and use the strength of our collective belief to pull the team up the Pennant Hill. Let's win three!
> Oof Wah,
> Ernie Banks

At 10:30 Friday morning, the Cubs boarded a bus outside Gate K. The question was, were they headed to their own 100-year funeral or the most inspired comeback in franchise history? I watched from the sun porch as a few fans—less than a half dozen—saw them off. Arizona Jeremy was there, getting his hat signed by Soto, Theriot, and DeRosa, among others. He waved to Dempster, and his neighbor waved back with a smile as he stepped onto the bus.

I had a couple guests the night of Game 2. Lee Smith struck up a friendship with Scoreboard Rick during his days closing games for the Cubs, so when Smitty's kid had two student friends from Louisiana Tech come up for the game Thursday night, Rick found them a flophouse for the night—at the Swank.

The three of us went to breakfast the next morning on Clark Street, and Rick gave them a mini tour of the ballpark. They found a baseball that must've fallen out of the ivy, and I found a penny embedded in the gravel along the right-field line. "Pick it up and bring it with you to L.A.!" Scoreboard Rick said excitedly. "That might be the lucky penny that turns the season around."

As we were walking out Gate K, Rick got a call from Smitty and put him on speakerphone. Like everyone else, Smitty wanted to know what's wrong with the Cubs. He'd watched the night before, noting Soriano's incessant hopping, the long faces in the crowd, and Zambrano's surly disposition. Then he said of one of my overnight guests: "Watch out for that Joel."

"Tell me about it," I responded. "He showed up last night wearing a Dodgers jersey!" Smitty chuckled and elaborated: "He's a preacher's son. Gotta watch out for those preacher's sons. His grandfather used to make me play baseball all day. I'd be collecting my red wigglers and crickets, getting ready to go fishing, and he'd drag me off to go play baseball somewhere. One time our pitcher shot his eye out in a huntin' accident, so that's why they put me out on the mound."

Smitty's fun-spirited story about his beginnings was tempered quickly by some bad news. I returned home and logged into my email, finding a note from Danny, my Toons proprietor friend, that his father had died after a nine-year battle with cancer. DB

Alfonso Soriano sits dejected in the Dodger Stadium dugout during Game 3.
Steve Green photo courtesy Chicago Cubs

had been at Game 2 the previous night in his season seats along the right-field line, toasting his father. Then I got a text from Harry the Rookie. Bob Romain, the father of Al's girlfriend, Miriam, who had shared his story about getting shut out on tickets for the 1945 World Series, died of a heart attack while playing tennis that morning. He'd been in his seats in the first row of the upper deck the night before—a terrible final Cubs game to endure. At least he didn't have it to remember long.

I called Miriam to offer my condolences, and she talked fondly about her father. She told me how the last Cubs game she missed was to attend his surprise 75th birthday party in late August. Willy B and I had scored tickets to Games 3 and 4 and booked last-minute flights to the West Coast. But it was tough to get motivated for a road trip after talking with Miriam. She was so sad. Baseball was supposed to be an escape from the everyday rigors, a place to forget. But here, Bob Romain's death provided some perspective. There were bigger losses than a couple of baseball games.

I tried to cheer Miriam up by sharing my story of finding a lucky penny on the field. She and Al had canceled their plans to go west for Games 3 and 4, but my lucky penny was making the trip, and this series was coming back to Wrigley for Game 5, I assured. "I can't go to Wrigley right now. It's never going to be the same," she said somberly. "Next round, I'll go to the next round."

I also had my last 20 bucks in my pocket. A nest egg that I'd hoped would get me through the season was dried up, and I had to take out a loan from my best friend to get me there and back. I was all in…the Cubs were going three-and-out.

· · · ·

THE BATTERY ON MY CELL PHONE died during the first inning of Game 3, perfect considering what little good news could be passed along. When I plugged in later, I had 17 text messages, mostly from friends and family making sure I was out of reach of any sharp objects or high ledges. There was a lot of anger, venting, and calls for mercy: "Nothing ever changes," read one. "I'm breaking up with the Cubs," said another. "I feel like I'm hungover, and I didn't drink," read a third. Arizona Jeremy checked in from Murphy's in

Wrigleyville: "Sorry you had to see that. We deserve better for all the hours we gave them this year."

But like Clint Eastwood said in *Unforgiven*, deserve's got nothing to do with it. Baseball is in the earning business, and the Cubs didn't play like the team that had earned home-field advantage. In fact, in two runs at the postseason under Piniella, they were 0–6 and averaged two runs per game.

"I don't think it has anything to do with the 100-year thing," Piniella said. "We can play postseason between now and another hundred years, and if we score six runs in a three-game series, it'll be another hundred years before we win."

More accurately, the Cubs' sloppiness and lack of clutch hitting cut them out at the legs. L.A. only had one more hit in the series, but walks and errors cost the Cubs in Games 1 and 2, and Chicago batted just .179 with runners in scoring position, compared to the Dodgers' .333. L.A. skipper Joe Torre, a veteran of 14 straight playoff appearances dating back to his days with the Yankees, thought the Cubs played like a team with a lot to lose. "Starting in Chicago might have been a benefit to us," he said. "There was a lot of pressure on them."

An email string created by the bleachers season-ticket holders had a lot of rants and pleads, but also some comic relief from Radical Tim, who asked, "Does anyone know of a good barber?" Mary Ellen pointed out that TBS had cut fatefully into *Titanic* to start Saturday's broadcast. Others noted that a third of the cost for next year's tickets were covered with money they'd put up for playoff tickets—and it was only 190 days 'til Opening Day!

Al blogged and then turned BleedCubbieBlue over to the vents of his readers: "This one makes me angry," he wrote. "This team was the one that was 'different,' that felt right, that set records and accomplished feats that hadn't been done in decades. And not only do they go out early, they go out with barely a whimper....Will I quit? Hell no. I'm a Cubs fan. That's how I grew up; if you're my age or older, you have many of these shared disasters. Now all of us have 2008."

Crankshaft reported that a shrine had been assembled at the bleachers gate on Waveland and Sheffield. They left empty Old

Style cans, flowers, and candles, and there were signs and notes with all sorts of sentiment. Workers at Murphy's helped put it together. "It was like a death," said one bartender. "The 2008 season died."

The bunting was taken down, and many players had cleaned out their lockers and were gone by the time my flight landed. Arizona Jeremy was gone, too. He and his wife packed up their car and left that evening. We never got to say good-bye the way we wanted to—with a smile and a toast to the summer we'd given up everything and followed the Cubs' amazing run to the World Series.

On Wednesday morning, I saw Scoreboard Rick driving a forklift down Waveland, taking the pads from the outfield wall to be stored. I had hoped to be writing my recap of the Cubs' Game 5 victory to overcome incredible odds and win the series. Instead, October 8 brought the first news of the off-season: the Cubs had picked up the $7 million option on pitcher Rich Harden, and hours after arriving home in the Dominican Republic, reliever Carlos Marmol had gotten a bump on the forehead and seven stitches in an automobile accident—another "Cubbie occurrence."

On the day the NLCS opened in Philadelphia, baseball at Wrigley was a boy's game again. Lilly and a few friends knocked some balls around on a tranquil field with nobody in the stands, and his dogs ran around the unlined confines. A few blocks away, Harry the Rookie waved to Demp, who was kicking it on his front porch with his son, and rookie reliever Jeff Samardzija was picking up a few things at the Jewel on Southport. A new digit was added to the sign at the Lakeview Baseball Club, and AC0063100 was unveiled by Tony and Mike Racke to little fanfare.

I got together with Al and Miriam for dinner in mid-October, and she had more distressing news. Her mother had been hospitalized recently with a kidney stone. Miriam added that her cat, Kelly, had a stroke recently and had to be put down. "Girl," I said, "you are having one baaad month."

Miriam had some good news, too. She had accepted a part-time gig with Examiner.com writing about Cubs baseball several times a week. Her dad knew she was interviewing for the job and said

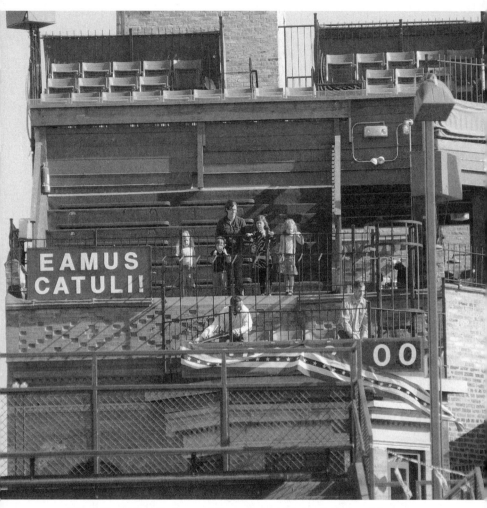

Mike (left) and Tony Racke unveil the newest addition to their sign at the Lakeview Baseball Club. *Photo by John "Nunu" Zomot*

to her shortly before he died, "I knew there was a reason you were going to so many games."

Baseball seems to bridge generations, and Miriam and her father bonded over the Cubs. She had lived in Atlanta for 20 years but returned every summer to take in some games with her father in his seats in the first row of the upper deck. She returned to

Chicago in 2004, and they went to about 25 games together the next season and a bunch more in 2006. Their routine sounded familiar. They always would start with a pregame meal at Tuscany, just like Dandy Don.

Just before the 2007 season, she met Al, and they bonded over their common love of baseball. Al's mother died when he was young, his sister passed away a few years back, and his dad lives in California. Other than his son, Mark, and daughter, Rachel, the only other family he had for her to meet was the one he spent summers with in the corner of Wrigley's left-field bleachers. Their first game together was in Milwaukee over the first weekend of the 2007 season. Al introduced her to Hawaii Jeff, and Peanut Tom and Ginger, who'd made the trip. But she was nervous about meeting the lion's share of Al's family during the first homestand.

"Everyone I sit with out there, I met in the bleachers," Al said. "I told her it'd be fine. As a born and raised Cubs fan, they would all understand that she 'got it.'" Then he laughed and looked over at his girl. "Now her and Jeff conspire against me. I told you it wouldn't be a problem, and it wound up being a problem... for me!"

Miriam was overwhelmed with the sympathy from the bleachers family after her father's death. Many of them came to the services and the two-day shiva that followed before Yom Kippur. Others sent cards and condolences and signed an online guest book. Her mother was particularly touched.

"That was Al's family, and two summers ago they greeted me with open arms and brought me into the fold so quickly, because we all share that same passion," Miriam said. "It's the passion, the loyalty, the bonding, especially in bad times, that brings at least that bleacher group together....I will never curse my dad for making me a Cubs fan, maybe because it really was my choice."

• • • •

A DAY AFTER THE CUBS were eliminated, I took some photos of the sunset on Venice Beach. Maybe it was just my first California sunset, but it seemed a paradox. I thought back to the sunrise behind the billowy clouds on Opening Day. My season was muted and ominous at the start, when there was such uncertainty. But here at the end, the sky was so beautifully full of colors. It was confusingly clear.

I pulled my lucky penny out of my pocket and wondered how it could've failed. I'd never considered the story of how it might've found its way onto Wrigley's foul line to begin with. In my mind's eye, I saw a disgruntled fan hollering some profanity and chucking it from the upper deck after the final out of Game 2. Minted in 2008, it had been his or her lucky penny once. It was carried through 162 games and two playoff losses. I took it to its final resting place in the rich Southern California sand.

Besides the games, I considered all that I had written about in the past 10 months—the births, deaths, weddings, and engagements. In a week I would become Peyton's godfather, a spiritual shepherd helping to guide a new life. Never mind that the first thing I taught her was to love a baseball team that always breaks your heart.

As I was finishing my baseball thesis, I was also packing up to move. The Swank will be no more, and I'll likely never live closer than 1,000 feet from Wrigley, much less home-run distance. Tuscany was closing, making room for a new establishment to take its place owned by 36-year-old Chicago nightclub mogul Billy Dec. I called Dandy Don with the news, and he was shocked but took it in stride. "I guess I'll have to find a new place," he said.

I thought back to a sun-baked August afternoon on Tuscany's outdoor patio, when Dandy Don's wife, Pat, succinctly summed up their decades of coming to Wrigley. "It's been more than just the Cubs," she said. "You make friends and have a lot of memories. But there are lots and lots of changes. It's always moving forward. You can't be stuck in reverse. You've got to go with the flow."

I needed to lay low, become a squatter for a little while until I got my financial feet back under me. Anxieties abounded. You've probably deduced by now that things didn't work out with my girlfriend, Sandra. Old loves haunt me in my dreams, and so do people I used to work with at the Cubs, whom I ask, "Is there life beyond the ivy?"

Unemployment was at a 34-year high, and the government acknowledged what we already knew—the world was in a recession.

"What's next?" people asked me. "Can you go back to the Cubs?" But "go back" just doesn't sound right and is not the advice Pat Dando gave: "It's always moving forward. You can't be stuck in reverse."

Wrigleyville's constant flow of change was ever-present, and the offseason was likely to become a gusher. It started with Woody not being re-signed. Offers for the franchise and ballpark would be coming in December, and a new owner might very well be in place by Opening Day. What changes would they bring about?

I originally thought the title of this book to be too cliché. But then I would tell people what I was doing—keeping a pulse of the team in the clubhouse, sitting with fans during games, and just basically inhaling Wrigleyville for a summer. "Oh," they would say, "you're livin' the dream." The title fit then, and it had to fit at the end. I'd been to 103 baseball games in one year and will never come close to doing that again. I needed to consider the 64 wins I saw and not dwell on the final three losses.

I had hoped all along that the dream would be chronicling the Cubs finally winning a championship and avoiding the 100-year shame. But moments can be fleeting. I began to realize the dream is Wrigleyville—the Disneyworld of baseball—and the family I've come to know there. As fall turned toward winter, I celebrated birthdays with Scoop Steph's group at Full Schilling on Clark Street, went to a Blackhawks game with Harry the Rookie, and had lunch with Dandy Don at Gibson's—in his neighborhood, for a change. I started growing my hair out, picking up the baton where Radical Tim had left it. I spoke to Arizona Jeremy on the phone and found he'd returned to the mortgage business in Scottsdale. More important, he and his wife were expecting their first child, a boy, in April. Suddenly, taking a week off for a 2009 homestand at Wrigley seemed a daunting task for him. Alongside friends I'd had for 10, 20, even 40 years, Big Joe loaned his brawn and Peanut Tom his company van to help move me out of the Swank. Somewhere along the way, I stopped telling these people's story and started living it with them.

So what's next for me? Another book? Another editing job? Freelance writing? Teaching? They're all directions I've weighed.

But on a whim, I headed west to Lake Tahoe with a Toons buddy, "Ziggy," who had been downsized from his job in the financial sector. We figured on finding jobs as ski instructors and spending a season in the mountains—living another dream.

But I'll be back in my hometown come spring, rooting on my Cubs with all my friends, old and new, hoping to end that streak at 100. We'll all be looking for those "signs" that 2009 will be special. The first one came less than a week after the Phillies won the 2008 World Series, when a new leader and resident of Chicago (never mind that he's a Sox fan) stood before hundreds of thousands in Grant Park, and delivered his mantra: "Yes we can!"

"Wait 'til next year" has been a cliché tied to the Cubs for years, and 2008 taught me why. The dream would have continued whether the Cubs won a championship or not. My journey was not complete and never will be. I hunger for that post–Opening Day snack. You know the one, that stale peanut out of Peanut Tom's bag.